AuDHD

AuDHD
Blooming Differently

Leanne Maskell

FOREWORD BY DR BECKY QUICKE

"When a flower doesn't bloom, you fix the environment in which it grows, not the flower." **Alexander Den Heijer**

Copyright © Leanne Maskell 2025

The rights of Leanne Maskell to be identified as the author of this work have been asserted by her in accordance with the Copyright, Designs and Patents Act 1988.

All rights reserved. No part of this publication may be reproduced, stored in a retrieval system, or transmitted in any form or by any means without the prior written permission of the publisher, nor may it be otherwise circulated in any form or by any means without such permission. Additionally, this book may not be distributed in any binding or cover other than that in which it was originally published, and a similar condition must be imposed on any subsequent purchaser.

Cover design by Ellie Perkins @ Write & Sunny
Design and typesetting by Danny Lyle

Disclaimer

The information provided in this book, *AuDHD: Blooming Differently*, is for general informational purposes only. It is not intended as legal, medical, or professional advice and should not be construed as such. The author and publisher are not responsible for any actions taken by individuals or organisations based on the content of this book.

The content is based on the author's research and personal experiences. While every effort has been made to ensure the accuracy and reliability of the information presented, the author and publisher make no representations or warranties, express or implied, regarding the completeness, accuracy, reliability, suitability, or availability of the information contained within.

Readers are encouraged to consult their own legal, medical, or mental health professionals before making decisions or taking actions related to ADHD, workplace accommodations, or any other topic discussed in this book.

The information in this book is not a substitute for professional advice, diagnosis, or treatment. The author and publisher disclaim any liability, loss, or risk incurred as a consequence, directly or indirectly, of the use or application of the contents of this book.

In no event shall the author or publisher be liable for any damages or legal claims of any kind. While every effort has been made to ensure the accuracy of the information, no responsibility is assumed for errors, inaccuracies, omissions, or any other inconsistencies.

The mention of specific products, services, organisations, or professionals does not imply endorsement or recommendation by the author or publisher unless expressly stated.

This book is based on the author's personal experiences and opinions. Any references to individuals or organisations are made in good faith and are not intended to harm reputations. The author and publisher do not accept responsibility for any interpretations made by readers.

Any resemblance to real persons, living or dead, is purely coincidental unless otherwise stated. Some experiences have been adapted and anonymised to protect privacy. Any resemblance to real individuals is unintentional.

This book is protected under international copyright laws and may not be reproduced, distributed, or transmitted in any form or by any means without prior written permission from the author and publisher.

By reading this book, you agree to the terms and conditions outlined in this disclaimer. If you do not agree with these terms, please do not use or rely on the information provided.

IF YOU FEEL FRUSTRATED BY A BRAIN THAT FEELS LIKE IT'S CONSTANTLY AT WAR, THEN THIS BOOK IS DEDICATED TO YOU.

I wrote it for the people who think differently to 'most'. The misfits, who feel like they never quite belong, no matter how hard they try. Everyone who feels as though they're 'too much', yet still never 'enough'.

It's for those who feel like their brain is pulling them in a million directions. The people who are lost, who have no idea what to 'do' with their life, as everybody else seems to have it figured out. It's for the people who have accidentally spent their entire lives making sure everyone around them feels comfortable, only to realise that they never felt comfortable the whole time.

It's for the children and parents who are being failed by their schools, the adults who have been failed by the healthcare system. It's for the people who are stuck on waiting lists for assessments, and those who have been 'diagnosed and dumped', wondering what they're supposed to do now.

It's for the loved ones of these people, who see how incredibly wonderful, sparkly, and brilliant they are, and so wish they could just see themselves the way you do. It's for the parents who are worried they're not good enough (you are), for the teachers who are at breaking point, and the doctors who feel helpless.

AuDHD: Blooming Differently

I wrote it after being diagnosed with autism in October 2024, 6 years after being diagnosed with ADHD. It felt like my brain was exploding with questioning every life experience up I'd had until that point, my methods of subconscious masking suddenly so glaringly obvious that it left me feeling like a shell of a person. I had no idea who I was without the strategies I'd created to survive.

Just like when I wrote 'ADHD: an A to Z', I needed to get it all out of my head. So, I locked myself away from the world for 10 days, writing non-stop, wondering if I'd ever go outside again (I did).

I wrote my life out and felt such pain and grief for not only myself, but everybody else who's struggling without access to the support they deserve. I pulled the pieces of me apart, and put them back together again, finally able to see who 'I' was.

I hope that this book encourages you to do the same, because you are just as capable as me. I hope you read it and remember that if you're struggling right now, this is temporary. You have no idea how good your life is going to get - and making friends with your brain is just the beginning.

Thank you to everybody who has helped me along the way, doing the best with what you had available to you. To those who saw things in me I couldn't see in myself, who helped me to stick around on this earth and be able to discover how what I thought were my 'weaknesses' were in reality, the brilliant things that make me who I am - an AuDHD-er.

You are not alone.

Prologue

I met my younger self for a hot chocolate.

She asked if she's still 'weird'.

I said yes, but it's the best thing about you.

She asked if she's broken.

I said no, the environment around you is.

She asked why she feels so different to everybody else.

I said it's because you think differently, but this isn't a bad thing.

She asked if anyone will ever like her.

I said yes, more people than you can imagine - you just need to find them.

She asked why she's told off for sliding down bannisters and hanging upside down from trees.

I said that she shouldn't be told off for these things, but she should be careful not to hurt herself.

AuDHD: Blooming Differently

She asked if she really is an attention seeking drama queen.

I said no, you feel things deeply - and that's a beautiful thing to share with the world.

She asked how she could just be normal.

I said that's the last thing you'd ever want to be - trust me.

I promised her that one day it would all make sense - until then, she just needs to remember that she's not the problem.

This is the conversation I wish someone had had with me at that age.

I wrote this AuDHD book for children like her to grow up feeling less broken - I hope you enjoy it.

Contents

AuDHD A-Z: Key Terms — xi

Foreword — xv

Introduction — xvii

1. What is AuDHD? — 1

2. Childhood — 16

3. Adolescence — 35

4. Learning — 61

5. Vulnerability — 86

6. Mental Health — 115

7. Trauma — 145

8. Support — 175

9. Employment — 203

10. Transitions — 230

11. Paradoxes — 257

12. Diagnosis — 284

13. Acceptance — 313

AuDHD A-Z: Key Terms

This glossary explains some of the 'language' around AuDHD used throughout this book. Feel free to refer back to it at any time!

- **AuDHD**: the co-existence of the two neurodevelopmental conditions, autism and ADHD, in the same person (who is referred to as an 'AuDHD-er')
- **AuDHD Inertia**: the desire to want to remain in a constant state (autism), but also feeling a need for novel stimulation (ADHD). It's also referred to as 'rotting', as we beat ourselves up in this state, stuck in 'freeze' mode.
- **Alexithymia**: difficulty identifying, feeling, or describing emotions, often leading to challenges in emotional expression. It loosely translates to 'no words for emotion' and is strongly linked with autism & ADHD.
- **Body Doubling**: when people do separate activities with each other, not trying to influence each others behaviour (also known as '**parallel play**').
- **Disclosure**: the act of 'officially' informing another person or organisation that you are disabled. This is most often seen within the workplace, where it is not compulsory.
- **Double Empathy Problem**: difficulty in mutual understanding between neurodivergent and neurotypical individuals, where both struggle to empathise with each other, such as language differences in visiting a foreign country.
- **Executive Functioning**: our ability to 'do what we know',

relating to the pre-frontal cortex part of our brains responsible for skills such as self-awareness, emotional regulation, and motivation.
- **Hyper-focus**: intense, narrow concentration on a single task, often at the expense of everything else, which can be situational and task-dependent. This is often associated with ADHD.
- **Hyper-empathy**: when an individual is overly in tune with other people's emotions, mirroring them to the same intensity. They may feel these emotions as their own. This is often linked with autism.
- **Hyperlexia**: a learning difference involving advanced reading and writing abilities compared to our peers.
- **Info-dumping**: sharing excessive amounts of information on a topic of interest, often without realising that others are not interested - sometimes known as '**monologuing**'.
- **Interest-Based Nervous System**: a concept where motivation and focus are driven by interest, rather than importance, as for neurotypical people.
- **Masking**: concealing or suppressing natural AuDHD behaviours, traits, or emotions to fit in or avoid judgement, as a social camouflage which is extremely energy-intensive.
- **Meltdowns**: an intense emotional outburst or breakdown, often triggered by sensory overload or emotional stress, often associated with autism.
- **Monotropism**: a way of cognitively experiencing the world with intense, sustained focus on one thing or limited interests, having a 'deep dive', 'all or nothing' attentional style. Immersing ourselves in this can sometimes be called a '**monotropic attention tunnel**', filtering out other stimuli.
- **Monotropic Split**: the painful experience of being

AuDHD A-Z: Key Terms

pulled out of intense focus, where sensory inputs that have been 'shut off' during deep concentration suddenly overwhelm an individual all at once, creating a jarring shift from calm to chaos.
- **Pebbling**: named after 'Penguin Pebbling', the act of sharing information or gifts with someone to display affection and connection.
- **Neurodivergent**: a person who thinks differently to '**neuronormative**' (i.e normal) standards. A group of people who think differently to one another are '**neurodiverse**'.
- **Nonspeaking autism**: an autistic individual who is minimally verbal (speaking fewer than 30 words), or doesn't speak at all.
- **Oppositional Defiance Disorder (ODD)**: a pattern of defiant, disobedient, and hostile behaviour towards authority figures.
- **Pathological Demand Avoidance (PDA)**: extreme avoidance of demands or expectations, often due to anxiety or a need for control.
- **Reasonable Adjustments**: changes that an organisation, such as an employer or school, is legally obligated to make to support a disabled individual. Also referred to as '**accommodations**'.
- **Rejection Sensitive Dysphoria (RSD)**: intense emotional pain or distress triggered by real or perceived rejection, usually lasting for a limited period of time.
- **Selective Mutism**: a clinically recognised anxiety condition where an individual may lose the ability to speak in certain situations, which is not within their control.
- **Shutdowns**: a response to overwhelm, where the person mentally "shuts down" and is unable to function or respond.
- **Stimming**: repetitive movements or behaviours, such

as hand flapping, used for sensory regulation or self-soothing.
- **Support needs**: typically relating to the level of support an individual may need to live independently, these may be referred to as 'high / level 1', 'medium / level 2', or 'low / level 3'.

Foreword

It takes a special combination of an interesting perspective and honest, real life reflections to maintain my own wandering attention, and this book had me hooked and engaged from beginning to end.

Leanne's incredible ability to help others feel understood and not alone through her writing pours through the pages as she weaves together her own AuDHD memoir with helpful information and advice.

This book is a generous offering of two books in one. The memoir sections are illuminating and fascinating and provide powerful self reflections via her own firsthand experiences. These sections are an emotional read at times and although everyone has their own unique lived experiences, they will give AuDHD readers a sense of being understood and united, which is a soothing balm to the inner turmoil and shame that can often be felt.

They will also give those who are supporting AuDHDers a true insight into the vulnerabilities and brilliance of this combined neurotype.

The memoir is then supported by informative sections on how AuDHD might impact many areas of life from childhood into adulthood. In true Leanne style, she leaves no stone unturned!

From education and employment to mental health and trauma, the information she shares helps readers make sense of what AuDHD is, the impact it might have and how to best support yourself and/or others as she coaches the reader through her tips.

This is a comprehensive and compassionate guide that shines a wonderful, rainbow coloured light on what it means to be an AuDHDer. It's an important gem of a book that I will be recommending to all of our clients.

I hope gets into the hands of many, as not only will it increase awareness and understanding but it will likely save some lives.

Dr Becky Quicke
Clinical Psychologist and Founder, Autistic Girls

Introduction

Warning: this book is not going the be the most cheerful one that you've ever read. It's not about how AuDHD is a 'superpower', but it's also not going to be the type of book that you could have just Googled.

That's probably an odd way to start off, but it feels only fair.

After being diagnosed as autistic last year, I was encouraged to write a 'guide' to AuDHD by people far more expert in these things than me. However, I didn't want to, at least not without sharing my story first. I coach people daily who are in the 'in-between' stages of figuring out whether they too, could be autistic and have ADHD.

As the two conditions have only been able to be diagnosed together since 2013, and accessing even one assessment is hard enough, the thought of navigating another can be extremely overwhelming. You absolutely do not have to have ADHD, be autistic, or anything else to read this book.

Instead of a 'how to thrive with AuDHD' guide, it's more of a 'you are not alone in your struggles' book, with the advice and information that I could have *really* used at the time. Essentially, it's an autobiography mixed with a 'stealth help' book of what **not** to do!

I'm extremely fortunate to be in a position to provide this advice, because I am ~~an AuDHD coach, have a law degree, National Specialist Coach of the Year, 4x best-selling author, trainer of 400+ ADHD coaches, founder, have been on tv,~~

~~presented to Directors of the World Health Organization~~ **alive to tell my story.**

I shouldn't be. As you will see, I have spent a lot of my life not wanting to be here. This is your **trigger warning**: this book talks about so many terrible things. From abuse, to trafficking (yes, literal trafficking), attempted kidnapping, depression, grooming, suicidal ideation, and the sheer state of support (or lack of it) available for neurodivergent people - it's quite dramatic.

If you're a parent, it's up to you whether you'd like to share it with your child, but I'd imagine there's far worse on the internet. I hope that this book can help them to see that they are not alone, whatever they might be facing right now, and can open up conversations between you that you may not have otherwise had.

This is because these topics are **so important to talk about**. They are the reality for so many AuDHD-ers who blame themselves for the failings of others, struggling in silence. I wish that I'd read this book when I was a teenager, to see how much better things can become with the right knowledge, support, and environment.

I have been very careful to edit my experiences to cause minimal damage, and have, if you can believe it, spared you from the very worst trauma of my life, but I have been honest. I have shared my experiences from being a little girl who hung upside from trees, to a grown woman wondering how her life ended up being like series 8 of a terrible TV show, completely out of control.

At the end of the day, I am just a human being, trying to make sense of my brain. The fact that you're reading this means you are **just as qualified to write your own book.** Nobody else has to read it, but this can be a great way to piece the puzzle of your life together.

Introduction

I am a female presenting, white woman, who can function relatively independently. My experiences will not cover the enormous range of differing experiences of AuDHD, such as those of transgender people, parenting, nonspeaking autistic people, or of people of a Global Majority background, and nor do they intend to.

I have done my best to make this as applicable to as many experiences as possible, but I am one perfectly imperfect person, who can only speak on behalf of herself. I am not a doctor, psychiatrist, therapist, psychologist, or academic researcher. Your experience is your experience. It is all completely valid, and your voice deserves to be heard, so please use it.

Truthfully, I am in a very privileged position that I never in a million years could have imagined when I was diagnosed with ADHD at the age of 25, 7 years ago. A woman at a school talk I once did exclaimed how I 'probably had a really good life growing up', and I burst out laughing.

I am (over)sharing my story with you because **you don't need to have had a good life in order to change it.** It's been incredibly lonely to grow up not knowing why I thought so differently to everybody else, or what was 'wrong with me', to the point that I have often wanted to end it.

This loneliness has given me a gift: the ability to make other people feel seen and validated, because I know the pain of not feeling as though you belong. If there's one thing I've learned from the 'better' years of my life, it's that **everybody struggles.**

It doesn't matter how famous or rich they are, how well their brain can meet neurotypical standards, what job they've got, or how happy they seem on social media. From the outside, my life has certainly appeared 'good', and this was the problem. I knew I 'should' be happy, but could never reach that point, feeling ungrateful and lazy. I just needed to 'pick something and stick to it', but this was impossible.

My life has almost certainly been very different to yours, but there's commonality in all of us, because we're all human. We've all had a childhood where we learned 'how to behave properly', gone through our standardised education system measuring our worth by how well we can regurgitate information, and tried to figure out what we're meant to be doing on this planet.

We've all felt the sting of rejection, compared ourselves to others, or experienced difficulties in life. However, the difference for AuDHD-ers, is that we so often grow up feeling 'broken' in some way, because we can't figure out how everybody seems so *normal*.

There are probably areas of this book that you don't agree with - and that's okay. We all think differently, after all! Feel free to drop me a message on *hello@adhdworks. info* if you'd like to raise these directly.

You can read this book **however you want to.** It's written in chronological order, but you don't have to start here. You can just take what you need from it, even if that's just using it as a coaster or laptop stand. Please don't beat yourself up for not reading it at all, or for not finishing. If you've read this far, that's enough.

It's a tough read at times, but if you stay around until the end, you'll see how much things can change. I am not a celebrity (although, very sadly, the world of LinkedIn might argue otherwise due to my current addiction), and I don't see myself as anything particularly 'special'.

However, I can say that for most of the time, I am happy, and incredibly grateful that I stuck around. Not because of the things I've gone on to 'achieve', but because I now understand how my brain works. I live a life that isn't constantly

Introduction

drowned out by a narrative of how stupid or lazy I am, but one where I am able to be kind to myself, most of the time.

I really hope that by reading this book, you can do the same. You deserve it.

If you'd like further support, I'd strongly recommend looking for an ADHD Works coach (although I am biased, as I trained them all!). They've been trained with the mindset and approaches throughout this book, on our Executive Functioning Coaching Framework, and as of April 2025, there'll be the training of the first **ever** cohort of AuDHD coaches. You can find a directory of coaches on www.adhdworks.info.

Finally, thank you. I know how hard it can be to read a book these days, especially if you're neurodivergent, and it means a lot that you've chosen to spend your valuable attention on this book.

Welcome to the chaos - I really hope you enjoy it.

1. What is AuDHD?

I'm Leanne, and I have AuDHD, which refers to the co-existence of Autism Spectrum Disorder (autism) and Attention Deficit Hyperactivity Disorder (ADHD) in the same brain.

You won't find AuDHD in any diagnostic or scientific manuals, because the two conditions have only been able to be diagnosed in the same person since 2013. Before then, it was only one or the other, despite significant cross-over in symptoms and co-occurrence rates, at approximately 50-70%[1].

Despite these similarities, these conditions are also extremely different from one another, like two opposing magnets in our brain, fighting for control.

It's extremely difficult to access an diagnostic assessment for one of these neurodevelopmental conditions, let alone both, with years-long waiting lists or private assessments costing thousands of pounds. This means that potentially millions of people have been failed by broken systems, going undiagnosed and unsupported.[2]

This also means that there's very little research on the co-occurrence of autism and ADHD. There's lots on both conditions, with a huge increase in recent years, as the

---
1 Hours, Recasens, and Baleyte, 'ASD and ADHD Comorbidity', https://www.ncbi.nlm.nih.gov/pmc/articles/PMC8918663/
2 You are perfectly entitled and encouraged to read this book, whether you're formally diagnosed with ADHD and/or autism, self-diagnosed, or 'normal', whatever that means.

numbers of adults seeking an ADHD assessment have risen by 400% since 2020, but not so much on them *together*.[3]

AuDHD can look very different from 'pure' ADHD or autism, and can be very difficult to untangle. Symptoms are often hidden under a lifetime of paradoxes, creative adjustments and masking, with certain traits showing up differently in different situations.

An individual may have traits of one or both conditions which could result in them meeting the clinical diagnostic criteria for a formal diagnosis - or not at all. Although neurodiversity is as natural as biodiversity, referring to the variations between all human brains, diagnostic criteria is man-made.

Humans aren't designed to fit neatly into boxes, and especially not outdated ones, which are largely based on presentations within little boys. However, there can still be great value in a label, even if self-appointed, as it can help us to understand ourselves and how we experience the world.

WHAT IS ADHD?

ADHD is a neurodevelopmental condition linked with symptoms of inattention, impulsivity, and hyperactivity, which can be external or internal. The diagnostic criteria requires a persistent pattern of symptoms of inattention, impulsivity and hyperactivity, which are present in two or more 'important' settings, such as home and school.

These symptoms need to result in a significant 'impairment' in a person's life, which is why not everybody has

---

[3] Topping, Alexandra. 'ADHD Services "Swamped", Say Experts as More UK Women Seek Diagnosis'. *The Guardian*, 13 January 2023, sec. Society. https://www.theguardian.com/society/2023/jan/13/adhd-services-swamped-say-experts-as-more-uk-women-seek-diagnosis.

ADHD, despite us all experiencing various challenges with attention. ADHD has only been diagnosable in adults since 2008 in the UK, and like autism, is often under-diagnosed in women and girls.

It's also linked with an approximately 30% developmental delay[4] in executive functioning skills, such as self-awareness, problem-solving, memory, emotional regulation, and motivation. This is why we may struggle to 'do what we know', despite our best efforts, and feel mentally younger than others our age. Autism is also strongly linked with differences in executive functioning skills, as both impact the pre-frontal cortex parts of our brains.

Hyperactivity

Despite the traditional association of ADHD with 'naughty little boys' disrupting classrooms, this hyperactivity may manifest internally and/or externally.

Internally, this mental hyperactivity may feel like having a brain with 500 radio stations playing at the same time. It can feel like having racing thoughts, *all of the time*, with a brain that will simply not be quiet. Having so many thoughts at the same time can translate to intense anxiety and overwhelm, which can also manifest as talking very quickly or excessively.

Externally, this physical hyperactivity may appear as physical restlessness, where we may feel as though we're being driven by a motor which makes us want to get up and walk around or fidget. It's like having a huge amount of electric energy in your body all of the time, which needs

---

[4] Petra, 'Developmental Delay, or Being a "Late Bloomer" - Implications for ADHD Across the Life Span' - https://www.petrahoggarth.co.nz/post/developmental-delay-or-being-a-late-bloomer-implications-for-adhd-across-the-life-span#:~:text=Using%20this%2030%25%20delay%2C%20a,a%2013%2Dyear%2Dold.

something to be done with it, resulting in intense discomfort if this isn't possible.

The benefits of this hyperactivity are having a huge amount of energy! If we have an environment where we can express ourselves fully, we can put this energy to extraordinary use, such as with me writing this book.

Impulsivity

The impulsivity associated with ADHD can feel like having a brain that acts before thinking. We may do or say things without knowing why, or wanting to. I've heard that 'most' people have the ability to think about what they say before the words come out of their mouth, which sounds like a wonderful skill to have.

This can make us very vulnerable to exploitation, danger, and decisions that we may later regret, such as quitting jobs or ending relationships. It's associated with challenges in time perception, experiencing time as 'now or not now'. We may also experience emotional dysregulation due to this impulsivity, not realising how we're feeling until it builds up and explodes through impulsive actions.

At the same time, our impulsivity can also make us brave, innovative, and creative. We might join up dots others can't see, acting on our 'wild' ideas before having the time to think them through fully and talk ourselves out of it! This is likely a contributing factor of why people with ADHD are 300% more likely to start their own business - we see beyond the status quo.[5]

Inattention

ADHD is linked with an intense difficulty with concentrating, and having a short attention span. This can lead us

---

[5] 'The DaVinci Method' by Garret LoPorto, 2005

to have 'monkey brains', jumping between thoughts like a monkey hopping from one tree branch to another without stopping, which can make things like listening or focusing very difficult.

However, ADHD isn't a *deficit* of attention as much as a challenge of *regulating* it. We're said to have interest based nervous systems, which means we're motivated by interest, not importance, as neurotypical people are.[6] This can result in struggles with delayed gratification, and the ability to hyper-focus on areas involving personal interest, novelty, or adrenaline.

We may find tasks very difficult that others find 'easy', such as cooking and administrative tasks. It may be difficult to get started on, or to complete tasks, depending on our level of interest. We may be great at the first 75%, but struggle significantly with the last 25%!

If we're in environments where our interest based nervous system is supported, then we can achieve extraordinary results. Understanding and accepting our challenges enables us to implement support for them, which will look different for each person.

WHAT IS AUTISM?

Autism is a neurodevelopmental condition affecting how individuals perceive and interact with the world around them. The diagnostic criteria includes 'impairments' in social interactions, social communication, and restricted and repetitive patterns of behaviour, interests, or activities. Symptoms need to be present from early childhood.

The 'impairment' aspect of these diagnostic criteria's are dubious, because they're ultimately based on neurotypical

---

6 ADDitude. 'ADHD & the Interest-Based Nervous System', 13 February 2018. https://www.additudemag.com/adhd-brain-chemistry-video/

standards, such as equating eye contact with being polite! Personally, I don't see my AuDHD traits as 'impairments', or 'deficits' - they are just part of who I am.

Just like ADHD, autism is a highly individual and situational condition, with traits significantly varying in impact. It's a 'spectrum' condition *once you are on the spectrum*. People are not a 'little bit' autistic - as with ADHD, these are distinct conditions that people are born with. Every individual will have their own unique presentation of symptoms and experiences of autism, ADHD, and/or both (potentially as well as other conditions!).

Social interactions & communication

Autistic people may experience differences in social interactions and communication in a range of ways. We may struggle with interpreting and reciprocating social cues like facial expressions or body language, making it difficult to understand others' intentions or emotions. We may take language literally and be very direct or literal with others, resulting in misunderstandings.

We may not perceive or connect with social relationships in the same ways as others. For example, this could include differences in how we make or keep friendships, handle periods of unstructured time and make eye contact.

Empathy is commonly stereotyped as lacking in autistic people, but some people may often experience the opposite - hyper-empathy, feeling the emotions of others. These differences are related to the 'double empathy problem', which essentially means that there's a mismatch in empathy between people who have very different ways of experiencing the world.[7]

---

[7] 'The Double Empathy Problem' - https://www.autism.org.uk/advice-and-guidance/professional-practice/double-empathy

This can also manifest through our communication styles, such as by not engaging in verbal communication or flapping our hands when speaking to others. We may be very interested in certain topics and want to connect over these as opposed to making small talk, seeking deep and meaningful interactions.

These differences can make autistic people very vulnerable to exploitation and misunderstandings with others, resulting in intense loneliness. Social connection is a core need for human beings, but our needs may not always align with what's considered 'normal' by our society.

This is ironic, given the honesty and clarity that accompanies these differences. Social norms are often founded on unwritten rules, but having these clearly established benefits everybody, in addition to a world where we all say exactly what we mean, instead of expecting people to be able to read our minds.

Restricted and repetitive patterns of behaviour, interests, or activities

Autistic people may experience the world through self-imposed 'rules', struggling significantly with a lack of structure or certainty, often being driven by intense anxiety. This can manifest as a strong preference for certain routines, such as eating the same foods, which can result in extreme distress if disrupted.

Whilst many autistic people find comfort in strict routines and repetitive behaviours, not all of these are equally beneficial. Some may involve positive habits, such as exercising, providing an outlet for sensory overload and anxiety.

Others may be more challenging, or harmful. For example, the fear of making mistakes can result in extreme perfectionism, or internalised behaviours could result in self-harm as a way to cope with overwhelming emotions.

We may also experience intense focus on specific topics, which contrary to stereotypes, don't have to be niche! The difference is in how *intense* our focus is, despite these often being referred to as 'Special Interests'. This is linked to differing attentional styles, such as the ability to only focus on one topic at a time, and struggling with interruptions, which could also manifest emotionally.

These ways of existing can come with significant strengths, such as deep concentration, strong attention to detail, and incredible expertise in certain areas. We tend to be extremely resilient, given how much energy it takes to manage this on a day to day basis, and can experience immense joy in our routines and interests.

Sensory sensitivity

Autistic people may be over or under sensitive to how they perceive and experience the world. This can mean everyday sensory inputs, such as sounds, lights, textures, or smells, can feel overwhelming or painful. These sensory needs may differ between senses, even within the same person. For example, I become extremely overwhelmed in social situations, but also seek out strong sensory experiences.

What may be a minor annoyance for some people can cause significant distress for autistic people, such as the feeling of labels on our clothes. I also believe emotional sensitivity is relevant here, as many autistic people may struggle with identifying or feeling their emotions, unless these are extreme, or delayed processing. Heightened sensitivity to justice and fairness is commonly seen within both ADHD and autism.

When we're unable to cope, we may find it impossible to regulate our emotions. External manifestations could include shouting, crying, or throwing objects, which is often known as a 'meltdown'. Internally, this could involve being unable to communicate or engage with others, resulting in overwhelming feelings that could involve suicidal ideation, often referred to as a 'shutdown'. Autistic people are up to 7 times more likely to die by suicide than the general population.[8]

These differences can be very difficult to live with, but can also bring great joy and unique perspectives. For example, we may notice details in our environment that others overlook, such as the unique tones in a piece of music.

WHAT IS NEURODIVERSITY?

As ADHD and autism are neurodevelopmental, they typically manifest during early development and are present from birth, lasting throughout life. Essentially, they affect the way our brain works - we just have different operating systems to 'most' people, but this doesn't make them wrong.

These are fundamental, natural differences in brain functions, as opposed to being illnesses that can be 'treated' or 'fixed'. As a result, these people are termed as 'neurodivergent', because their brain wiring diverges from those which are able to meet the neuronormative (i.e. 'normal') standards imposed by our society.

Living in a world designed for people who have a 'typical' brain structure, referred to as 'neurotypical', can be very difficult. As both conditions are rooted in differences in brain structure, they're just part of who we are, like the colour of our eyes. However, just as we can get glasses if we're

---

[8] Susan, Willgoss. 'Suicide and Autism, a National Crisis.' - https://www.rcpsych.ac.uk/docs/default-source/improving-care/nccmh/suicide-prevention/workshops-(wave-4)/wave-4-workshop-2/suicide-and-autism---slides.pdf?sfvrsn=bf3e0113_2#:~:text=Population%2Dwide%20studies%20in%20the,autistic%20people%20without%20intellectual%20disability.

struggling to see, support can be very helpful for those experiencing difficulties as a result of the neuronormative society we live in.

Challenging ADHD *symptoms* can be improved with medication, because ADHD involves certain neurotransmitters. The medication works by adjusting the levels of these neurotransmitters, helping to improve focus, attention, and impulse control - but it doesn't change the structure of the brain.

In contrast, autism doesn't primarily involve a specific neurotransmitter imbalance that can be targeted by medication. This is because it affects social communication, sensory processing, and behaviour patterns rooted in brain structure.

Unfortunately, both conditions are characterised by 'deficits', 'impairments', and 'disorders'. This framing makes it unlikely that children who internalise their symptoms, often due to societal conditioning, will be diagnosed. Given the difficulty in accessing an assessment for even one of these conditions, the reality is that many neurodivergent people, especially women and girls conditioned to be 'good', go undetected and unsupported.

Until the internal experience becomes visible externally, these people are unlikely to receive understanding or support for how their brains work. No amount of conditioning or 'telling off' will enable them to change their brain structure.

Now, consider why zebras haven't been domesticated like horses, despite their physical similarities and the fact that both belong to the Equidae family. Horses have a more hierarchical structure that humans were able to tap into, allowing them to 'break in' horses, establishing a clear leadership dynamic. In contrast, zebras have a looser herd structure, meaning that they do not naturally submit to authority or follow a leader as easily.

Zebras are also much harder to control than horses because they evolved in environments with a high density of predators. This led to the development of intense survival instincts, such as a strong flight response. In comparison, horses faced fewer predators, resulting in less extreme survival behaviours. Ultimately, zebras are wired for constant self-preservation, making them resistant to domestication - or our human society's standards.

Just as zebras are more likely to be considered 'bad' at conforming to these standards, neurodivergent people will struggle to fit into conventional societal norms. Imagine a zebra growing up in a herd of horses, unaware of its distinct wiring; it's easy to see how challenges, often labelled as 'deficits', might arise.

The pressure to conform to standards we will never be able to meet due to uncontrollable factors that aren't our fault can result in misunderstanding and under-appreciation of our inherent strengths and differences. This pressure is what turns creative zebra children into repressed horse adults, who despite the best effort of those around them, cannot be broken in. To me, this is a sign of strength.

WHAT IS AUDHD?

Instead of a horse or zebra, imagine a unicorn. Not quite a horse or a zebra, but also a mystical creature that doesn't quite fit in anywhere, one that most people don't believe in. You shine with creativity and innovation, but are deeply misunderstood. Showing your true self is likely to confuse others, who doubt your reality.

You try to fit in, but despite your best efforts, always feel a little bit 'too much'. Your complexity and magic is all rolled up into one horn, bang in the middle of your head, but this seems to be invisible to everybody else.

AuDHD: Blooming Differently

Autism and ADHD are highly distinct conditions, so living with both can be extremely challenging - and extremely magical. It's a lifetime of constant contradictions, which nobody else can see.

ADHD thrives on novelty and seeks out new experiences, often leading to boredom, while autism needs routine and consistency, resisting change. ADHD can mean missing details in tasks, whereas autism may be hyper-aware of them.

ADHD experiences time as 'now or not now', struggling with perceiving time and planning ahead, whereas autism needs to be exactly on time, sticking to schedules. ADHD often feels under-stimulated, craving sensory input, while autism can feel overwhelmed by sensory experiences.

ADHD seeks stimulation from others, whereas autism requires solitude to recharge. ADHD wants to try everything, moving on to new interests quickly, autism wants to deeply immerse themselves in special interests.

ADHD thrives on risk-taking and impulsivity, whereas autism requires logic and caution. ADHD thrives in mess and chaos, autism needs organisation and structure. ADHD says yes, autism says no.

If you're exhausted reading this, just imagine what it's like to live it.

People often discover that they're autistic after finding out that they have ADHD. This is because supporting ADHD symptoms, such as with medication, means that the autism traits which may have been deeply hidden can appear.

For me, AuDHD feels like half of my brain is wildly trying to escape the other half, which just wants to figure out the rules and fit in. Together, they can be intensely stressful to manage, but with understanding and acceptance, they also offer the strengths and benefits of both - a unicorn brain.

What is AuDHD?

Tips: AuDHD-ers

- If you're exploring AuDHD, be kind to yourself and recognise that there are no 'right' answers. If traits resonate with you, this is valid - you don't need a formal medical diagnosis.

- Remember that AuDHD doesn't change who you are, although it might feel like a whole new identity!

- Give yourself time and space to process and explore AuDHD and what this means to you - your experience will be unique to you.

- Question what you would do if you had a formal diagnosis, and how things might be different. You can start now by understanding yourself and making any necessary changes.

- Remember that autism and ADHD share a lot of symptoms and ultimately involve man-made, outdated diagnostic criteria. Don't stress yourself out trying to pick these apart!

- Research credible resources that resonate with you and your experiences, to learn more.

- Seek out support from people you trust, such as family, friends, or professionals such as AuDHD therapists or coaches.

- Join a support group where you can meet others who have had similar experiences.

- If you're in the UK and are self/employed, apply for Access to Work, which can fund support such as coaching. This doesn't require a formal diagnosis.

Tips: loved ones

- Practice patience, compassion, and non-judgement. The AuDHD experience can be very overwhelming to navigate, and supporting your loved one throughout with validation and collaboration is extremely important.

- Remember that your loved one is simply who they are - not a label or condition.

- Respect their preferences, including their curiosity about AuDHD, recognising that these labels can be extremely helpful to process their experiences and understand who they are.

- Encourage open communication, asking open-ended questions about their experiences with an intention to learn. Check in on them regularly, as this can be an overwhelming process.

- Try to avoid sharing your own judgements or opinions, unless asked for, especially around sensitive topics such as medication.

- Remember that your loved one will be unlikely to be able to explain AuDHD to you, especially at first. They are not medical professionals, and they're probably trying to understand it themselves.

2. Childhood

MY EXPERIENCE

As a child, I felt like a selfish, attention-seeking drama queen. My favourite hobbies included sliding down the bannisters, hanging upside down from the apple tree in the garden, and climbing up door frames. I quickly learned that these were 'wrong', often finding myself in trouble for reasons I couldn't understand.

For example, one Christmas, I opened all of my presents at 6am. I excitedly thanked my relatives when they woke up hours later, and couldn't understand why I was suddenly being told off. All month, I had been told I had to wait until Christmas Day to open my presents, which is what I did. I didn't understand why other people needed to watch me open them, especially as the presents were supposed to be for me, not them.

I also learned that the way I expressed myself verbally, as well as physically, was wrong. I spent hours in a speech and language therapist's office, trying to get rid of my lisp and mumbled speech, feeling like it was utterly pointless.

I felt extremely misunderstood, finding solace in books, and writing my own versions in the back pages. These books became an escape from real life, where I could create my own world, with a sense of certainty.

In my early years of education, I was laughed at for reading in the playground, but I couldn't figure out what

Childhood

else I was supposed to do during this unstructured time, filled with overwhelming noises.

The thought of strolling up to someone and assuming they'd like to hang out with me felt impossible, and I'd often end up reading in a bathroom cubicle to pass the time. However, this was also very stressful, as others started to make awkward comments about what I was doing in there for so long.

At one point, I had scabs on my shoulders from falling over, which a girl demanded to eat, saying she'd pull them off if I didn't, so I handed them over. I'd assumed that this transaction had made us friends, joking that I'd always remember her due to the still present scars on my shoulders.

So, during the next break time, I tried to talk to her, but she didn't respond. I thought maybe she didn't hear me, so I waved my hand in front of her face, and she bit it. With teeth marks etched onto my hand, and blood oozing out, I asked the teacher if I could go home, hoping this qualified me as 'sick'.

The teacher was horrified, and asked who had done it. The girl was suspended, and I felt incredibly guilty, not meaning to get her into trouble. I didn't even realise that she had been bullying me.

Other children expressed their dislike for me more clearly, taunting me for having 'yellow' skin, a lisp, and for being tall. I couldn't figure out what I was supposed to do about these things, or why this seemed to be a problem.

Eventually, I made some friends by studying and copying the behaviours of 'popular' kids, applying the same conversation strategies to others who were also being bullied. I realised that I only really needed 'one' friend, which would provide someone to sit with in class, although I was conscious that they weren't helping my popularity.

My time outside of school was dedicated to figuring out how to be 'cool'. I'd listen to the radio obsessively to try and understand what kind of music was popular, and pored over magazines to learn what clothes were fashionable, begging my parents to buy me a whole new identity.

I tried to make face-masks out of butter and sugar, making my face break out into spots. I cut my hair with scissors, leaving an awkward sprout at the top of my forehead, meaning I had to get a fringe. At one point, I was obsessed with trying to make sure there were never any bumps in my hair, wetting it down in the bathroom at school, only to return to a laughing classroom.

At home, I found companionship in our pet chickens. It was my responsibility to feed them, until one morning, when they escaped. They would usually return back into the pen after dark, but that day, everyone was leaving the house. When I got home, I raced down to the chicken pen only to trip over one, which was now headless. A fox had taken the others and left that one for later.

I felt overwhelming grief, shame, and guilt. I was unable to get the image of the headless chicken out of my head, believing that I was a murderer and a terrible person, so no wonder no one wanted to be my friend. I often sat by the front door, crying and rocking in a ball, trying to will myself to run away to create a new identity. I'd stare at the golden metal handle for hours, but I couldn't do it.

This was mainly because I believed that that men would hurt me if I went out alone. I picked this up from hearing about the kidnapping and murders of children my age on the radio, which terrified me. I became terrified of white vans, feeling frozen with fear whenever anyone happened to pass by when I was out.

I took a knife to bed in case one broke in, keeping it under the pillow my head rested on every night. I struggled to get to sleep due to my intrusive thoughts about somebody breaking into the house, and usually woke up due to nightmares. Then, I'd go out of my bedroom to sit at the top of the stairs whilst everybody was asleep, curled into a ball for hours, hyper-aware of every sound, terrifying myself with imaginary scenarios.

In the daytime, I was obsessed with trying to turn off the explosion of thoughts constantly invading my brain. I didn't understand how I was supposed to be 'happy' or 'good' when there were no clear instructions. I'd often sit outside doors to listen to conversations, trying to understand how I could change myself to fit in.

However, everyone and everything seemed to have conflicting messages, and I felt like the problem for not being 'normal'. I turned to the media, becoming obsessed with magazines filled with messages about how being 'fat' was the worst thing anybody could be, even celebrities. As a result, I developed intense eating disorders, terrified of my body changing.

These unhealthy behaviours turned into self-harm, as I tried to cut myself with a maths compass, having seen this in a movie. At one point, I found some tablets, and tried to overdose, but woke up the next morning, frustrated that I couldn't even do that right.

I was an expert at hiding how hard I was working to be 'normal', scared of giving anybody even more reasons not to like me. Even so, anger would often hit me unpredictably, and I'd act in ways I couldn't control, such as once tipping a bowl of tomatoes over a family member's head as they watched television, staining the new cream carpet.

My brain and body felt like a trap that I couldn't get out of. All that appeared externally was a little girl, but inside, it felt like I was a monster.

The AuDHD Lens

As ADHD and autism are neurodevelopmental conditions that people are born with, symptoms may become apparent in early childhood. For example, we may not hit developmental milestones, such as speaking or walking at a certain age, and struggle to interpret social cues such as facial expressions.

The co-existence of both means that these may interlink, such as impulsive, 'naughty' behaviour masking the underlying causes of anxiety. We may not develop the social tools to express this, or to be able to identify that it's not 'normal' to struggle so much with the world around us.

It's unfortunate that our society holds even babies to these standards from such a young age, which parents may understandably feel very anxious about. Parents obviously want their children to be happy and healthy, and their failure to meet certain expectations so early on can be concerning.

However, it's important not to project this onto the children themselves - they're just different, not broken. Our society doesn't acknowledge our unique strengths early on, just whether we can meet the pre-defined standard of 'normal'.

As young children tend to be less self-aware and commonly engage in 'parallel play' alongside, instead of with each other, AuDHD symptoms may also be less evident at this stage. Their repetition of words (known as 'echolalia') or discomfort with changes to routine, such as going to nursery, may be viewed as normal experiences, rather than related to AuDHD.

This is particularly so if one or both parents have undiagnosed autism, ADHD, or AuDHD themselves, seeing their traits

Childhood

as normal. The heritability rate of both ADHD[9] and autism has been estimated to be 80%[10], with a strong genetic link.

'Naughty' Behaviour

AuDHD symptoms may become more apparent in the ways that children begin to engage with the world, such as by showing limited interest in social interaction. This shows their independence, and isn't necessarily a bad thing, but our society may argue otherwise.

Differences may become more apparent as expectations of reciprocal behaviour are placed on children, such as waiting to take turns during conversations. They might not respond when spoken to, due to audio processing differences, or find following social 'rules' confusing, such as having to ask to go to the bathroom. They may also experience sensory and emotional dysregulation that could arise through various forms such as bedwetting or aggression.

Pathological Demand Avoidance

'Naughty' behaviour is especially likely if a child experiences Pathological Demand Avoidance (PDA), as coined by psychologist Elisabeth Newson. This involves a persistent and marked resistance to everyday demands, driven by anxiety and a desire for autonomy. This avoidance can apply even to simple tasks, like brushing our teeth - which I rarely did throughout my childhood.

PDA isn't clinically recognised, but is an experience recognised by many people in reality. It's said to be a lifelong

---

[9] 'Is Autism Genetic? | Autism Speaks'. Accessed 2 February 2025. https://www.autismspeaks.org/science-news/autism-genetic.

[10] Grimm, Kranz and Reif - 'Genetics of ADHD: What Should the Clinical Know?' https://pmc.ncbi.nlm.nih.gov/articles/PMC7046577/#:~:text=The%20formal%20heritability%20of%20ADHD,mechanisms%20explain%20this%20huge%20difference

condition[11], and can be extremely difficult to live with, as we battle against ourselves for reasons we don't understand.

Oppositional Defiance Disorder

Oppositional Defiance Disorder (ODD) is a condition that is seen in 55-90% of people with autism and ADHD combined.[12] This includes a frequent and ongoing pattern of anger, irritability or vindictiveness, in addition to arguing and defiance towards parents and other authority figures, including seeking revenge.[13]

This can be diagnosed in children and adolescents, but can continue into adulthood without support. ODD is said to involve 'deliberate' attempts to annoy or defy others, often limited to specific people or places, whilst PDA stems from an intense desire for personal control in all areas of life.

Emotional Dysregulation

The emotional regulation differences in AuDHD-ers may result in extreme challenges, which may begin to present during childhood.

We may experience anxiety on a near-constant basis, due to overwhelm from processing the world around us. This can mean that we're often in survival mode, automatically reacting with 'fight, flight, freeze, or fawn' responses to our internal and external experiences.

---

[11] LCSW, Alex Bachert, Adrienne Duhon. 'Differences between PDA and ODD & 7 Ways to Offer Support'. Rula, 6 September 2024. https://www.rula.com/blog/pda-odd/
[12] https:Mayes, Susan D., Sara K. Pardej, and Daniel A. Waschbusch. 'Oppositional Defiant Disorder in Autism and ADHD'. *Journal of Autism and Developmental Disorders*, 27 July 2024. https://doi.org/10.1007/s10803-024-06437-9
[13] https://www.rula.com/blog/pda-odd/#:~:text=Extreme%20Demand%20Avoidance%20Questionnaire%E2%80%99%20(EDA%2DQ)

Alexithymia

Alexithymia is a term loosely translated to 'no words for emotion', which means we may struggle to feel, process, or identify our feelings - but we do have them. If we can't feel them, we can't regulate them, and distress within the environment may build up without us realising, resulting in a very painful explosion. When combined with the impulsivity of ADHD, this can be extremely dangerous, as we become incredibly overwhelmed.

This may become complicated if an AuDHD-er experiences 'hyper-empathy', where we may experience how *other* people feel so intensely that it becomes overwhelming, placing their needs ahead of our own. In contrast, some AuDHD-ers may also be unable to imagine themselves having somebody else's experiences at all, which can cause different ways of responding than may be expected.

Teaching children about emotions and helping them to identify how these come up for them is important, recognising and validating that this may not reflect 'normal' experiences.

Rejection Sensitive Dysphoria

'Rejection Sensitive Dysphoria' (RSD) is a non-clinical experience commonly associated with ADHD, although every AuDHD-er I've worked with has recognised this within themselves. Coined by Dr William Dodson, RSD is said to be extreme emotional pain at real or perceived rejection, lasting for a set period of time.[14]

It can be so painful that suicidal ideation may occur. For me, it's an invalidation of my own feelings, often triggered

---
14   Dodson, William - 'Emotional Regulation and ADHD' - CHADD - https://chadd.org/wp-content/uploads/2016/10/ATTN_10_16_EmotionalRegulation.pdf

by something 'small' such as believing that someone doesn't like me. This can quickly spiral into a tornado, where I extend this belief to everybody I know!

This may be complicated by autism, such as assuming that we need to be explicitly invited to social gatherings when in groups, even though the intention may have been to include everybody. As a result, we may consistently engage in the 'fawn' survival response, engaging in people pleasing behaviours and hiding or ignoring our own needs in the hope of avoiding rejection.

Simply knowing about RSD can be enormously helpful, as it can enable people to identify warning signs, and when it's happening. This validation of their own experiences can enable them to distance themselves from their thoughts, calming the tornado and emerging from the survival state of fear.

With this regulation, they can then challenge these thoughts, or engaging in healthy coping strategies such as doing an immersive activity such as watching a movie.

The intense feelings may pass within a few hours, days, or even weeks, but it's important that AuDHD-ers are reminded that these are temporary and normal, with communication lines kept open.

Meltdowns

Meltdowns are a common experience for AuDHD-ers, often mistaken for tantrums. They may occur due to overwhelm, such as high demand from our environments, such as sensory overload or experiencing change. They can also be related to our basic needs, such as being overtired or in pain, often resulting from a build up of factors.

These are external manifestations, which may be expressed verbally (e.g crying or shouting) physically, (e.g kicking or punching) or a mixture of both. For example, 68% of autistic

Childhood

children and teenagers have been found to have displayed aggression to a caregiver.[15]

I think of meltdowns as the manifestation of the 'fight' survival response. They aren't intentional or controllable - they're an inability to cope. They are not a choice, but unimaginably intense and painful experiences where we are unable to express ourselves another way.

Similarly to RSD, labels can be very helpful for us to identify and process our experiences. It can be helpful to talk about these, in identifying warning signs for an individual, such as repetitive questioning or pacing.

To help someone experiencing a meltdown, it's important to try and avoid judging them, regulating your own emotions first. Providing reassurance, letting them know that you're there for them, avoiding asking questions, advising, or restrictive methods, such as removing privileges can help.

Physical restraint should obviously be avoided wherever possible, unless it is absolutely the only way to keep a person safe, including yourself. Creating a safe, calm environment without overwhelm can give an individual space and time to recover.

Discussing this with an AuDHD-er is crucial, as it normalises their experiences and enables you to collaboratively create a safety plan, such as identifying triggers and practical strategies that help them. These will be different for everybody, so it's important that a plan is tailored to the individual, as we may not be able to follow a 'typical' one!

Shutdowns

Similarly to meltdowns, shutdowns are typically triggered by stress, sensory or informational overload, but occurring

---

15   Kanne S.M. and M.O. Mazurek J. *Autism Dev. Disord.* 41, 926-937 (2011) PubMed

internally. I think of this as the 'freeze' survival response, where we can become withdrawn, unresponsive, dissociative, or numb to our environment. People experiencing a shutdown are not sulking or being emotionally manipulative - they cannot control it.

We may experience Selective Mutism (SM), which is a clinically recognised anxiety condition commonly co-occurring alongside autism. Around 70% of children with SM may also meet the diagnostic criteria for ASD, although less than 1% of children are currently diagnosed with SM.[16] We may lose the ability to speak in certain situations, such as during a shutdown, which is not within our control.

This is temporary, and not the same as general verbal difficulties which may occur with autism. For example, 25-30% of autistic children are said to be minimally verbal (speaking fewer than 30 words), or don't speak at all - this is often referred to as 'nonspeaking autism'.[17]

Other signs of a shutdown could include wanting to hide, a complete loss of energy, and an inability to make decisions. We may struggle to regulate our emotions or body temperature, feeling like our brain is on fire. Warning signs may include heightened anxiety, and finding it difficult to speak or think clearly.

Similarly to meltdowns, it's advisable to explain to AuDHD-ers what shutdowns are if they don't already know, learning about their particular experiences, triggers, and needs. This enables you to create a safety plan, including if this isn't something they typically experience, helping to provide a sense of certainty for if it does.

---

16 Children with autism spectrum disorders and selective mutism (Steffenburg et al., 2018)
17 Brignell, Chenausky, Song, Zhu, Suo & Morgan - 4/11/18 - Cochrane Library https://www.cochranelibrary.com/cdsr/doi/10.1002/14651858.CD012324.pub2/full

A person experiencing a shutdown will need a quiet, safe space to recover. Matching your energy to the person will enable you to co-regulate, and reassuring them that this is okay to experience, and will pass, is key. Expecting the individual to be able to control these uncontrollable experiences, or blaming them, will only make it worse.

Augmentative and Alternative Communication methods (AAC) may be extremely helpful for AuDHD-ers who can only or prefer to communicate non-verbally, including during shutdowns. This could include using visual supports, such as picture exchange systems, sign language, or writing, for example.

AAC can be tailored to the individual's needs and preferences, which can be extremely beneficial if their use is normalised in day-to-day life for AuDHD-ers - I much prefer to communicate by writing than speaking!

It's important to remember that emotional dysregulation is not intentional, whether it occurs in AuDHD children or adults. Creating low-demand environments and flexibility, presenting tasks as choices, with a collaborative, fun approach can be extremely helpful. For example, instead of telling a child to brush their teeth, you could say, 'shall we brush your teeth before or after the bath?'.

As parents, you can also model emotional regulation and share your feelings with your child. These may often be hidden or repressed, but helping your child to see that you understand how they feel, and have adapted your behaviour to cope, is key. You don't need to have experienced AuDHD, RSD or PDA to do this - we all have feelings!

Environment

It can be very difficult to adapt to one environment from a sensory perspective, so change and transitions can be extremely difficult to manage, especially if unpredictable. As a result, AuDHD symptoms may become more apparent as a child's environment changes, such as moving from primary to secondary school.

As we are constantly experiencing and processing our environment in multiple ways, these needs can be difficult to identify. They are limitless, including potential reactions to certain lights, sounds, textures, experiences and people.

For example, AuDHD children may experience hyper-sensitivity to certain experiences, such as textures of food. This can emerge as Avoidant / Restrictive Food Intake Disorder (ARFID), seeing children avoid certain foods or types of food.

They may experience overwhelm in certain situations without understanding why, such as whilst grocery shopping. The noise, temperature, and high potential of getting lost in a supermarket can be extremely stressful for an AuDHD-er.

These needs may also arise in relation to clothes, especially if they have to wear school uniform. The clothes labels or textures that feel imperceptible to 'most' children may feel overwhelmingly painful for an AuDHD-er, causing constant distress throughout the day.

Understanding AuDHD can help adults to accept these sensory differences and figure out tailored strategies to change the environment, instead of their child. Being able to explain the purpose behind certain environmental expectations in an accessible way, such as the point of eating vegetables, can help children with collaboratively identifying solutions.

Accepting and helping your child to identify the 'why' behind their discomfort, without their having to justify it - such as texture or lighting, for example - can also result in strategies to meet their needs. It can also be helpful to share your own experiences as a parent, to model how you would adapt to certain situations, and demonstrating that they are not alone.

Sensory differences may also arise as hypo-sensitivity, resulting in an under-sensation to certain experiences. For example, I was often seeking out strong sensory experiences as a child, such as hanging upside down and wrapping myself up in our long velvet curtains.

This can be concerning for parents who don't understand the reasons behind their child seeking such extreme experiences, which may also pose a risk to themselves and/or others. For example, we may be climbing onto high surfaces, hanging upside down, or putting ourselves in danger in other ways.

Taking a compassionate and collaborative approach can help to work with the AuDHD, instead of against it. Understanding their own neurodivergence can empower them to take responsibility for this, becoming more aware of their own vulnerabilities, tendencies, and needs.

Sensory needs are not preferences - they are needs. They aren't choices, and there's no 'one size fits all' approach that will work for everybody. Children who are supported to identify and advocate for their needs early on will be able to meet these as they develop, benefitting everybody.

Telling a child about AuDHD

As parents, it can be confusing to know whether to tell a child about their neurological differences. Many decide not to out of fear of 'labelling' or limiting their child with a condition, but these are ultimately words to help them better understand their experiences.

Education is empowering, and information about ourselves provides a 'reason' for us feeling different from others.

AuDHD: Blooming Differently

However, it can also feel challenging when you don't fully understand conditions like autism or ADHD, or how these interlink, which isn't your fault.

Finding age-appropriate ways to communicate these differences to your child, with or without a diagnosis, is ultimately up to you. Personally, it would have saved me a lifetime of feeling broken if I had known I was neurodivergent during my childhood.

It's understandable to feel as though these conditions may cause a child to hold themselves back from trying, but they can also give them the tools to understand how to reach their full potential. Using metaphors can be very useful, such as by referring to operating systems like Apple vs Google.[18]

Professionals can also help with this, such as specialist therapists and coaches. Having coached many AuDHD children myself, I've seen first-hand how empowering it's been for them to have someone they can relate to, who can help them to reframe their neurodivergence in an empowering and positive light. However, it's very important to fully vet anybody working with children, such as by requesting a DBS certificate and references.

Ultimately, to support a child who may be AuDHD, my best advice is to accept them as they are, and collaborate with them as a team. Sharing information isn't limiting - it is empowering.

---

18   Here's a template of a presentation I've used to explain ADHD to primary school children: https://www.canva.com/design/DAF9WSRVPEA/6B_SAs6UyvtSwwYLE7FJUQ/view?utm_content=DAF9WSRVPEA&utm_campaign=designshare&utm_medium=link&utm_source=publishsharelink&mode=preview

Childhood

Tips: AuDHD-ers

- Explore your own strengths and challenges, including how these may show / have shown up in childhood, and the impact this has had on you.

- Map out your needs and preferences, identifying areas of particular challenge or difficulty. Being as specific as possible can help to establish tailored strategies that can help.

- Remember that AuDHD isn't a bad thing - it's simply the way your brain works. It's not your fault, and there are great strengths and benefits, along with challenges.

- Focus on your strengths and interests, identifying things you like to do, even if these feel unusual. If you're an adult, reflecting on what you enjoyed as a child can be very helpful to connect back to this part of yourself.

- Create a self-care toolkit, identifying tools that can support you when you're feeling overwhelmed. For example, this might include sensory soothers such as noise-cancelling headphones, breathing techniques, or movement breaks.

- Set boundaries to protect your energy, such as by limiting the number of social engagements you attend in a week.

- Create a plan for emotional regulation challenges, such as soothing activities and space to decompress.

- Try to connect with other neurodivergent people your age, who can help you to understand yourself better and validate your experiences.

- Be kind to yourself, and remember that your differences are your strengths!

- Remember that you are not alone, and neurodivergence is nothing to be ashamed of. Your brain works the way it's supposed to!

Tips: loved ones

- Learn about AuDHD, and how this presents in a child who may be displaying symptoms.

- Help your loved one to understand their own challenges and strengths, potentially within the context of AuDHD and neurodivergence.

- Work with other adults to collaboratively identify solutions, involving the child in these conversations as much as possible.

- Engage in open conversations with your child about their experiences, whilst sharing your own that may resonate.

- Explain the reasoning behind certain requests or decisions, enabling the child to feel in control.

Childhood

- Remind your loved one that they are always loved unconditionally, and AuDHD is just a part of who they are - it doesn't define them.

- Remember that the child is not 'broken' or 'disordered' - their brain simply works differently, and that's okay.

- Try to accept the child's experiences and needs without requiring them to justify this, acknowledging their experiences and equipping them with language to use in the future.

- Remember that you're doing your best, and are likely not a medical professional - or superhero! It's okay to get things wrong, but it's not a reflection on you or your abilities.

- Help your loved one to see and use their strengths, encouraging their interests and the things that bring them joy.

- When faced with challenges, try to adopt a coaching approach to collaboratively identify specific needs and preferences, establishing tailored strategies and boundaries to support your loved one.

- Identify areas of challenge, such as shopping, and try to interlink these with areas of enjoyment.

- Ensure that your loved one has space to adjust and adapt to any changes or difficulties.

AuDHD: Blooming Differently

- Remind your child regularly that they are loved and matter, and that you're on their side no matter what.

- Create a plan for emotional regulation challenges, such as soothing activities and space to decompress.

- Seek out professional and peer support for yourself and your loved one - you are not alone!

3. Adolescence

As a teenager, I moved to Cyprus with my family. I was relieved to be able to start over with completely new people, creating a new identity for myself.

In one way, school in Cyprus was moderately easier to cope with than England, because we finished at 1:40pm, meaning there were only two 20 minute break times to survive each day, instead of an hour long lunch break.

However, I got the bus to school. This started every morning off with intense anxiety, as I had no certainty about whether it was on time. Every time I got on, I was met by a chorus of boys screaming insults at me, hissing and calling me a husky dog for my blonde hair and blue eyes.

This experience wasn't exclusive to them; every time I went outside alone, I would get heckled in the street by passing cars, their horns blaring, making me jump out of my skin. I knew that I felt extremely uncomfortable, but didn't see the point in telling anybody else. I was just embarrassed, feeling like it was my fault.

On the first day in my new school, I became overwhelmed in a Greek class where I couldn't understand the language, and everyone was shouting. One child asked to borrow my Tippex, which I happily handed over, mentally noting a transaction which could potentially result in companionship.

Instead, they threw it back at me, hitting my forehead, everybody bursting out laughing as blood trickled down my face. Embarrassed, I impulsively threw it back at them, but it hit the teacher, who sent me to the disciplinary officer. I was terrified of getting into trouble, so was hysterically crying, begging them not to expel me, which resulted in me getting my first ever detention.

I was so upset that my new opportunity to reinvent myself was out of my control, leaving me as the 'weird' one, yet again. However, as there were lots of expats in Cyprus, I soon found a group of fellow misfits to hang out with.

I started to spend a lot of time at their houses, finding it much easier to play a 'role' of the guest than being at home, as myself. I was very overwhelmed by the messiness of my bedroom, which was essentially a 'floordrobe', meaning I was constantly losing and breaking my belongings after accidentally tripping over them. Every time I cleaned it, it was messy again within minutes.

When the house was burgled, the police were horrified that a teenager's bedroom had been trashed so badly. I had to explain that I did it myself - the burglars had just rather impressively found my pocket money stashed in what should have been a drawer for socks.

I always felt cold. I hated showering because it made me even more cold, especially when I had to get out. There was no shower gel, but I hated the slimy feeling of the soap bar on my skin, so I never used it, not realising this was odd. I couldn't stand having wet hair, but I also hated the sound of the hairdryer, feeling like it was etched into my brain. I never washed my face and rarely brushed my teeth.

I hated getting dressed because of the coldness of the morning, so I'd sleep in my school uniform. When I stayed at other people's houses, it felt much easier to participate in these 'normal' activities in the way that my friends did, body doubling together with the toothbrush I kept at their house.

Adolescence

Being in other people's homes enabled me to see into their lives, with clear information about how to make them like me, such as posters on the walls, signifying what musicians I should listen to. It was a relief when the responsibility of deciding what to 'do' in the unstructured time outside of school was taken by other people.

At 14 years old, this started to include going out clubbing in Ayia Napa, which often required sneaking out, lying, and hitch-hiking to clubs. We'd edit our passport details on 'Paint' and print them out, which served as easy access to any club we liked. I'd pick up half-drunk cocktails from the road and chain-smoke cigarettes, which helped me to feel less uncomfortable, until my brain switched off from alcohol.

This was because the clubs themselves felt like my nervous system was under attack, with loud music ringing in my ears, and crowds of sweaty people, which I'd often stand on tables and podiums to avoid. This was very dangerous, especially as there were often foam parties. I once fell off a bar I was dancing on, hitting my head on it as I went, and my friend dived under the foam to save me, whilst wearing a snorkel mask.

There was also the expectation to dance, which I had no idea how to do. Once, a stranger told me they felt sorry for me and had to teach me how to dance, because I was too embarrassing to watch. Every time I went clubbing, I couldn't wait to go back to bed, becoming so bored that I'd play games with myself, seeing how many men I could kiss in a night. This felt much easier to do than dance, even with my lesson!

I'd often get too drunk, and collapse on the pavement. Not wanting to go home, my 'friends' would stick their fingers down my throat in an attempt to make me sick. To cope, I'd often pass out or fall asleep in the club as they carried on dancing. I'd often be woken up as the sun rose, told that it was finally time to leave.

Being hungover felt strangely relaxing, as my normally endless cycle of thoughts was drowned out by a singular focus on how bad I felt. However, I could still be shaken out of this.

One morning, I was standing at a bus stop when a flurry of quad bikes beeped at me, with men shouting insults about my appearance. A second later, one crashed straight into a lamppost. I was overwhelmed with guilt and shame, feeling like I was responsible. I didn't know if I should tell the police, or whether I could be arrested for murder, going into panic mode.

A stranger standing next to me said that the bus would be cancelled, and asked if I wanted a lift with her friend. I nodded, in shock as she climbed into the back seat, leaving me to sit in the passenger seat by the male driver. Within minutes, I realised that the two people actually didn't know each other at all.

I felt in serious danger, saying I'd actually forgotten something and needed to get out on the side of the motorway. The male driver said that this wasn't possible, and things could be 'easy' or 'hard'. I chose easy, answering his questions about my life, whilst trying to stop shaking.

Miraculously, when we arrived at the town we were supposedly driving to 40 minutes later, he said I could get out of the car - but only after I gave him my phone. He typed his number in, called it, and gave it back to me. Bizarrely, he texted me jokes every day for the next month.

I don't remember telling anyone else about this incident, unsure how to put it into words and not seeing the point. I felt guilty for overreacting when nothing bad had actually happened, feeling like I was just being dramatic and ungrateful to these strangers who had offered me help. I was also so mortified about the quad bike crash, unsure whether the person had died, anxiously checking the news every day for weeks.

I also started to do modelling around this age, after being signed up to a model agency and not knowing how to say no. On my first job, which ended up being published in international editions of *Vogue*, I had two men appointed to get me dressed. I didn't know how to express my discomfort, trying to cover up my non-existent breasts as they pulled tights over my legs.

They looked up to see me, and burst out laughing, explaining that they were gay and didn't care about my body. I felt extremely guilty and embarrassed, and that experience taught me to make sure I never showed any discomfort again on a photoshoot, out of fear of offending somebody.

Nearly every month, I found myself being undressed by different strangers on jobs, which involved having to do things I didn't understand, such as being told to stand in sexually explicit poses, or hang inside car windows - all for fashion magazines. I hated it, but it also taught me to learn how to repress all of my discomfort, learning how to pick up the non-verbal signals from others that would enable me to meet their expectations and win their approval. This was largely because everybody else spoke Greek on these jobs, which relieved the pressure of having to make conversation.

However, when I once expressed doubt about an outfit, I quickly learned that my opinion didn't matter. I was met with horrified looks, and realised that pretending to love everything was the quickest way to leave.

Despite becoming an expert in masking my needs and feelings from modelling, my binge drinking of alcohol became out of control. For example, I once convinced a friend to stay awake all night and to get drunk before going to school, taking in water bottles filled with vodka and cranberry juice. Predictably, we fell asleep and decided to take it to school in flasks, which then spilled in our schoolbags on the way, leaving our books ruined, and smelling disgusting for months.

One night, I was out clubbing when a much older stranger picked me up off the floor with the intention of wanting to 'help'. I was then groomed into a friendship, being plied with even easier access to alcohol and cigarettes, which became a relationship.

Very quickly, I lost control of my life, unable to see a way out of this situation, and blaming myself for not being happy. At one point, I tried to end my own life by banging my head against the wall repeatedly for hours, resulting in a giant green bruise on my forehead for days afterwards.

I was extremely lucky to get out of this situation, although this came with multiple threats. As a teenager, I'd been obsessed with freedom and independence, but I simply couldn't see all of the ways that I was being trapped and controlled.

I was immensely vulnerable, open for anybody to take advantage of, all whilst blaming myself to maintain a sense of control - but I was just a child. If I and the people around me had known that I was neurodivergent, it could have saved me years of pain.

THE AUDHD LENS

Having AuDHD as a teenager can be very dangerous, even more so if nobody knows about it. We can be very vulnerable to exploitation by others, and may experience challenges in fitting in with our peers as social expectations develop.

We may also experience difficulties with regulating our behaviour and emotions, especially as we experience hormonal changes, such as puberty, meaning that symptoms may be incorrectly dismissed as immaturity.

PUBERTY

The developmental changes that accompany adolescence can be very challenging for AuDHD-ers, as our body changes in uncontrollable ways, and hormonal fluctuations intensify symptoms. The impact can be so severe, that one group of researchers proposed adolescence as the 'second hit' of autism, impacting an individual's capacity to transition successfully to adulthood.[19]

Hormones

People with AuDHD may also disproportionately experience hormonal-related issues, as these can be impacted by AuDHD symptoms. For example, Premenstrual Dysphoric Disorder (PMDD) affects up to 92% of autistic women, and 46% of those with ADHD.[20] Autistic girls have been said to experience higher rates of abnormal hormone changes, resulting in irregular menstrual cycles, cramps, polycystic ovary syndrome, and severe acne.[21]

Changes in hormones such as oestrogen and testosterone can impact brain function and emotional regulation, potentially impacting the efficacy of ADHD medication, and

---

19 Picci G, Scherf KS. A Two-Hit Model of Autism: Adolescence as the Second Hit. Clin Psychol Sci. 2015 May;3(3):349-371. doi: 10.1177/2167702614540646. Epub 2014 Aug 4. PMID: 26609500; PMCID: PMC4655890.
20 ADDitude - https://www.additudemag.com/pmdd-autism-adhd/#footnote7
21 'PMDD, Autism and ADHD: Premenstrual Dysphoric Disorder as Comorbidity'. Accessed 2 February 2025. https://www.additudemag.com/pmdd-autism-adhd/#footnote7.

manifestation of symptoms such as anger and impulsivity. This impacts our ability to regulate our emotions, which can manifest as extremely intense mood swings and mental health conditions, such as depression. Of course, this can show up throughout our life, as hormones fluctuate through menstruation cycles and menopause, for example.

The ways that we experience and regulate stress can also be impacted by puberty. Research has shown that the hypothalamic-pituitary-adrenal and autonomic nervous system may be functioning in an atypical way for an autistic teenager.[22] This means that AuDHD teenagers may experience a higher level of emotional dysregulation and stress, which can result in higher cortisol levels, also potentially impacting their physical wellbeing, such as through sleep.

Executive Functioning

During puberty, the brain undergoes significant changes to neurological networks to facilitate the essential tasks of adolescence, such as independence and forming supportive friendships. The primary areas include the pre-frontal cortex, relating to executive functioning development, which is also impacted by AuDHD.

The changes that accompany puberty generally involve the need for new routines, such as around menstruation or shaving. This can be overwhelming for AuDHD-ers, who may not know how to ask for help with navigating these experiences, or what the 'rules' are.

The transition from primary to secondary school can also be overwhelming, especially as children are expected

---

[22] Makris, Gerasimos, Agorastos Agorastos, George P. Chrousos, and Panagiota Pervanidou. 'Stress System Activation in Children and Adolescents With Autism Spectrum Disorder'. *Frontiers in Neuroscience* 15 (13 January 2022): 756628. https://doi.org/10.3389/fnins.2021.756628.

Adolescence

to take on more responsibility for managing their own schedules. Most of the time, they're not actually taught *how* to do this - there's rarely accessible education available on executive functioning skills like time management from schools!

They're also likely to be in new environments, with new people, which can feel overwhelming. Similar experiences may apply with life transitions such as finishing school, going to university, or starting a new job.

Relationships

This can also be seen in navigating new kinds of relationships. Limerance is an intense experience commonly associated with AuDHD, where we may feel supercharged hyper fixation on another person, and an intense rush of overwhelming feelings as 'love'.

Limerance is mental activity, which can result in obsessive and disruptive focus on another person, regardless of whether they share our feelings back. The fantasy of a relationship itself may prove more stimulating than the reality, becoming a sense of comfort and emotional regulation lacking the normal ups and downs of 'real life' relationships. It can result in a sudden surge of neurotransmitters such as serotonin and dopamine that can be highly addictive - but can also cause great pain when this wears off.

On the flip side, relationships are often filled with pain and rejection, especially as a teenager. Those with AuDHD may experience intense fear about the future and whether something will 'last', resulting in a significant change to our environment and a yearning for control.

The onset of hormones during puberty may also result in hyper-sexuality for AuDHD-ers, which can be intensified by impulsivity and result in potential dangers such as unwanted pregnancy. Conversely, they may also experience hypo-sexuality, with a lower than average sex drive, feeling like there's something 'wrong' with them, as their peers focus on this.

AuDHD-ers are also more likely to be of a divergent sexual orientation, which may feel confusing and overwhelming, especially in contrast to societal expectations. They might have had sex education on one form of relationship in school, but it's unlikely to cover the endless possibilities of sexual preferences, such as asexuality.

Evidence shows a link between gender dysphoria / nonconformity and AuDHD, which may become more difficult to manage during puberty.[23] It's crucial that these children are able to access tailored, affirming support to help them navigate this alongside AuDHD.

It's extremely important that AuDHD teenagers are able and encouraged to have open, informed discussions about puberty in the ways that work for them. Being able to understand what's happening to their body and what this means can be empowering, facilitating autonomy and independence. Without this, we may experience intense shame and isolation, which may continue into adulthood.

Friendships

As 'child's play' transitions from largely parallel play during primary school, into 'socialising' during secondary school, AuDHD children may find this transition very difficult. They've likely not been literally taught 'how' to make friends or socialise, leaving them vulnerable to bullying and exploitation.

---

[23] ScienceDaily. 'Wishing to Be Another Gender: Links to ADHD, Autism Spectrum Disorders'. Accessed 2 February 2025. https://www.sciencedaily.com/releases/2014/03/140312103102.htm.

Adolescence

This is exacerbated by communication differences for AuDHD-ers. For example, when hearing about a person's experience, we may impulsively share our own, in the hope of showing that we understand and making a connection. However, this could easily be misunderstood as an attempt to focus the conversation exclusively on ourselves, or as invalidating of the other person's experiences.

We may also have a literal interpretation of words, not understanding jokes or 'banter' amongst our peer groups. For example, I'd never assume I was invited to a social gathering unless I was specifically and personally invited, even when I was a part of a group where an invitation was shared.

This, in addition to misunderstanding social cues, such as facial expressions and tone of voice, can result in significant challenges navigating friendships. As friendships become more based around concepts such as popular trends rather than shared activities, AuDHD teenagers can struggle to keep up. Instead of having 'fun' when socialising, they may experience it as immensely stressful, whilst hyper-aware of the heavy neuronormative expectations to fit in. Difference isn't often welcomed during this time.

An AuDHD child who develops strong masking skills may have a lot of friends, but feel exhausted, constantly repressing their symptoms. They may not feel as though they're liked for the 'real them', having to portray a socially acceptable version of themselves.

The ADHD parts of their brains may seek out stimulation from others, finding it distracting from their overwhelming thoughts, and accept all invitations offered to them without thinking ahead to how difficult they may find it, or to check other commitments. The autistic part may battle against this, attempting to create rules and structures around unstructured relationships and experiences.

This can be especially complicated for girls, who are socialised to have a 'group' of friends, including a 'best' friend. In contrast, boys are often encouraged to bond over shared activities, such as football. If an AuDHD child has a 'special interest', they may try to repress speaking about this to others, especially if it's unusual. This may feel painful, because their brain is strongly pulling them towards it.

Managing such intense internal struggles can result in impulsive or 'odd' behaviour around others, resulting in arguments and misunderstandings. AuDHD teenagers may not necessarily tell the adults in their life about this, presenting an image of everything being 'fine'. Alternatively, they may become very withdrawn, refusing to engage in social interactions, possibly for reasons they're unable or unwilling to explain.

Given the strong presence of social media and the internet in teenagers' lives today, AuDHD teenagers may have a strong preference for online interactions over face to face ones. These can feel easier to manage, with more time for processing and planning. The internet offers a world where they may be able to find others who think like they do, sharing similar 'weird' interests and feeling understood. Whilst this can be positive, it can also be very dangerous, as they can be very vulnerable as a result of their neurodivergence.

The online world tends to lack boundaries, existing as a tempting escape from reality that we can plug ourselves into 24 hours a day, especially if we have the ability to hyper-focus that accompanies AuDHD. When we're in this mode, we might not feel time passing at all.

Outside of it, time can feel endless. This also complicates the stresses that AuDHD teenagers may encounter, as they may experience time as 'now or not now'. If all they've ever known is a school environment, this setting may be all they're literally able to imagine in the future, interpreting that they will always be ostracised.

The friends that they make may not necessarily be the same age. As AuDHD is linked with a developmental delay in executive functioning skills, it can make us mentally 'younger' than our peers. At the same time, AuDHD adolescents may prefer the company of adults, not recognising the social norms or expectations around concepts like age or hierarchies. These relationships can offer comfort, but also could pose serious danger.

Bullying

Due to these factors, signs of AuDHD in teenagers could include being bullied or rejected by their peers. Secondary school[24] has been found to be the most common times an AuDHD-er will experience bullying, affecting up to 94% of autistic people[25]. Children with ADHD were found to be 3-17 times more likely to be classified as a victim of bullying, a bully, or both, compared to their neurotypical peers.[26]

Symptoms of impulsivity and hyperactivity may appear as bullying, but they may not necessarily be intended as this. Bullying others may also arise as a defensive mechanism or coping strategy, especially if we've experienced bullying ourselves. AuDHD can explain these situations, but it doesn't excuse them.

---

24   Bullying Victimization is Associated with Heightened Rates of Anxiety and Depression Among Autistic and ADHD Youth: National Survey of Children's Health 2016–2020 - https://link.springer.com/article/10.1007/s10803-024-06479-z
25   Bullying of children and adolescents with autism spectrum conditions: a 'state of the field' review -https://www.tandfonline.com/doi/citedby/10.1080/13603116.2014.981602?scroll=top&needAccess=true&role=tab
26   Study: Children with ADHD More Likely to Bully — and to Be Bullied - ADDitutde - https://www.additudemag.com/bullying-and-adhd-research/

In contrast, AuDHD could also look like the most popular child in the class, who prioritises their friendships over everything else in their life. They might prefer 1:1 interactions to groups, developing very close relationships with one or two others.

As a parent, this can feel concerning, given the expectations on teenagers to be 'social'. I imagine it's every parent's worst nightmare to think of their child in pain, but supporting, accepting and taking an interest in the ways that they naturally prefer to socialise can help to learn more about it, opening up conversations.

If your child is being bullied, or bullying others, it's important to understand the full context and to take action as soon as possible, such as by involving their school. Taking the time to understand their experiences and validate their emotions can be extremely helpful, reminding them that you're on their side - no matter what.

If you're a teenager reading this, please know that your way of socialising is absolutely valid, but you are also vulnerable, and need to make sure you're protected.

Seeking out friends with common interests, especially those who are also neurodivergent, will help you to see that you are not, and never have been, the problem. You are simply existing in a structure that isn't made for the wonderful, unique ways that your brain works - but it is temporary, as painful as it might feel right now. There are so many people in the world waiting to be your friend, who will accept and celebrate you exactly as you are.

Behaviour

Being unable to control our environment, thoughts, relationships, and bodies can be an incredibly overwhelming experience, along with multiple competing new expectations to meet and experiences to process.

Adolescence

These challenges may be complicated further by experiences of PDA or ODD, as explained in 'Childhood'. These can create additional conflict for AuDHD teenagers as they work to process and navigate their environment with far more difficulty than their peers.

This overwhelm can become externalised, manifesting as challenging or rebellious behaviour. Naturally, this could result in children getting into trouble. From being accused of not listening, to acting out in class as a way to cope, they may find themselves being told off a lot. One child told me how they didn't attend chapel in the morning, because they preferred to have detention, which enabled them to do their homework. This made sense to me, but obviously the school wasn't happy!

This behaviour could look like getting into arguments, aggression, or running away from home, for example. The possibilities of AuDHD struggles are endless, easily confused with general teenage angst and hormonal changes.

AuDHD-ers are also likely to be highly intelligent and creative, developing strategies to get around any rules imposed on them that they don't agree with. I remember a 'light bulb' moment when I realised that my parents couldn't actually do anything to me if I misbehaved or was caught lying.

What I really needed was someone to talk to about *why* I was acting like this. I needed to feel safe enough to feel like I wasn't going to get into even more trouble if I opened up. The AuDHD brain may be very 'all-or-nothing', and previous mistakes we've made, or passing comments we've heard, might be mentally filed as evidence for why we can't possibly ever ask for help.

School
AuDHD may not be easily accepted within school environments, such as with shame around children needing

additional support or taking medication. Teenagers with one or both diagnoses may not understand these conditions, significantly impacting their confidence.

As a result of these various challenges, AuDHD children may find themselves suspended or excluded from school. Autistic pupils are three times[27] as likely to be suspended than pupils with no special educational needs, and 39% of children with ADHD have had fixed term exclusions from school. 11% have been excluded permanently.[28]

Alternatively, some AuDHD children may be extremely anxious about getting into trouble, aiming for perfection and putting themselves under extreme stress without realising that this isn't normal. For example, they may feel that they have to get 100% in a test, with no adults around them realising that they are holding themselves to such unrealistic standards.

These challenges may culminate in children simply refusing to attend school, with their parents in impossibly difficult positions. The reasons for this may vary, with 68% of AuDHD children more likely to have experienced school refusal behaviour due to bullying.[29] One study found that 42% of autistic students were presently absent from school.[30]

If you're a parent of an AuDHD child, it's important to explore how your child experiences school, even if they

---

27   Autism Education Trust, 'School Exclusions' - https://www.autismeducationtrust.org.uk/sites/default/files/2021-09/exclusions_a_guide-for-parents_i-s.pdf
28   Waters Creative. 'ADHD and Exclusion in Schools | The UK ADHD Partnership'. Accessed 2 February 2025. https://www.ukadhd.com/ adhd-and-exclusion-in-schools.htm.
29   'School Refusal Behavior in Children and Adolescents: A Five-Year Narrative Review of Clinical Significance and Psychopathological Profiles'. *Italian Journal of Pediatrics* 50 (30 May 2024): 107. https://doi.org/10.1186/s13052-024-01667-0.
30   'School Absence and Refusal High among Students with Autism'. Brain Sciences, 18 May 2020. https://www.ucl.ac.uk/brain-sciences/news/2020/may/school-absence-and-refusal-high-among-students-autism.

seem to have no issues. It's good idea to discuss things like exams, the sensory environment, and social interactions on a regular basis, opening up conversations about what makes school feel challenging.

If your child is refusing school, it's important to stay calm and to validate their feelings. Punishment may reinforce negative feelings, so focus on understanding rather than controlling. It can be helpful to break attendance up into chunks, such as by going in for a single day, rather than a week. Coaching can also help with this, in helping children to identify the purpose and how this can link into enabling them to do certain things they want to do in the future, such as travelling.

It can also be extremely helpful to consider hybrid or online options, with schools such as Gaia Learning[31] making learning accessible for all. This is especially so if children find that they can engage better at home, such as by teaching themselves, as I did.

Ultimately, these children can't be forced into compliance - they need to trust that someone can and will help them. They may find it hard to think beyond their school years, but you can help them to realise that there's so much more to life.

Boundaries

Nobody *wants* to get into trouble, and AuDHD children may be excessively anxious about this, becoming hyper-compliant. This makes them extremely vulnerable to exploitation by others, being friends with anybody who 'picks' them, and open to potential manipulation from those who may treat them inappropriately.

---

31   https://www.gaialearning.co.uk

Loneliness can feel all-encompassing for any teenager, but especially one who is AuDHD. They might be unable to stop thinking about friendships, but struggle with them significantly. As a result, they can easily fall into the 'wrong crowd', where they may be easily influenced to do things like smoke or drink alcohol.

They also may struggle with the concept of boundaries, especially as the nature of relationship dynamics change from friendship to something more. If nobody has taught us about how to be in a romantic relationship, it can be difficult to know how to approach them, resulting in us being easily controlled.

This is especially so when it comes to sex and our bodies, which may be changing in ways we don't understand. There's immense pressure on teenagers around sexual advancement, especially within our pornography-filled age and in social media. In contrast, sex is still an uncomfortable topic for our society to address openly, resulting in children learning about it in other ways.

If no one has taught an AuDHD-er how to or when they should say 'no', especially if they struggle with sensing their own emotions, they may learn to trust the opinions of others over their own. This is especially concerning given the possibly isolated nature in which they're growing up, feeling like others don't understand them. If they come across someone who does, trust can be handed over very quickly. This makes us especially vulnerable online, where people can easily conceal their true identities.

Our struggle in understanding social cues can lead to difficulties in recognising when a boundary has been crossed, or when to set limits. This can result in feelings of confusion and shame around relationships, especially if we experience delayed emotional processing. I have had many

Adolescence

situations where I felt 'fine' at the time, but overwhelmed with grief and regret afterwards, realising that I was uncomfortable the entire time.

Consent can be very difficult to provide if we have impacted self-awareness. AuDHD-ers may also struggle with changing their mind after it has been provided, feeling 'bad' and as though they may be accused of lying. This can feel important for someone who has a strong sense of justice and hyper-empathy towards the feelings of others, over their own.

Ultimately, AuDHD-ers may not understand the unwritten social rules that accompany relationships, meaning potential struggles with understanding the boundaries of ourselves and others.

Support

I can't imagine how difficult it must feel as the parent of an AuDHD child who seems to be getting into trouble or hurting themselves, essentially being in harm's way. However, by getting help for yourself and the emotions this brings up in you, such as with therapy, you will be best placed to help them.

If they're experiencing challenges, collaborate with the school. Schools should have Special Education Coordinators to provide support, implementing adjustments such as flexible schedules or sensory-friendly spaces. A few small changes can make a big difference. For example, I once wrote a letter for a child who found they could focus much better when listening to music, explaining how this was linked to their ADHD, which the school then accepted as 'valid'.

If you're in the UK, you can also apply to the Local Authority for an Education, Health, and Care Plan. This is a legally binding document outlining support a child with special educational needs or disabilities will receive, such as provisions for them to go to a specialist school. These decisions are often successfully appealed at tribunal, with a 96% success rate for parents and carers[32], so it is definitely worth seeking legal advice if you're unhappy with the outcome.

Identifying 'safe' adults that AuDHD children can speak to is vital to ensure they have support if they need it. It can be helpful to explain explicitly the circumstances in which they might wish to speak to a designated adult, as otherwise they may not understand what the 'point' is. Teaching your children self-advocacy skills can also be very helpful to enable them to speak up, especially if they're experiencing challenges with other students.

Next up, I *strongly* recommend explicitly telling all children, especially those who are AuDHD, about what kinds of support is available, the ways in which they can be helped, and how important it is that they do. I didn't ask for help because I didn't understand the point, even if I was in pain.

However, just because I didn't know what *could* help, didn't mean I didn't need it. I needed the emotional support that came with a hug and reassurance, validation of my experiences, and guidance in difficult situations. Children need to know *why* they should risk the vulnerability of being rejected by asking for help.

Creating routine and predictability for children is also a great way to help them transition to and from school, such as by having a visual schedule and preview of any changes happening in the future. They may benefit from sensory and emotional regulation tools, such as fidget toys, and

---

[32] SEND Tribunal Appeals at a record high - Disability Rights - https://www.disabilityrightsuk.org/news/send-tribunal-appeals-record-high

Adolescence

movement breaks. It's also ideal if they can access therapy to help them process their emotions and build confidence, as school can be such a challenging time.

Being explicit about concepts like privacy and consent is key, especially for AuDHD-ers who may struggle with all-or-nothing thinking. Talking about things like periods and sex is key to ensuring they feel comfortable and safe, as they may not say anything themselves. Teaching them self-care, even about the 'simple' things that you might assume they know, but notice resistance towards, such as showering, can be enormously helpful.

AuDHD-ers may need to be explicitly and regularly asked about their experiences, because they might not be able to describe how they feel about them. They may feel scared to talk about any challenges they've experienced due to not wanting to hurt or disappoint others, or fearing any repercussions. It's crucial for them to know that they will never be in trouble for seeking help.

Explaining what kinds of actions could be taken if there was a problem can help them to see the 'point' of this, including how you can help. Whether this is simply by offering them a space to unload, or taking more serious action such as by talking to the police together, reassure them that you won't do anything without their permission.

Talking to teenagers about their AuDHD and how these kinds of challenges can manifest can help them to identify such situations in the future, understanding their own vulnerabilities.

Asking them to help you understand their experiences without judgement can provide safety and trust for conversations to take place. This might not happen immediately, but building a regular routine of talking about issues like this, or providing a regular opportunity for these to happen, such as with therapy or coaching, can help. Asking questions instead of reacting can help AuDHD teenagers to reflect on their own experiences and make decisions.

They may feel as though they are 'adults', strongly resisting being told what to do or who to see, but helping them to simply understand that there are people who may use this against them is important. It's important to reinforce healthy relationships, and that this doesn't necessarily mean everybody!

If you're a young person experiencing these challenges at school, please know that things *do get better*. It might feel like school is awful, but this is not your fault. Talking to your parents and teachers may feel awkward and scary, but they can help.

Accepting their support means being able to create environments which will work better for your brain, instead of fighting them by yourself. You have a highly unique set of skills, and brilliant opportunities ahead of you, and the grades you get in school do not define your future - but you have nothing to lose from trying - and everything to gain.

Tips: AuDHD-ers

- Learn about AuDHD, linking this to your experiences to understand how your brain works. This can help you to feel empowered and less isolated.

- Try to identify, recognise, and accept your needs, such as those relating to sensory experiences and socialising. You don't need to change yourself!

- Create a toolkit to support yourself, such as grounding techniques that help you to calm down, and routines that can reduce overwhelm such as breaking your day into manageable chunks.

- Try out different tools that could help with feeling overwhelmed, such as fidget toys.

- Seek safe friendships with those who understand and accept you as you are.

- Remember that trust is earned, not automatically granted.

- Recognise your own vulnerabilities and ensure you protect yourself.

- Seek support from trusted people in your life in the ways that work for you, even if you're not sure how to ask for it.

- Try not to place pressure on yourself to fit in - your differences are what make you, you!

- Set boundaries such as saying 'no' when you're feeling uncomfortable, remembering that it's okay to prioritise your wellbeing.

- Learn about puberty and the changes that may happen in your body, including how hormones can intensify AuDHD traits.

- Remember to be very careful around romantic relationships, and to take things as slowly as you can. These feelings are nothing to be ashamed of, but it's important to ensure you can trust them.

- Be careful of people who seem to want things from you, or who make you feel uncomfortable.

- Monitor how long you spend online, as this can become overwhelming and impact areas of your life, such as sleep.

- Limit overcommitment where possible, ensuring that you have time to yourself to decompress.

- Embrace your strengths, passions, and interests. You don't need to have a 'normal' job!

- Celebrate small wins, recognising that some things may be more difficult for you than others - and deserve to be celebrated!

- Find like-minded communities, such as with other AuDHD-ers.

- Access professional help, such as from an AuDHD coach or therapist, who can provide guidance and support.

- Remember that it's okay if you don't know what your future looks like: it will all work out!

Tips: loved ones

- Learn about AuDHD, and how this presents in a young person who may be navigating puberty.

- Practical radical acceptance, recognising that your loved one's behaviour stems from genuine challenges and differences in how their brain functions, not defiance or immaturity.

- Create open communication channels, encouraging your loved one to share their experiences, thoughts, and feelings without fear of judgement.

- Validate your loved one's emotions, helping them to identify them and practicing empathy.

- Remember that social misunderstandings can often occur due to mutual differences in communication styles. Trust your loved one to communicate in the ways that work best for them.

- Provide structure and predictability, especially as AuDHD teenagers navigate puberty. Creating routines and clear expectations can be very helpful to foster a sense of control.

- Have open, pro-active conversations about puberty and sex, ensuring that your loved one understands what changes may occur and how they can support themselves during this time.

- Address diverse sexual orientations and gender identities to ensure your loved one feels understood and supported.

- Normalise their social preferences, such as 1:1 interactions, instead of pushing traditional expectations of group socialisation or being 'popular'.

- Engage in regular communication around online interactions, ensuring your child feels safe to discuss and share this world with you, in addition to being able to recognise potentially dangerous behaviour from others.

- Empower self-advocacy by supporting your loved one to understand their needs and requesting support, such as through scripts to do so at school.

- Recognise masking and its effects, such as over-exerting themselves to appear 'normal', reminding them that they are great as they are.

- Work with the school and other professionals to ensure your loved one is sufficiently protected.

- Seek out professional support for yourself to process your own experiences of this.

- Share your experiences with your loved one, reminding them that they aren't responsible for your feelings.

- Seek to understand the reasons behind challenging behaviour, instead of telling your loved one off.

4. Learning

Everybody I knew seemed shocked when I received straight A's in my external school exams, with one teacher having asked an entire class if I had cheated.

I felt like I *had* cheated, but I didn't mean to - I was just as surprised. I could never concentrate in school, my mind always focused on break times and whether people liked me or not. To cope, I'd hide headphones up my shirt and listen to music, read fiction books hidden in my academic textbooks, or obsessively make origami birds out of paper. I couldn't understand how I'd gotten these grades, because I still felt stupid.

In reality, they were the result of a pattern-based brain. When I learned that marks couldn't be deducted in exams for writing incorrect information, I chose only exam based subjects. I knew that I could write huge amounts in very short periods of time, as my mind instinctively switched into a different mode, writing things I didn't even know I remembered. Under pressure, I could absorb and memorise substantial amounts of information, but I couldn't do coursework.

Word based exams felt fun, because they were predictable. I understood the structures that I needed to follow, such as introducing topics, presenting for and against arguments, and concluding. It felt like a different part of my brain took over when writing, guiding my responses.

A month before the exams, I used exam preparation books that provided clear instructions, criteria, and templates, and everything somehow made sense in my brain. I found it much easier to teach myself than to learn from a teacher in class, but couldn't motivate myself to do this until the deadlines were close enough to cause me to stress out.

I naturally enjoyed subjects like English, but when
I had to stand at the front of the class and present, I burst into tears immediately. I'd also find myself racing ahead, having read entire books in days that we had to plough through and painfully read out loud line by line, each student taking turns. I rarely put my hand up to answer a question asked by the teacher, and was often shook out of my daydreams by accusations of not listening. I was often so bored that I fell asleep on the desk, which was very embarrassing.

Logic-based exams were much harder, so I avoided them wherever possible, dropping maths and science as soon as I could. I hated having to 'show my working out', as the numbers overwhelmed me and I couldn't figure out how I'd gotten to the answer I had.

'Fun' subjects like drama were no better. I first realised I was 'different' from other kids when we had to act as animals, and I assumed everyone else would feel just as awkward as I did, but instead, everyone immediately pranced around the room growling and roaring, as I froze to the spot. For my GCSE options, I had to choose between art or Greek.

I couldn't speak Greek, and froze up in oral exams, so I picked art, telling the teacher how useless I was and apologising in advance. Upon seeing my attempt at drawing half a pepper, they said, 'see, you *can* do art.' Those classes were enjoyable, allowing my mind to switch off as I painted mindlessly, happy in the knowledge that I 'could' do art.

However, I was also frustrated, because I was acutely aware that this wasn't a 'useful' subject. I was even more frustrated when it came to the exams. I got an A in art, but the students who sat on my table and loved it passionately, replicating perfect images of what they saw, were graded with B's. This was except for one, who got an A*. They'd turn up to every class and simply pour paint onto the page before sitting on their phone, disengaged.

It made me angry that the levels of passion and obvious skill weren't reflected in the grades, shaping how I thought about subjective marking and 'creative' subjects. One person's interpretation of incredible was another's interpretation of not good enough - so how could these be measured objectively?

P.E was hell. I hated having to get changed, and to do sport. I was extremely badly coordinated, to the point that a tennis teacher told me I could leave the tennis club I joined as a child as a special circumstance, because I was so bad. I avoiding joining any extra-curricular activities at school again.

School based learning felt off-limits to my brain, as I was either too quick, and bored, or too slow, and confused. However, this changed when a new teacher came to the school to teach law. I'd picked the subject because my friend did, but this teacher was different from the others. She was kind and patient, seeming to understand my brain. She encouraged me to sit at the front of every class with my friend, and in those classes, learning felt fun.

Law wasn't just about dry text or endless analysis of poems - it was about people and real life, with practical and useful information that could be applied outside of the classroom. I made stories up in my head to help me memorise case names, and for the first time, I felt fully engaged, even putting my hand up to answer questions, basking in the glow of positive feedback and validation provided by the teacher. Her affirming teaching style enabled me to get 100% in my exam.

This led me to pick law to study at university, although I felt completely overwhelmed by the idea. I simply could not picture myself in a future environment as my friends could, and had no idea what to 'do' with my life. I picked the university to go to based off where a friend went in London, relieved that I'd know at least one person.

I avoided applying for any universities that required a verbal reasoning test called the LNAT. I didn't know I was neurodivergent, but I knew that I simply could not do verbal reasoning tests, beating myself up for not being able to do these seemingly 'easy' and 'obvious' assessments.

Initially, I missed the grades to get in, scoring a 'B' in History. I was extremely angry and upset, as I'd understood from my school that AS Levels would be considered the same as one A Level, but I was wrong. Within minutes, I was making plans to kill myself, but fortunately, someone in my life fought very hard for my exam to be remarked, and it went up by 14 marks - an examiner had missed out 2 pages!

However, moving to London also terrified me. I arrived armed with legal pepper spray and a basic phone, convinced I'd be attacked every time I stepped outside. It took months before I felt comfortable enough to go out without them.

I shared a university residence flat with a few other students, including one was also studying law, so we'd initially go to lectures together. Every time, I'd emerge feeling like the lecture had been in Chinese, realising that I hadn't been able to taken in anything at all. I tried different strategies, such as writing notes, but it was extremely confusing and theoretical - nothing like my experience at

A Level. So, I skipped most lectures, which seemed to be a waste of my time, attending only the mandatory tutorials.

When I attempted to read the 100 pages of reading we'd been assigned each week for these, I found myself equally disengaged. I'd look at the pages I'd highlighted, angry that I couldn't recall anything that I'd read. I turned up to the classes with my laptop, googling the answers to questions and reading them from Wikipedia when called upon, seeming to get by.

During Fresher's week, I realised that there were no extra-curricular groups I felt like I could join, so I didn't. I instead went out clubbing, having been invited by club promoters who'd found me on social media, sending daily invitations.

I didn't understand the dynamics behind this, believing the promoters were my friends, but I used this as a 'reason' for other people to be my friend, inviting anybody and everybody along. This worked quite well, as we were given lots of free alcohol.

Beyond the velvet rope, I found these clubs extremely boring. We'd queue up for hours in the freezing cold, just to get into a dark room crammed with people and music that was too loud.

When we returned from summer to the second year of university, other students asked me which vacation schemes I'd applied to. I assumed they meant a literal vacation, thinking this was related to some kind of trip abroad I didn't know about. Upon Googling this, I learned that they meant legal internships, a common requirement in becoming a solicitor, involving multiple rounds of interviews.

I'd already missed most of the deadlines, but was completely overwhelmed by the idea of applying anyway. I had no idea how to make my shameful career of modelling sound like something that was vaguely professional on a CV, and I had no other work experience.

In the third year, the buzz was about training contracts. I learned that this was another hoop to jump through to start an actual career as a lawyer, often requiring at least one vacation scheme (if not more), work experience, and a dedication to 'commercial awareness', a phrase that plagues me to this day.

At an open day at a top law firm, I was asked about my extra-curricular activities. I vaguely answered that there weren't many at my university, which was met with surprise. So I said that because of this, me and my friends were setting up a chess club. The recruiter was delighted, and asked me lots of questions about it, which I promptly made up answers to on the spot.

I returned to university and told my friends we had to set up a chess club, as I'd lied about it to a law firm. I did play chess with one of them, but only as a drinking game before going clubbing (taking tequila shots whenever a piece that wasn't a pawn was captured). Before we knew it, we had founded the chess club, of which I was ironically the President.

We assumed no one would join if we didn't promote it, but lots of male students found it. They were pretty surprised to see a group of girls welcoming them with freshly baked brownies! Everyone thrived in their accidental roles, and incredibly, we ended up competing in a London tournament.

Somehow, I managed to graduate from university with a 2:1 degree in law. I did this by largely memorising my friend's notes that were made throughout the year, upon realising it was going to be impossible for me to even read the thousands of pages of law I had to catch up on. At my graduation, I felt like a fraud, with a degree I didn't deserve and had no idea what to do with. At least I could say that I had been President and Founder of the Chess Club.

THE AUDHD LENS

Traditional learning environments can be a minefield for AuDHD-ers, who may have unique ways of learning, processing, and memorising information that doesn't fit into a 'one size fits all' approach.

School and university can be extremely overwhelming from a sensory perspective, navigating harsh lighting, social expectations, and the constant fear of getting into trouble. Autism may appreciate the structure of full time education, whilst ADHD may rebel against it.

LEARNING DIFFERENCES

It's notable that 'learning difficulties' primarily apply to standardised skills, such as reading or writing, in comparison to art or drama. These are all forms of their own neurodivergence, including:

Hyperlexia

I didn't understand why I have always been able to write and read so fast, until I came across the term 'hyperlexia' in the brilliant Professor Nancy Doyle's book on neurodivergent leadership.[33]

This is associated with advanced reading and writing abilities, often noticed in children who have taught themselves to read! I's not a diagnosable condition in and of itself,

---

[33] Learning from Neurodivergent Leaders: How to Start, Survive and Thrive in Leadership - Dr Nancy Doyle, Professor Almuth McDowell
- https://www.amazon.co.uk/Neurodiversity-Leadership-Nancy-Doyle/dp/1805011421#:~:text=Learning%20from%20Neurodivergent%20Leaders%3A%20How,.uk%3A%20Doyle%2C%20Dr.

likely because there's no 'deficit' involved, although 84% of hyperlexic children are said to be autistic.[34]

However, we may be able to read a huge amount of information very quickly, but this doesn't necessarily mean that we're processing it. We may be able to regurgitate it, as I did for my exams, but that doesn't necessarily mean that we understand it. This can prevent us from being able to fully engage with the material, creating a sense of confusion and imposter syndrome.

Equally, it can result in boredom. I found being in classrooms where pages were read out painfully slowly, child by child, so boring that it was almost painful, skipping ahead to the end. It can also result in challenges speaking, where we may be much better able to process and understand our thoughts by writing them out.

Dyslexia

Dyslexia is a neurodevelopmental condition relating to vision, as the visual system struggles to process the fine details of words, and/or track words on a page into sentences and paragraphs. It has three core elements: word reading accuracy, reading rate, and fluency and reading comprehension.

Dyslexia is essentially the opposite of hyperlexia in terms of being able to read and interpret written information, or difficulties with spelling and grammar. This can understandably be extremely difficult for children who are being judged on how well they can present themselves through words, such as in the majority of exams. Their written work may not reflect their knowledge or ability, and they may understandably avoid tasks involving writing or reading.

---

34   'Hyperlexia: What It Means, What the Symptoms Are, and More'. Accessed 3 February 2025. https://www.webmd.com/children/what-is-hyperlexia.

For this reason, dyslexic children are often given extra time in exams, allowing them to better process the information as their fellow students are able to. In the 'real world', there are so many tools to help dyslexics thrive, from spellcheck to ChatGPT, and dictation software to Google. The same applies for non-dyslexics, as the majority of adults in the UK have a reading ability at or below Level 1, which is what is expected of the average 11-14 year old.[35]

Given this, it's bizarre how much pressure there is on children to be able to spell and read 'correctly' in education systems. Between 18-45% of people with dyslexia also meet the criteria for ADHD,[36] and some studies have suggested up to 50% of autistic people may also have dyslexia.[37]

Dysgraphia

This neurological condition is related to challenges with turning thoughts into written language for their age and cognitive ability, despite having the education to do so.

I once saw a dysgraphic person struggle with writing a birthday card, spending an hour deliberating over the best words to use. This was a light bulb moment for me, as I assumed this was obvious. It's important to remember that there is no such thing as 'normal', and everybody has their own challenges, processing information very differently from one another.

It primarily affects writing skills, involving difficulty with letter formation, spacing, and handwriting. However, again, this may not accurately reflect their knowledge or ability.

---

35 Health literacy 'how to' guide - NHS England - https://library.nhs.uk/wp-content/uploads/sites/4/2020/08/Health-literacy-how-to-guide.pdf
36 The overlap between dyspraxia, dyslexia and ADHD - Psychiatry UK - https://psychiatry-uk.com/the-overlap-between-dyspraxia-dyslexia-and-adhd/
37 'Autism and Dyslexia: The Link Between - Apex ABA Therapy'. Accessed 3 February 2025. https://www.apexaba.com/blog/autism-and-dyslexia.

This is especially relevant given how much of our life we spend typing on keyboards, rather than writing on paper, especially after school.

These types of conditions can understandably have a significant impact on children's self-esteem. It's estimated that more than 60% of AuDHD children have dysgraphia.[38]

Dyspraxia

Dyspraxia is also known as Developmental Co-ordination Disorder (DCD). It's a sensor-motor issue, causing challenges with sensing where the body is in space and controlling movements, especially those such as fine motor movement.

This can cause children to perform less well than expected in daily activities for their age, and to be clumsy. For example, they may struggle to learn to ride a bike whilst others their age are doing so. Dyspraxia affects up to 6-10% of the general population, with up to 2% severely affected. There is a large crossover of dyspraxia with AuDHD, with over 90% of us experiencing weakness in our fine motor skills.[39]

I was so clumsy as a child that I was taken to the doctors, who said it was from a build-up of earwax, but the clumsiness remained throughout my life. Dyspraxia can emerge in many forms, from struggling to write and hold a pen, to manipulating objects such as tools in woodwork or pottery.

Dyscalculia

Dyscalculia is a specific and persistent difficulty in understanding number-based information, which can result in

---

[38] 'High Prevalence of Dysgraphia in Elementary Through High School Students With ADHD and Autism - Susan D. Mayes, Rosanna P. Breaux, Susan L. Calhoun, Sara S. Frye, 2019'. Accessed 3 February 2025. https://journals.sagepub.com/doi/10.1177/1087054717720721

[39] Elkin, Rachel. 'The Overlap between Dyspraxia, Dyslexia and ADHD'. Psychiatry-UK (blog), 3 October 2022. https://psychiatry-uk.com/the-overlap-between-dyspraxia-dyslexia-and-adhd/

challenges with maths, as a result of maths-related concepts being processed differently in the brain. However, like all of the other learning differences, this doesn't mean that people with this condition are less intelligent or capable than people who don't have dyscalculia.

Dyscalculia can result in significant stress when faced with numbers-based information, which is definitely something I experience! My challenges include recognising and remembering numbers, to doing calculations in my head, figuring out tax, and even simply transferring money from my bank account. 31% of students with ADHD are said to have a math disability, a rate 5 times higher than the general rate of math disabilities, which falls between 6-7%.[40]

This can have a significant impact on us throughout our life, as it may impact our ability to manage our finances and fully understand concepts such as debt or savings in the future.

ATTENTION DIFFERENCES
Interest Based Nervous System
Due to an interest based nervous system, people with AuDHD may experience the ability to 'hyper-focus' on tasks that are of interest to them. This can feel like being in a state of 'flow', where time and space cease to exist around us. It's often triggered by adrenaline, interest, and novelty.

For this reason, we may be *really* good at focusing on the first 75% of a task, but struggle with completing it. There may be some parts our brains simply won't allow us to start or finish, such as repetitive, detail-orientated administration tasks. This can be extremely frustrating, because we may appear as though we are capable of extraordinary work,

---
[40] 'ADHD and Math: What's the Connection?' Accessed 3 February 2025. https://www.healthline.com/health/adhd-and-math#dyscalculia.

but struggle with parts others would find 'easy', especially as the novelty fades.

We may also be able to hyper-focus with increased levels of stress, such as me before my exams. I was able to memorise entirely new subjects in the space of a few weeks, because I was so stressed in knowing how I'd not learned anything at all during the year. This can lead us to perform well under pressure and in fast-paced environments, although it can be unhealthy to put ourselves under so much stress. Using this as a strategy to 'finish' work is unsustainable, as it can lead to burnout!

Monotropism

In this way, ADHD is a struggle of *regulating* attention, rather than a deficit of it. Monotropism has often been linked with autism, which relates to a highly focused attentional style, restricted to a few interests or areas. For me, this is one of the key parts of my own AuDHD.

Monotropism feels like a heightened version of hyper-focus, because when I'm interested in something (like this book!), it is *all that I can think about*. To do any other tasks feels frustrating, and it can be extremely unhealthy, seeing me work for 10 hours at a time when I can be uninterrupted, such as on the weekend. This can result in the 'Special Interests' often associated with autism.

Catherine Asta, the brilliant author, podcaster and therapist, described monotropism as scuba diving, in comparison to neurotypical people who may be happy with a surface swim.[41] This is exactly how my brain feels: I wouldn't just

---

[41] In her book, 'Rediscovered: A compassionate & courageous guide for late discovered autistic women (and their allies) - Catherine Asta - https://www.amazon.co.uk/Rediscovered-Compassionate-Courageous-Discovered-Autistic/dp/1805011502

Learning

go for a 'quick dip', because as soon as I'd get myself in the water, I'd only be able to think about how long I 'should' stay in, or being cold again minutes later when I'd get out, having to dry off again.

Instead, I'd love to deep dive down to the bottom for hours, submerging myself in a new world - then it would feel 'worth' the pain of a transition from dry to wet. The challenge with this is that coming up to the surface, especially too quickly, can be very painful!

The indicator of monotropism isn't how niche the interest is (such as train-spotting or collecting stamps!), but of how *intense* it is, especially within girls who may mask these symptoms with 'socially acceptable' interests, such as reading. I'd often be so engrossed in reading that I'd be walking down the street whilst reading a book, or running on the treadmill at the same time!

It can feel very painful to stop when I'm interested in something, as I have no idea if the same level of passion will be there when I return, and everything else is blocked out of focus around me.

At the same time, this attention style can result in great expertise and extraordinary, self-created joy. To dive deeply into certain topics and understand them in detail, as opposed to having lots of interests, can result in specialist knowledge and fulfilment.

However, this can be very challenging to navigate within a traditional educational environment. If we struggle with motivation or focus on areas that aren't of interest, attending mandatory classes can be exceptionally hard. Whereas neurotypical people tend to have a motivation style focused on 'importance', such as the importance of learning across a range of subjects, we may not see the point, or be able to motivate ourselves.

For this reason, it's extremely important that AuDHD-ers understand their strengths and passions, and create environments where they can indulge in these. Tailoring teaching styles to the interest based nervous system can be very helpful, such as by gamifying learning or bringing in short term goals to foster dopamine and accountability.

Monotropism can also be challenging for students if they don't see any of their interests reflected in 'traditional' hobbies. As there's a focus on extra-curricular activities during school and university years, especially as a way to bond with others, this can feel isolating. I couldn't identify or accept my own interests until adulthood, as I was so focused on masking my symptoms during adolescence, which made life very hard.

AuDHD-ers should be reminded that their interests are valid, no matter how restrictive or niche they are. My music interests extend to one artist only: Taylor Swift. I will happily listen to her music on repeat, but this means I have no idea about popular culture or other musicians. This can make me feel quite alienated and 'weird' in comparison to others, especially during conversations about music.

It can also feel quite challenging to engage in conversations around topics that aren't of interest, and I will often relate these back to my experiences. This isn't because I'm not interested in other people, but because it's the only way I know how to connect without my brain disengaging.

This may not always come across during conversation, and friends may understandably become bored of hearing about my interests, which I've also turned into my work! The strong, magnetic pull of our interests can also lead to 'info dumping', where we share a monologue of experiences or information with others, despite not realising that they're not necessarily as interested as we are. As a result, conversations can become quite one-sided.

Learning

This also makes me pretty terrible at small talk, often diving in with 'deep' questions, such as asking what someone would do if they won the lottery.

However, there's absolutely nothing wrong with having a few (or one!) intense interest(s), rather than spreading our attention across lots, which is known as polytropism, more commonly seen in neurotypical people. Finding people who share our interests is important for a sense of community and shared experiences, reminding us that we are not 'weird' - we're passionate!

PROCESSING STYLES
Monotropic Split

This educational difference relates to how we process our environment, and its impact on our ability to pay attention. This can emerge in a few ways for AuDHD-ers, interacting uniquely with our other learning styles. For example, when a monotropic person is deeply engrossed in a task, their other senses may 'shut off'. This means they may become unaware of their surroundings, inner body sensations such as hunger or needing to go to the bathroom, noise, lights, and anything else.

If they are pulled from this without warning, they may experience a 'monotropic split'. Imagine a spotlight of attention that is suddenly disrupted by the main light being turned on in a theatre. All of the sensations overwhelm us at the same time, and it can be very distressing to experience, causing us to lash out. Equally, it can be quite unhealthy to ignore our own bodily needs!

Throughout my life, I've had the catchphrase of 'one minute!', as I remain so deeply immersed in whatever it is that I am focusing on, not wanting to return to the 'real world' and all of the sensory overload it brings.

Bottom Up Thinking

These differences can also show up as 'bottom up' thinking styles[42], meaning we process the details before the context of a situation. For example, in walking into a playground, an AuDHD child may be overwhelmed by stimuli such as voices, people, temperature, games, and other activity around them before being able to process that they are in a playground.

In contrast, a neurotypical person may experience 'top down' thinking, drawing on prior learning and memories, experiencing a 'concept-before-the-detail' approach.

This detail-orientated thinking can make it harder to focus on specific tasks or goals until all of the sensory input has been processed and organised. This can make it very difficult to prioritise or respond quickly, such as if we are asked a question in class by a teacher.

Problem Solving

This can also contribute to 'almost effortless associative thinking skills'.[43] As a 'bottom-up' thinking style doesn't constrain itself by seeing a set of symptoms and fitting these into a prior box. Instead, we can find innovative solutions and draw upon multiple stimuli and information to connect the dots.

This is a great benefit of our often 'squiggly' career backgrounds, as we can bring a huge range of skills and experiences to our present moment. Research[44] has linked innovative problem solving styles and creativity with ADHD and autism, resulting in endless ideas. Autistic people have been found to be 40% faster at problem solving than non-autistics.[45]

---

42   Extra with Temple Grandin on autism innovation: the secrets of Silicon Valley (2015) | The New Idealist
43   ibid
44   ibid
45   'Study Finds Autistics Better at Problem-Solving | EurekAlert!' Accessed 3 February 2025. https://www.eurekalert.org/news-releases/719241.

As a result of this attentional style, we may be great at pattern-recognition, even on a subconscious level. This can be disconcerting for those around us, where our brain may be working on overdrive to identify potential situations and outcomes, such as whether they still like us!

This can emerge as an analytical thinking style. For example, autistic people are said to have an 'unusual enhancement on logical consistency.'[46] This means that the way options are framed can impact our response, resulting in challenges when completing psychometric tests, for example. We may be reliant on logic, rather than emotions or interoceptive signals, which can result in misunderstandings in situations where we're expected to act a certain way, such as on birthdays.

Sensory Processing

AuDHD-ers may also experience sensitivities to their environment which heighten the intensity of stimuli. For example, bright lights, loud sounds, or even the texture of clothing can pull attention away from a task or interaction, as the brain prioritises managing sensory discomfort over situational context. We may be hyper-sensitive in some ways, such as sensitivity to sounds, or hypo-sensitive in others, needing certain stimulation to our surroundings.

Environmental unpredictability can also challenge our ability to focus, such as a lack of structure or inconsistent routines. This can make it harder for us to regulate our attention and feel secure in our surroundings, experiencing a constantly heightened state of anxiety or withdrawal as a coping mechanism.

---

[46] Shah, Punit, Caroline Catmur, and Geoffrey Bird. 'Emotional Decision-Making in Autism Spectrum Disorder: The Roles of Interoception and Alexithymia'. *Molecular Autism* 7, no. 1 (13 October 2016): 43. https://doi.org/10.1186/s13229-016-0104-x.

School and university can be hugely overwhelming because of this. From the intense noises, being in close contact with others, having to sit still for hours on end, and *then* do homework afterwards - it can be a nightmare. AuDHD children may use up a huge amount of energy masking at school, resulting in emotional outbursts when they arrive home.

This can be very difficult for their parents in terms of getting them a diagnosis, as Autism or ADHD assessments will generally require evidence of challenges within 2 or more important areas, such as home *and* school.

It can also be extremely challenging for parents to effectively advocate for their children within such broken systems. From navigating rules like when they can go to the toilet, to being made to go outside at break-time, school presents a mountain of difficulties. AuDHD children may also develop effective masking skills, such as my own in 'stimming' during class whilst making origami birds, which prevent their challenges from being picked up by others.

Audio Processing
Auditory discrimination is another important aspect of AuDHD, especially within schools. We may struggle to discern between different sounds, experiencing them all at the same level, such as various conversations in a dining room, and the sound of a fan. This can make it very difficult to be present, resulting in overwhelm. Similarly, we may struggle to respond to people when they are talking to us, such as not recognising when our name is called.

This is related to Auditory Processing Disorder (APD), which has been linked with an up to 50% occurrence alongside ADHD[47], where we can struggle with processing sounds. Up to 80% of reports by parents suggest that autistic children process sounds in atypical ways.[48]

I have APD, which was diagnosed after I completely forgot to press the button as directed upon hearing sounds in an auditory assessment! Not because I didn't hear them, but because I had zoned out. This has led to situations such as me not leaving a building when the fire alarm was going off, as I didn't register the sounds as an alarm, but I did hear them.

APD can make educational environments very challenging, as it's often an 'I speak, you listen' approach in class. Writing notes, doodling, or fidgeting can help with this, dependent on the individual. It's important to recognise that everybody will have a different way of processing information, and not everybody learns in the same way

Thinking styles

Temple Grandin has suggested three categories for autistic people's thinking styles: visual, verbal / logic, and musical / mathematical thinkers.[49] In my experience, these can also be applied to those with ADHD.

Visual thinkers think in pictures and need to see things to process information, such as by having a photographic memory. They may see things physically or in their mind to process information, making links between certain concepts that may seem confusing to others. For example, I would

---

47   Comorbidity of central auditory processing disorder and attention-deficit hyperactivity disorder - https://pubmed.ncbi.nlm.nih.gov/8083142/
48   Auditory Processing Disorder - Sophie Schwartz - Autism Speaks - https://www.autismspeaks.org/expert-opinion/auditory-processing-disorder#:~:text=We%20know%20that%20autism%20and,process%20sounds%20in%20atypical%20ways.
49   Temple Grandin's three types of Thinkers in Autism - Life With Aspergers - https://life-with-aspergers.blogspot.com/2011/08/temple-grandins-three-types-of-thinkers.html

focus on 'mentally photographing' the words that I needed to remember, linking the letters to other words that were similar, even though they had no context.

Verbal / logic thinkers may excel in learning languages, and have a passion for words, literature, and speech. They may think in lists, with a huge memory for facts and information, especially related to statistics.

Music and math thinkers may think primarily in patterns. This could relate to patterns in all areas of life, such as across numbers and relationships. As a result, AuDHD-ers with this thinking style may excel in pattern and/or formula based subjects, such as coding and music.

My belief is that we all share certain strengths, challenges, and thinking styles, but some of these may be more dominant than others. The Genius Finder[50] tool provides a great way of measuring a person's 'spiky' profile, helping to identify tailored strategies to support with areas as relevant to the individual.

Our dominance in certain areas may mean challenges in others. For example, I struggle severely with 'imaginative' thinking and play, finding it very difficult to get out of my head. I can feel overwhelmed at requests to act in a certain way, or to create something artistic with no reference point, for example. However, I can write this book!

Understanding how our brains naturally think can help to build self-confidence, identify strategies for learning, and process information effectively. This is especially important in educational environments, where students are generally expected to fit into an approach that may not work for everybody, with expectations around exams and tests, which can cause significant anxiety.

---

50   https://geniusfinder.com/products/individuals

Learning

Tips: AuDHD-ers

- Try to identify, recognise, and accept your learning styles and differences. You don't need to change yourself!

- Consider what you need from your learning environments.

- Consider disclosing your neurodivergence to your educational institute, because they may be able to help - even if you're not sure what is available. Seek out support for this, such as by taking a family member along with you.

- Personalise your learning style, such as by gamifying tasks or setting short-term goals.

- Minimise distractions by putting your phone as far away as possible! I always used to get someone to change the passwords on my social media accounts during exam time.

- Do what you enjoy, not what you think is a 'good' subject or career. You likely have great abilities in the areas you can hyper-focus on, so use them!

- Remember that your learning journey doesn't have to look like everybody else's. It's okay to be different.

- Try to build in time to align with your learning style, accommodating for transitions. For example, if you're monotropic, having lots of 'deep focus' time scheduled in your calendar can be useful, but build in time to transition out of this and change task - or eat lunch!

- Use timers, such as Pomodoro timers, to help shift focus if needed.

- Body doubling can be extremely effective for AuDHD-ers - try out online resources such as Focusmate.com.

- Leverage your strengths, and don't worry too much about your 'weaknesses' - you can find support for this, such as through tutoring.

- Navigate sensory overload by using tools such as earplugs or fidget toys as needed.

- Balance hyper-focus and burnout. We may have lots of deep interests that bring us joy, but we are still human beings that need to take breaks!

- Do one task that is not of interest before doing tasks that are of interest each day - your energy will be greater when you wake up.

- Embrace and validate your interests, even if they're niche, and find communities that share these interests. Be selective about who you choose to tell, if others aren't as keen!

- If anybody makes you feel uncomfortable, tell an adult you trust. Bullying is sadly very common, but it shouldn't be happening, and you can do something about it.

- Explore options of tools that can help with specific learning differences, such as speech-to-text software.

- Try to remember that school and/or university can be difficult, but it is just one part of your life. This might feel like your whole world right now, but you have so much ahead of you and don't have to 'achieve' or 'be' anything other than yourself.

- Explore options for support, such as Disabled Student's Allowance, if you're at university.

Tips: loved ones

- Help your loved one to explore how they naturally prefer to learn, and develop strategies to utilise their strengths.

- Support your loved one in advocating for accommodations that can help them within education, such as by using noise cancelling headphones.

- Encourage your loved one to follow their interests within education, reminding them that they don't need to do a 'normal' job!

- Support them to explore tools that could help, such as electronic notebooks or dictation software.

- Listen to your loved one's sharing of 'special interests', validating their experiences.

- Identify areas of challenge within education for your loved one and identify potential support, such as additional tutoring.

- Explore options for support, such as Disabled Student's Allowance for UK university students, and Education, Care and Health Plans, helping your loved one to access these.

- Remember that if you've met one neurodivergent person, you've met one neurodivergent person. Your loved one has their own unique experiences that they may not even understand themselves yet, so try to avoid making assumptions.

- Help your loved one to manage their focus and attention by breaking up tasks into chunks, and supporting them with transitions. Remember that if they are interrupted from a deep focus, they may become very distressed due to sensory overload, so try to help them such as by having a clock or sand timer within eyesight.

- Explore online quizzes with your loved one, helping them to identify what kinds of thinking styles they may have. The website EmbraceAutism has endless, excellent free resources for this.

Learning

- Help your loved one to navigate sensory overload during education periods by understanding their needs and strategies to support them through this, such as having 'wind down' time after school.

- Try to ensure there are breaks between high demand tasks, such as school, and other tasks that require high energy levels, such as going shopping.

5. Vulnerability

When I moved to London for university, a stranger approached me in a shopping centre and asked if I'd considered modelling. I mentioned I had done it before, and wasn't interested in starting again. However, I provided my phone number, and before I knew it, found myself at the agency office.

During this meeting, I was measured and told I needed to lose a few inches off my hips to join them. I left in tears, my existing eating disorders made worse by these strangers pushing me into a job I didn't even want to do. Even so, when the person who scouted me called to say that they were at risk of being fired if I said 'no', I ended up trying it out, which apparently just required me to 'stop eating bread for a few weeks'.

Those weeks became months, where I'd find myself working for free, often being pressured to get undressed to take photos for my portfolio in men's homes. I also discovered that my agency had planned to get me into debt by covering a hair appointment I didn't want in advance, 'on my account'. Fortunately, a family member found out and stepped in, strongly advising that I never let anybody get me into debt.

When I finally met the agency's weight requirements after months of starving myself, I was immediately asked to lose more. It felt like my soul - and literal agency - had been

Vulnerability

kidnapped. I was furious with myself, because I couldn't stop doing this 'job' I hated. The more I tried to change my body, the more I hated it - and I didn't even want to do modelling! This was especially so after learning that most modelling jobs didn't even pay any money, which was previously my only justification, as models were usually expected to work for free for 'exposure' in the type of high fashion niche which that agency specialised in.

It was only after I was pressured to do a lingerie campaign against my wishes ('they want curvy girls!' I was told), that I finally realised they didn't care about me at all, and quit.

However, after graduating from university, my life fell apart. The loss of structure provided by full time education had a significant impact on my well-being, even though I'd rarely attended class. I found myself unsure of what to do, spending my days worrying about how I'd survive financially, feeling like I had no prospects, despite having a law degree.

I applied for countless jobs doing anything at all, but was met with rejection after rejection. So, I joined another model agency, who were more 'commercial' and less restrictive than my previous one. After seeing a photo of the Whitsunday Islands in Australia, I impulsively booked a ticket to go a few months later, when it would be hot. I reasoned with myself that I'd have 'fun' for a year, and then return to complete another qualification in law, which could help me to become more employable.

However, modelling was far from fun. It was absolute chaos for my brain that was desperate for predictability, but addicted to novelty and adrenaline. I had to wait until 6pm every day to receive a 'Daily Schedule' email, outlining my next day. There was no option to refuse or ask questions - just a list of addresses to visit. Usually, this involved attending unpaid auditions, where I'd traipse around London with a heavy portfolio and heels, before often queuing for hours in lines with other models, sometimes spilling out all the way along a street.

I found these auditions, known as castings, very difficult. They involved talking to strangers and being scrutinised for my appearance, often being asked to undress in front of them. I struggled with travelling, usually getting lost, and dressing myself, even though I wore the same outfit of tight black clothes every day, as instructed by my agency. Lining up in hours-long queues of cold, hungry models standing on the pavement, I repeatedly questioned what I was doing with my life.

I did manage to book jobs, but these were also extremely stressful. The high of booking a job was immediately replaced by the belief that I'd never work again, as I obsessed over how to be 'perfect' and rebooked.

I didn't receive any money for several months, living off my teenage modelling income. This was partially because models are typically paid 3 months after doing a job, and partially because I had no idea how I was supposed to be paid. It was only when I ran out of savings that I meekly asked my agent whether they needed my bank account details, flushing with embarrassment.

Only then I discovered that I was expected to 'check in' with the accountant, who I didn't even know existed, every month to ask if any money had come through for me, which felt extremely embarrassing.

For a lot of the time, however, the 'Daily Schedule' emails didn't arrive at all. I would be paralysed with fear for the next day consisting of nothing but refreshing my emails repeatedly in case something came in, constantly on call. The boredom was intolerably painful.

Vulnerability

I usually spent the days applying for literally any 'real' jobs I could find, begging anybody to let me work for free for them. Friends of friends managed to get me work experience, but somehow I inevitably quit everything I started a few days in. I failed at everything from transport law to restaurant PR, feeling more and more hopeless each time.

Every rejection email I received would send me into an anxiety spiral about how unemployable I was, as I obsessed over each passing day of how I was 'too old' for modelling, despite only being 21 years old. I was convinced that I was already late to life, especially in comparison to my peers who'd all started their graduate schemes and career paths. Ironically, I was often on the websites they were shopping on during their breaks!

To cope with this uncertainty, I developed a habit of going out with club promoters and getting drunk if I had nothing to do the next day. I found that being hungover allowed me to exist without having non-stop anxiety about never being able to get a 'real job', giving myself permission to watch entire seasons of television shows all day.

One night, I felt attracted to someone. I was so torn up with shame about *mentally wanting to cheat* on my boyfriend of 5 years, just by this feeling (no actual cheating involved!), that the next day, I broke up with him.

Suddenly, I found myself in a hurricane of impulsive decisions. I moved into a shared flat, one of many, none of which I'd stay in longer than a few months - if I was lucky. In that one, I lasted until a friend stayed whilst I went on holiday, and I felt too awkward to ask for it back when I returned, instead finding a new place to live.

I immediately became addicted to dating. I'd swipe yes to everybody on dating apps, hooked on the dopamine highs of getting a 'match', hardly even looking at their profiles. I'd go on dates with anybody who asked to meet up, the anxiety of which I found settled immediately if I started them off with a mutual tequila shot.

Unsurprisingly, this usually ended up in dangerous situations with strangers. From me being in A&E nursing what I thought was a broken nose after falling off a table at a 'supper party', to dancing under the London Eye with a stranger, hours before he went to get an 'L' tattooed on his wrist... it was like living in a terrible television show.

These chaotic dates kept turning into very intense, short lived relationships, even though I didn't particularly want to be in them. The anxiety of a 'seeing' stage of dating was extremely painful, as I didn't see the difference between 'exclusive', 'dating', 'official', and 'in a relationship' - so I ended up moving far too fast with everybody who was unlucky enough to go on a date with me. Very quickly, these burned out, such as one that lasted for 3 weeks, where I went to see the same circus show *every single night* that the person was performing in, until I exploded with RSD.

Any attempts I made at 'sober' dating seemed to go badly wrong. Once, I suggested a first date at an immersive sensory exhibition that took place in complete darkness. I arrived late, finding that I had to give up my phone before being led into a dark room with two men - the guide and my date. Five minutes in, I had a huge crying panic attack meltdown, begging them both not to attack me, which didn't go down very well, especially as it was my idea!

Another saw me impulsively agree to go on a desert trip with a stranger I met when I went on holiday to visit a friend for a week, leaving their house for several days, where I was worried that I was 'in the way'. This seemed like a much better option, before I found myself sitting in the back of the car with no phone signal and two men I hardly knew,

Vulnerability

realising how incredibly dangerous this situation was. I had a huge panic attack, genuinely believing that they had planned the whole thing and were taking me to be murdered. Fortunately, we were fine, and they didn't take the accusation too personally!

If I wasn't on dates, I was clubbing, essentially getting drunk every single day. However, the clubbing invitations had started to include dinners with strangers, which I'd misunderstood as being hosted by these top London restaurants for PR purposes.

I only realised that there was potentially something wrong when an 18 year old model was once openly offered £10,000 in cash to sleep with a very wealthy man she'd never met before at the dinner table. There was also a clear expectation to go out clubbing afterwards, with the experiences starting to feel uncomfortably like an obligation. One night, my drink was spiked with drugs by the promoter, which they enthusiastically confirmed when I asked.

I also started being offered 'free' trips labelled as 'model holidays' to places like Dubai by both my agency and club promoters. I knew this felt very dangerous and too good to be true, and usually said no, blaming my schedule. However, during one bad moment, I impulsively accepted a trip to a club opening abroad from a promoter I had grown to trust and saw as a friend.

Immediately, I changed my mind, and was told that I'd have to pay for my flights if I wanted to cancel. My fellow model friend who'd first told me about it begged me to come, saying how afraid she was to go alone. So I went, only to find out that I'd been misled about the nature of the trip. It wasn't a club opening - it was a stag do.

I probably wasn't the best 'guest', shrieking about how I'd been lied to and trafficked to the men on the trip the entire weekend, who were all visibly uncomfortable and insisted they had no idea how the situation had come about. I honestly cannot believe that I survived.

During another 'free' dinner, a much older stranger invited me on a trip, travelling by private jet, to which I said a firm 'no', saying that I had to work. However, a few days later, I was sent to a modelling casting for a job in the same location, on the same dates, as the trip I'd declined. Naively, I thought it was a coincidence.

I then received excessive gifts from the stranger that costed more than an entire year's salary, making me feel extremely uncomfortable and as though I should be grateful, even though I didn't want them at all. Out of confusion, guilt and fear, I ended up going on the trip, unable to understand how I'd gotten there.

This led to a relationship that I was certain that I didn't want, but couldn't figure out how to escape. I felt trapped, yet guilty, watching my 'friends' benefit from the situation with presents and holidays, while I questioned what was wrong with me for being so unhappy. I eventually managed to get out of this situation when my partner told me how many other girls would kill to be in my position, and I impulsively answered that I didn't want to be at all. This relationship costed me the majority of relationships in my life, as I saw how so many people didn't seem to care about me or my wellbeing.

Seeing into this world showed me helped me to decide not to pursue a legal career just because 'it paid well'. Money very clearly could not buy happiness, but I wasn't sure what I was living for, my future stretching ahead of me like a void where things could only become even worse.

This saw the start of a very long period of becoming suicidal. I felt utterly trapped by my own brain, unable to

Vulnerability

stop putting myself in stupid situations and hurting people. It felt like being a ghost, with no identity, and nothing tethering me to the ground. I knew something was wrong, but I couldn't figure out what - I just felt like I was ungrateful and stupid. As a doctor told me, I had the 'world at my feet', but I felt like I was suffocating.

After believing I'd hit 'rock bottom', I went to see a therapist. I had never been so mortified in my life, believing that I'd be hospitalised. Ironically, I was extremely annoyed to learn that the therapist couldn't diagnose me with anything, or even give me any medication.

All I was told is that I was exceptionally vulnerable, despite my insistence that I'd actually had a 'really great life'. I couldn't understand the point of paying £75 for someone to simply 'listen' to me - I said that I may as well talk to a lamppost!

I was strongly recommended to stay in the same place and continue going to therapy, as I was at 'serious risk'. Of course, I ignored this advice, and went off to Australia alone to reinvent myself, yet again.

THE AUDHD LENS

AuDHD-ers are more vulnerable to harm and risk than others, because our brains work differently to 'most'. This means that we're living life from a different rulebook than others around us, potentially experiencing exploitation and abuse without even realising it.

This is especially so for women, as 9 out of 10 autistic women have experienced sexual assault.[51] It's extremely

---

51   Cazalis, Fabienne, Elisabeth Reyes, Séverine Leduc, and David Gourion. 'Evidence That Nine Autistic Women Out of Ten Have Been Victims of Sexual Violence'. *Frontiers in Behavioral Neuroscience* 16 (26 April 2022): 852203. https://doi.org/10.3389/fnbeh.2022.852203.

important to ensure AuDHD-ers receive education and safeguarding in ways tailored to their brain wiring, enabling them to protect themselves.

As we may experience struggles in identifying our own feelings due to alexithymia and impacted self-awareness, we may be unaware of our own needs or when we're being mistreated, resulting in experience challenges in self-advocacy. We may feel 'fine' 99% of the time, unable to understand how the same patterns keep repeating themselves where we end up in danger or emotional dysregulation. Just because we can't always feel fear, doesn't mean it's not there.

This can also affect our sense of self, identity, and future goals, as we may struggle to know who we are, what we want, or what is 'normal'. As a result, we may end up unconsciously handing our agency over to other people.

SOCIAL VULNERABILITY

Misunderstanding social cues, others' intentions, and our own needs or boundaries can make us extremely vulnerable. This can be confusing to experience, especially as we might find ourselves in situations we didn't want to be in, but blaming ourselves for not saying no.

The delayed processing speeds associated with autism and ADHD mean that we may need more time to understand how we feel about something, such as a request. The impulsivity associated with ADHD means we can often say 'yes' immediately, without checking in with ourselves. The struggles we may experience with communication, including for those who are nonspeaking, can obviously exacerbate these challenges significantly.

For example, if someone asks me if I 'can' do something, I automatically answer yes. I generally can do anything if I put my mind to it, and avoid sleeping or eating! This is

Vulnerability

very different to *wanting* to do something, which I usually don't even know until I've already agreed. This can leave me constantly overwhelmed, overcommitted, and trying to do everything for everybody whilst beating myself up for being 'weak' or 'stupid'.

This can also be very dangerous if others can spot this vulnerability and use it to their advantage. For example, previous boyfriends have made direct requests of me to do things I didn't want to do, but I had no idea how to literally say no, because I *could* do them - I just didn't want to. That didn't feel like a valid response, but I now understand it's because it didn't match the question I was asked.

This vulnerability can impact our lives in a range of ways. For example, we're likely to experience bullying by others, with 1 in 5 neurodivergent people experiencing harassment or discrimination at work.[52] We may also struggle to control our own emotions and behaviour, resulting in bullying others, or being hyper-aware to the possibility that we could be.

This can also relate to other aspects of AuDHD, such as sensory overload. I once shouted at someone I hadn't seen for many years after they didn't turn the radio down when I asked, resulting in a huge argument.

We might easily find ourselves arguing with others and cutting off relationships, due to the complex and impulsive nature of AuDHD. This can be very overwhelming, especially if we struggle to understand our own emotions, or how these situations have happened. I have had multiple people throughout my life simply stop talking to me overnight, for

---

[52] One in five neurodivergent employees have experienced harassment or discrimination at work because of their neurodivergence - CIPD - https://www.cipd.org/uk/about/press-releases/one-in-five-neurodivergent-employees-experienced-harassment-or-discrimination-at-work/

reasons I still don't understand, other than that I am the common factor.

The impact of AuDHD on our self-esteem can also be debilitating, meaning that we're very vulnerable to anyone who wants to be in our lives, regardless of how they might treat us. I felt like I had no choice over who I was friends with, or who I dated - they picked me. I felt 'bad' to reject people, despite knowing that I definitely didn't want them in my lives, blaming myself and trying to force myself to like them.

For me, one of the hardest parts about being AuDHD, is how vulnerable I am to abuse. I hate how much I struggle to understand other people's intentions, automatically assuming that I need to be 'useful' in order for them to like me. It can often feel like I do this myself, subconsciously figuring out how to best meet their expectations and offering myself up for exploitation, without even realising. This may be a method of trying to keep control in situations that felt uncontrollable.

AuDHD-ers may find themselves in a range of abusive situations, including domestic violence and toxic friendships. We may struggle to understand what is 'normal', and trust the behaviours of those around us over our own. For me, it's felt like a lifetime of gaslighting myself, unable to figure out whether I am the problem, or those around me.

We can easily struggle with our own boundaries, especially in handing trust over to complete strangers. This, especially in combination with our executive functioning struggles, can result in codependent relationships, involving unhealthy reliance on another person. I have had repeated relationships like this through my life, putting all of my energy into one person and becoming extremely vulnerable to them as a result.

Vulnerability

It can be very difficult to leave any abusive situation, which may be further complicated by AuDHD. On average, it takes 7 attempts before a woman is able to leave a domestically abusive relationship[53], which may lead us to repeatedly return to relationships we know aren't good for us. I've done this for *years*, unable to imagine a life without this magnetic pull back to the toxicity, but I am living proof that you *can* get out - the pattern will just repeat until it's broken.

Support

If this resonates with you, please seek out independent support so that you have someone to talk to who you can trust. Having a neuro-affirmative therapist or coach can be extremely helpful to have someone objective, who can share an insight into what is 'normal' or not. Most of all, trust your intuition.

Although it can feel complicated and overwhelming to try and navigate your way out of situations that you don't want to be in, it is *always* worth it. This is especially due to the change and transitions involved, and difficulty in forming and maintaining relationships, but there are people out there who will make you feel safe, happy, and respected.

It can be very helpful to talk to other people in your life about what you're experiencing. From personal experience, I know how difficult this can be, especially in not wanting others to think badly of someone that we may change our minds about in the future, but you deserve a second opinion, and are allowed to change your mind - as many times as you want!

If you're the loved one of an AuDHD-er and worried about their social relationships, or them potentially being

---

53   Refuge. 'Facts and Statistics'. Accessed 3 February 2025. https://refuge.org.uk/what-is-domestic-abuse/the-facts/.

taken advantage of by others, please try to maintain open lines of communication. They might not reach out automatically, and can easily become isolated, so making the effort to stay in touch is going to help them remember that there are other people who care about them.

Signals may be hard to spot, but they may include signs of exploitation, changes in mood, chronic self-doubt, unhealthy coping strategies, isolation, or a seemingly total reliance on others. AuDHD-ers may experience frequent misunderstandings or arguments with others, and quickly form very close relationships with other people.

For me, I have come to understand my own symptoms of being in abusive situations. These include severe emotional dysregulation, suicidal ideation, feeling totally reliant on another person, intense paranoia, and withdrawal. I will usually avoid socialising with others, overwhelmed at how to explain the challenges I am feeling, and stop doing things like exercising or self-care, usually dissociating with work. If you have AuDHD, you may wish to reflect on what your own warning signals are.

As a loved one, the best thing you can possibly do is offer unconditional support and reassurance. You could ask whether they'd like you to listen or to provide advice, being aware that they may take your words literally and overthink your opinions. For example, if you tell them to leave a situation and they don't, this might prevent them from reaching out again in the future. So being accepting, supporting, and there no matter what, will ensure that when they're ready to ask for help, they will.

ADDICTION

AuDHD-ers are also more vulnerable to engaging in risky behaviour, and may be easily influenced by others. This can

Vulnerability

lead us into 'the wrong crowds', with people who we incorrectly believe care about us, reinforcing these behaviours.

These behaviours may impact us differently to others, as we may be more vulnerable to addictive substances, such as alcohol and drugs. Studies show how 43%[54] of people with ADHD are at risk of developing alcohol use disorder, with another showing up to 36% of autistic people experience challenges with drugs or alcohol.[55]

These substances may be a form of masking, allowing us to better cope with AuDHD symptoms such as struggling to maintain eye contact or conversation in social settings, and sensory overload. Due to my impulsivity and impacted self-awareness, I had no concept of how much alcohol I was drinking, and struggled to know when to stop.

We also may be more vulnerable due to the nature of our dopamine-seeking brain, convincing ourselves that we need a drink to 'relax', calming the barrage of thoughts in our head. Other addictions, such as smoking, might activate these areas with nicotine.

For example, studies have found that people with ADHD are more likely to try or take up vaping, which can also offer a form of 'stimming' and excuse to take a break from socials situations for our autistic side, tricking us into believing we're more relaxed.[56] Nicotine also causes our brain to release dopamine, explaining why we may 'feel

---

54 'Alcohol and ADHD: How They're Linked | Gateway Foundation'. Accessed 3 February 2025. https://www.gatewayfoundation.org/blog/adhd-alcohol-relationship/.
55 SPARK for Autism. 'Alcohol, Drugs, and Autism: What Risk Do Autistic People Face?', 17 April 2024. https://sparkforautism.org/discover_article/drugs-alcohol-autism/.
56 Vaping and Young People with Special Educational Needs and Disabilities: Desktop Review - Healthwatch Brighton & Hove - https://www.healthwatchbrightonandhove.co.uk/sites/healthwatchbrightonandhove.co.uk/files/Vaping%20and%20Young%20People%20with%20Special%20Educational%20Needs_%20Desktop%20review%20findings_Final_.pdf

better' after smoking, but this is also extremely unhealthy, and expensive!

The social communication challenges associated with AuDHD mean that we may be highly vulnerable to peer pressure. This is important to watch out for within teenagers, when their friends may be experimenting with alcohol and drugs, for example.

Developing such habits at a young age can mean they become coping strategies throughout life, forming as habits and masking the true reasons at the core of the addiction. The effects of this can be devastating, and can prevent people from understanding or accepting that they may be neurodivergent.

For example, when I was diagnosed as autistic, I was met by surprise and disbelief by many people I knew. This makes sense: throughout my life, I have been 'social'. I would deliberately socialise by clubbing, where I could get drunk and become a different version of myself. I'd be the person organising the nights out, with many of my friendships based on alcohol.

Ironically, it was taking ADHD medication that enabled me to stop doing this. I'm not sure how this medication can be considered 'addictive', given that it helped me to regulate my behaviour in other areas, and I can often forget whether I've taken it or not! Personally, I'd much prefer to take legally prescribed medication that helps my brain, instead of being addicted to substances that are destroying it.

I commonly hear this concern from parents, anxious about putting their children on medication. Considering my experience, if I had taken this medication from a younger age, I would have been much better placed to avoid the terrible situations that alcohol placed me in.

Vulnerability

Support

If you're the loved one of an AuDHD-er with addiction issues, the best thing you can do is to be supportive and compassionate, avoiding blame and judgement. Seek to understand the behaviour, including where it's coming from, instead of shaming it.

You can also support AuDHD-ers by consciously engaging in non-alcohol or drug related socialising. I stopped drinking alcohol when I dated someone sober, making friends who also didn't drink alcohol. It was a revelation: I realised that until then, I had no idea how to socialise without this crutch. Whilst you may be able to control your limits, be aware that an AuDHD-er may not. Avoiding situations where they may be tempted to mask out of anxiety, such as pubs or clubs, can be extremely helpful.

If you're an AuDHD-er with substance challenges, please take some time to reflect on *why* you're using these things. For years, I felt that my 'drunk' self was much cooler and better liked than my sober self, but it wasn't until I discovered I was neurodivergent that I realised this was by everybody else - not me. I much prefer being in control of my life, behaviour, and actions.

A good way to understand if you may need help is by trying to simply 'go without' the relevant substance, such as alcohol, for a week. The next time you're in a social situation, try to have just one drink, or none at all. If you find yourself being unable to do this, please understand that this is *not your fault*, but it also may not be healthy for you to continue.

Seeking help from an organisation like Alcoholics or Narcotics Anonymous can be a great way to find a community and replacements for this behaviour, including friends who understand your experiences. It's never too late to meet your real self, the person behind the highs, and I'm sure that your life will improve. You deserve to have relationships that aren't based on your own vulnerability. These substances have been made to be deliberately addictive, and your unique brain wiring means that you're unfortunately more vulnerable than most, so please take care.

EXECUTIVE FUNCTIONING

Executive functioning challenges linked with AuDHD mean that we may struggle to do 'basic' things like food shopping, cooking, and/or cleaning. For me, this feels like self-neglect, and is very painful to recognise or accept, as I feel like I'm constantly failing at 'adulting'.

When a pie in my oven set on fire, I called 999, asking them how to put it out. They shouted at me to leave the building immediately, but I argued back, insisting that I could put it out. Eventually, I emerged from the front door, still in my pyjamas at 2pm. Fire officers came into my flat and told me I didn't have a smoke alarm - I hadn't even realised.

I've experienced everything from having hot water bottles explode in my face after failing to follow instructions about boiling water (don't use it!) to repeatedly falling down my stairs, lying on the floor, unable to move. Having AuDHD means I'm very messy, but need cleanliness and order. I often don't even realise how much the mess is affecting me until it builds up emotionally into a meltdown or shutdown.

Struggling with the 'basics' means that we can be extremely vulnerable in terms of our general safety and health. This also makes us vulnerable to dependence on others. For example, when I once crashed my car, I realised that I had no idea who I was insured by, as my partner had organised it.

This is also partially why I have repeatedly moved into people's houses after dating them for short periods of time. It felt easier to adapt to someone else's habits and routines, rather than create any myself, and was a relief not to have to transition from their home to mine. Obviously, it's not a good idea to repeatedly give up the stability you have to move in with someone you don't know, and I repeatedly found myself in dangerous situations that were very difficult to get out of.

Support
If you have an AuDHD-er in your life, please know that they're not lazy - they have neurological differences that make these types of 'easy' tasks extraordinarily difficult. They need help, not judgement. You can make a huge difference by teaching them basic life skills, such as the friend who once taught me how to cook using a slow cooker and wrote me out easy recipes to follow in a journal.

Helping them to build self-care habits, and encouraging them to make adjustments that will support them, such as by getting a cleaner or weekly food delivery organised, can truly change their lives. They may not think to ask, or be embarrassed about this, but try to open up conversations, sharing your own challenges in return, normalising their experiences without shame.

If you're an AuDHD-er who struggles with executive functioning and tasks such as general day to day administration and self-care, please know that this is not your fault. You are not lazy, or stupid. Your brain is simply chasing stimulation and dopamine, and it's okay to be overwhelmed by things that others seem to be able to do just fine. However, just because you struggle to do them, doesn't mean that self-care or an environment where you can thrive should be off limits to you.

Help is available, and you deserve it. I felt such shame about getting a cleaner, but after the repeated encouragement of a coach, I did - and it was life changing. Spot the internalised ableism and judgements against yourself, and try to replace them with kindness and compassion. Treat yourself as you would a friend who was unwell. You are not a failure, and we all have different strengths and challenges.

FINANCES

AuDHD-ers may be extremely vulnerable financially, easily finding ourselves in difficult financial situations, such as debt, or struggling to budget and running out of money.

I've coached multiple people who have 'given' their bank accounts to friends or family, as a strategy to stop them from spending all of their money - but this makes us very vulnerable, even to people we trust.

Finances can seem like an elusive concept, with lots of jargon and bureaucracy around things like bank accounts and interest rates. It might feel as though certain things aren't worth looking into, like investing. Alternatively, it might feel as though these things are *the only* thing you should be doing, putting all of your day-to-day money away and leaving yourself without anything to live on!

Naturally, this also makes us vulnerable to others. I once offered someone to have access to all of my savings, thinking this would help with a visa application. Another time, I offered all of my credit and debit cards to a stranger whose car I'd crashed into, as I had to go to a modelling job and was terrified of being late. They asked me if I was on drugs!

I will often buy things for people without thinking, such as picking up meals, and spending a huge amount of money on those I care about, such as by sending them gifts for no reason, but feel guilty to spend anything on myself.

Vulnerability

As AuDHD-ers may struggle with planning ahead and financial planning, we may simply avoid doing this. For years, I had no pension, writing off the idea because I 'probably wouldn't be alive at 60.' We may also find ourselves in difficult situations involving owing money to others, especially if we have the habit of not opening our post or forgetting to pay bills!

Support

If you have an AuDHD-er in your life, please recognise their vulnerability in this area, and look out for them. This could include not accepting their offers to pay for things (and making sure you repay them if this does happen, as we may forget to ask!), and opening up conversations about money.

Although it's not something we typically discuss openly with others, this can be extremely helpful to talk about for an AuDHD-er who may not realise what's 'normal' when it comes to finances. Having these conversations regularly, such as by helping them to create financial routines, can be extremely helpful.

Help them to build accountability and learn how to do these things in the ways that work for them, instead of doing it for them. For example, me and a friend used to review our bank statements together each week, which was extremely helpful for me to actually look at them - even though this was an idea I had for her benefit, as she was struggling financially! The accountability enabled me to cancel impulsive subscriptions and to strengthen my budgeting skills.

If you're an AuDHD-er, I strongly recommend learning about financial management in the ways that work for you. It might seem boring (and I've met endless AuDHD-ers who have told me how they're 'not financially motivated'!), but you do need money to live. Having savings is crucially important, because this equates to independence and freedom. On the balance of probabilities, you probably will be alive at retirement age - you've made it this far!

Having a few accounts that you can easily keep track of, and manage your finances with things such as savings pots and standing orders for money to be diverted out of your account for the end of the month, can be extremely useful. The first step is awareness. Many of us may avoid looking at our bank accounts where possible, as even thinking about money can feel overwhelming, but this will show you where your challenges lie.

If you find yourself spending impulsively on takeaway deliveries, for example, you may wish to choose to delete the apps. When I realised I was buying myself things off an online shop with next-day delivery so much that I often forgot ordering them in the first place, I removed my membership enabling me to have free shipping.

Simply building in a small moment of time can help us with thinking about whether we actually need or want an item. Having routines, such as checking your bank accounts on a monthly basis, can help to ensure you are financially secure. Personally, I have found having 'rules' such as not lending money to others to be helpful. Harnessing the autistic part of your brain that thrives on set rules is important here, taming the dopamine seeking ADHD impulsivity.

For more information on this, I recommend reading 'F is for Finance' of my book *ADHD: an A to Z*.

LEGAL VULNERABILITY

Given our inclination towards taking risks and general vulnerability, AuDHD-ers may be vulnerable to being victims

Vulnerability

and perpetrators of crime, with an estimated 25%[57] of the prison population thought to have ADHD.

This can result in a number of ways. For example, when a friend's parent taught me to steal from shops as a child, I copied this behaviour, not realising the implications until I was caught - I never stole anything again! Being neurodivergent means that we may not understand or respect certain laws, leaving us vulnerable to exploitation.

The executive functioning challenges linked with AuDHD can also result in misunderstandings and challenges around things such as paying tax.

Further to this, we may also experience legal vulnerability due to experiencing harassment or discrimination at work. I receive messages on a near daily basis from people who are struggling with these issues, seeking legal support.

Unfortunately, the legal system is not always very accommodating towards neurodivergence. Given the extreme stress we may feel about getting into trouble, we may mask in such situations, saying what we assume the other person wants to hear. Alternatively, we might be extremely honest, interpreting questions such as whether we're sorry for our actions, literally. In parole considerations for people in prison, for example, answers to such questions are often an indicator of whether they will be released or not.

Support

It's extremely important to ensure that if you find yourself navigating a legal challenge that you access support. Although our passion for fairness and social justice can mean we're tempted to take on battles by ourselves, you

---

[57] https://www.theguardian.com/society/2022/jun/18/uk-prisoners-attention-deficit-disorder-adhd-prison

don't need to do this; and it's extremely stressful. Court cases can drag out for years, ruining your life in the process.

Finding a neuro-affirming lawyer who understands neurodivergence is key. For example, we often work with Tom Haines of In-House It Solutions and Sam Walkley of XVO Legal, who I've found to be extremely kind, understanding, and upfront. Asking upfront for fixed costs of fees, limiting this in advance, can help with misunderstandings such as being charged without realising for sending lots of emails that you believe are helpful!

If you have an AuDHD-er in your life, making sure that they understand how to access support where needed is extremely important. Advocacy can be exhausting, as can being discriminated against and exploited, so providing support to AuDHD-ers experiencing challenges in this area is key, even if they claim to have it all covered.

You may disagree with their actions, but shaming them for this is unlikely to work, so try understanding and being there for them throughout, with unconditional positive regard.

HEALTH

Unsurprisingly, AuDHD-ers are extremely vulnerable to health challenges. This could be due to the variety of factors discussed in this book, including co-occurring conditions such as chronic illness, burnout, and substance abuse.

Burnout is common in AuDHD-ers, especially because we may not realise our own limits and capacity. We may say 'yes' to everything without realising how much we're taking on, masking throughout and becoming too exhausted to do anything at all.

It's also highly likely that we will experience mental health challenges, such as depression and anxiety. This

Vulnerability

can make life very stressful to navigate, and we may not even realise that help is available. It may be very difficult to engage with health services, such as visiting the GP, which can be exacerbated by RSD and communication challenges. This is especially because even if we do seek help, this may not be understood properly within the context of our AuDHD.

We may also experience health challenges in relation to our executive functioning and self-care skills. For example, when I started experiencing temporary blindness during one period of extreme stress, I booked an eye test. The optician couldn't believe that I hadn't had an eye test in over a decade! Things like going to the dentist or having check-ups seem overwhelming, including the various steps such as figuring out a time, and planning ahead.

Support

If you know an AuDHD-er, you can support them by helping to create regular routines for things like going to the dentist. You can also help by talking to them about any health challenges they may be experiencing and sharing your experiences. For example, it was only when a friend commented on how unhappy I was after visiting me on holiday that it hit me - I hadn't realised that crying every day wasn't normal.

Staying alert to any health challenges they may experience now or in the future is also important, taking these seriously. Noticing any changes in mood, for example, or patterns of behaviour can help to indicate any potential concerns that the person themselves may be unaware of. Don't take it for granted that they will get help when needed - pro-actively take steps to support them, such as by visiting them at home, or making them appointments with medical professionals. You can make adjustments to help them, such as by having nights in together instead of going out, conserving energy.

It can also be very helpful to accompany them on visits with medical professionals, supporting with advocacy and ensuring that their needs are taken seriously. If not, you can help them by seeking out a neuro-affirmative practitioner - please don't give up.

If you're an AuDHD-er, I'm sorry for how confronting this chapter (and book!) might feel. However, accepting your vulnerability is absolutely crucial to ensuring your wellbeing and safety. Your neurodivergence means that you may be less aware of when you need support than others, and despite there being many brilliant strengths and positives of AuDHD, it does make you vulnerable.

This doesn't mean that you have to hide yourself at home for the rest of your life, but prioritising your health, safety, and wellbeing is key. Notice how the people who you spend time with make you feel and treat you. Identify any patterns that are feeling out of control, and make regular appointments with yourself to check in on your health.

This might feel like 're-parenting' yourself, especially if you experience similar challenges to me around areas like cooking or cleaning. However, it's okay to accept that you have learned to do things differently than others, with 'creative adjustments', but you deserve to be safe and healthy. You don't need to live on chicken nuggets - you can learn how to do these things in the ways that work with your brain.

Tips: AuDHD-ers

- Automate as much of your life as you can, such as by setting up regular dentist and doctor appointments in your calendar, or by using budgeting tools for finances. Every decision takes up valuable energy, so automate decisions where possible, to save it.

- Break down goals into smaller, more manageable steps to avoid overwhelm, such as by putting a timer on for 5 minutes of cleaning. Some is better than none!

- Ask for help, such as by having an accountability partner. Your friends and family are there to support you.

- Seek external support where necessary, such as Alcoholics Anonymous, or therapy.

- Keep a diary, and 'brain dump' in it before bed. This can be very helpful to track how you're feeling over a long period of time, and putting information such as in relation to what you've eaten that day can help with nutrition awareness.

- Use visual and automated reminders to help you prioritise yourself. I had a sign by my door for months that I'd painted which read 'Protect Yourself!'

- Identify safe spaces and people that can support you when feeling overwhelmed. It's important to have someone you can trust who you feel comfortable asking for advice and support.

- Identify your own signs of vulnerability, drawing on any previous situations that may have left you feeling unsafe or uncomfortable. Pro-actively take steps around this, such as by not going to places that serve alcohol.

- Create social scripts and 'rules' to help you navigate social situations, such as not paying for other people!

- Ensure that you don't become overly reliant on other people. Although this can feel tempting, it's extremely important to ensure your independence and autonomy. Notice any warning signs, such as needing to ask another person's advice or opinion before making small decisions on a regular basis, or areas of your life that you may be unsure about, like finances.

Tips: loved ones

- Reach out as much as you can - remember that your loved one may not always respond as expected, but they will definitely appreciate it.

- If you're worried about an AuDHD-er, try to speak to them about your concerns in a way that feels comfortable for them, such as by writing them a letter. Reminding them that you're there and can handle anything they're feeling is important, as they may not want to 'burden' you, or see the point in talking about it.

- Support your loved one with 'basics' such as booking health check-ups and financial management. Ensure that they understand the dangers of things like debt or buy-now-pay-later schemes!

- Try to engage with your loved one in ways that don't involve alcohol, such as by meeting up at a park instead of a pub.

- If your loved one is struggling with addiction, remember that this isn't their choice. Supporting them to break it down and identify small changes they could make in collaboration will be extremely helpful.

- If you'd like an AuDHD-er to do something, give them specific, detailed, and direct instructions. For example, instead of saying 'please lay the table', you could say, '[their name], please put out the knives and forks on the table'. Don't assume they will know what you mean!

- If you're concerned about someone your loved one is socialising with, tell them at the time. They may not realise this, and simply addressing what you've noticed can help to spark a realisation within them for the future.

- If your loved one is struggling with legal aspects, such as unpaid bills, make an effort to sit down and support them with this, ensuring they have appropriate support.

- Body doubling with your loved one, such as by creating shared routines to go to the dentist, or food shopping, can be extremely helpful, and provide a consistent touchpoint for connection.

6. Mental Health

After changing my tickets numerous times, I finally made it to Australia, despite a lost suitcase on the plane. I headed straight for Bondi Beach, sitting by the ocean and felt a moment of happiness, before me and my one bag of belongings were drenched by a giant wave.

I initially stayed with a friend's family, who I had gone to school with whilst living in the UK 10 years previously. I felt frustrated at being unable to remember any of the shared memories they spoke about, wondering what repressed trauma had 'happened to me' to cause this memory loss.

Living in Australia felt like a persistent wave of anxiety, because I was on a one-year working holiday visa, and couldn't be sponsored to stay longer as a model. The brief happiness I'd felt on my first day quickly gave way to constant dread, as I anxiously watched the days pass, terrified of the prospect of returning to the UK, every waking moment spent worrying about the future.

At the time, I didn't realise that I was struggling with my mental health. One day I broke out in a red spotty rash all over my body. Alarmed that this could impact any potential modelling jobs, I went to the doctor, who said it was stress related. I insisted that I wasn't stressed, explaining how I was the happiest I'd ever been.

I didn't recognise that my internal experience wasn't healthy, or even that it amounted to being unhappy. For me, it was normal. He asked what I'd eaten that week, and I realised that I'd been living on smoothie bowls and alcohol. I laughed when I was advised to get a massage, but to my amazement, it made the rash disappear instantly.

I'd left behind a complete mess in the UK. My modelling back there had descended into me bizarrely becoming a top maternity model, at the grand age of 22. I felt terrible about this, especially as a relative explained how pregnancy changed a woman's body in ways such as their ankles swelling, which obviously wasn't reflected on my size 8, non-pregnant, anorexic frame.

Every maternity job felt like I was misleading pregnant women into comparing themselves to me, but they were all I seemed to get booked for, and I didn't know how to say no. Ironically, I worked harder than ever to lose weight, assuming I was being booked as a maternity model because I was too 'big'.

So when I arrived in Australia, I was terrified. However, my model agency there immediately booked me onto campaigns for some of the biggest brands in the country. For the first time in my life, I agreed to do swimwear modelling, because I'd decided not to pursue law, believing this was 'one or the other'. Seeing myself in billboards made me feel uneasy, because I realised that the option of working in law was now definitely 'gone'.

I couldn't imagine anything beyond the present moment, feeling like only darkness lay ahead. I was convinced that I'd be an unemployable, unattractive, and lonely old woman with zero job prospects. To cope, I compulsively applied for any job I could find on a daily basis. Every rejection hit me like a gut punch confirming my fears, descending into suicidal ideation.

At a party a stranger on the beach invited me to, I met a man three times my age who ran a successful business.

When I asked him for a job, he arranged a meeting, and I *took him brownies*. He happily offered to sponsor me to stay in Australia, before insisting on driving me home, because he couldn't possibly have me take the bus.

Somehow I then ended up in his flat he'd just 'wanted to show me quickly', begging him not to murder me, to his surprise. I managed to leave, feeling uncomfortable, scared, and guilty, as though I'd accidentally led him on. An immigration advisor later advised me against the sponsorship, suggesting that it may be related to ulterior motives. I was crushed emotionally, realising that it was hopeless that anyone would ever seriously want to hire me.

I became obsessed with taking my own life. A taxi driver had once pointed out a local cliff edge called 'The Gap' that was notorious for people ending their lives, which became a fixation. Every day, I'd repeatedly scour the internet to understand whether anyone had died there, collecting research about the viability of the method. It was a macabre daily ritual that kept me mentally locked in darkness.

I also became obsessed with researching mental health conditions, unable to understand how I seemingly had ALL OF THEM. I was convinced that if anyone truly knew was going on in my brain, I'd be committed to a psychiatric hospital against my will, which would be even worse. This also prevented me from actually trying to kill myself, because I couldn't be 100% sure that I'd succeed, meaning that I'd likely end up in hospital.

Researching the 'success rate' of different suicide strategies was the only time my brain seemed to switch off, bringing a numbing sense of calm and hope. The rest of the time, I was plagued with guilt and shame about it. Suicide simply seemed like a logical 'off' switch to my disaster of a life, but I knew that it would hurt people in some way, such as my housemate.

AuDHD: Blooming Differently

I felt like I needed to find a reason, or suitable compromise before allowing myself to attempt an exit, my brain grappling between life and death. I tried to volunteer abroad, but even those applications were met with rejections. It felt extremely unfair to have to live and find a way to survive, when I hadn't asked to be born.

I also felt so selfish, because as one doctor told me when I vaguely tried to explain what was going on, I was a healthy young woman who could do anything. I had a law degree. I was a model. I made enough money to survive. I just needed to pick and stick to one thing. I agreed and left smiling, whilst knowing that it wasn't healthy to spend all of my time trying to figure out how to die, but I couldn't seem to communicate my shameful reality or inability to do this in full.

The most frustrating thing was that I had moments where I felt okay. I'd write out suicide letters all night, before waking up and tearing them into tiny pieces so my housemate wouldn't find them, extremely embarrassed. The routine repeated itself on a daily basis, and was utterly exhausting.

I was still incapable of controlling my day to day life and decisions around this. When I learned that an ex-boyfriend was visiting Sydney, I booked a trip away to avoid seeing him, impulsively inviting my new boyfriend of a few weeks along, just in case they happened to bump into each other when I was gone.

There, we went skydiving in the Whitsunday Islands, after which I burst out crying because I spent the entire minute and a half wishing that the parachute wouldn't open and I would die. I felt extremely guilty for wishing this, recognising that would have meant the death of the man I was attached to as well. It was symbolic of the mental torture I was in - wanting to die but being strapped to life and other people against my will.

Mental Health

At that point, things became unavoidably obvious externally as I explained why I was crying to my then boyfriend. He was understandably very concerned and we left the trip early so I could go to the doctor.

I finally booked a psychiatrist appointment for hundreds of dollars, understanding by then that these professionals were the only ones who could diagnose me with the myriad of serious mental health conditions that I obviously had.

In the meantime, a friend advised me to go to hospital to remove my contraceptive implant, explaining that this could be the cause. There, the emergency room doctor questioned my decision. He suggested I cancel the psychiatrist appointment, as he could give me medication to help, without even officially diagnosing me with anything. I was told to return to the emergency room a week later and to tell the reception that I had a wound that needed stitching.

I cancelled the appointment, before looking the medication up online to discover a warning about an increased risk of suicide. I felt overwhelming joy at now having a valid 'reason' to die. My death could be linked back to this medication, saving everybody I knew from feeling like it was their fault. Finally, I could plan and action my suicide without guilt. I never even tried the medication.

I set my plan for a week later, ensuring that it'd cause as little disruption as possible. I still had a modelling job to complete, belongings to pack, and ironically, a mental health group to attend which I volunteered for.

I'd stumbled across this group after being taken by a stranger who was supposed to teach me 'mermaid swimming'. When I turned up to the beach at 6am, I found a group of brightly dressed people sitting in a circle talking about mental health in the pouring rain. It'd been set up after the founder was hospitalised for Bipolar Disorder, and

I thought that volunteering could help me to see if I had it too (it didn't). It also felt too embarrassing to attend just because I needed it - I needed an excuse.

Once I'd made my plan, I finally felt at peace for more than a minute. I experienced an entire week without my daily routines of googling suicide or feeling crushing guilt, because it was all in hand. Instead of obsessing about the future, I enjoyed the present, walking along the beach and being able to enjoy it for the first time, taking it all in. I ate chocolate almond croissants for breakfast every day, because it no longer mattered if I put on weight, experiencing the pleasure of food. I reached out to my friends to hang out (and say goodbye, though they didn't know that), and had fun.

I did my modelling job without my usual sense of shame and fear, having an incredible experience with wonderful people, wearing beautiful clothes on a tiny island in the middle of the ocean. I didn't have a single fear about what job to do in the future, just gratitude for the moment. For the first time, I felt the *'lucky'* feeling I'd been 'supposed' to feel for so long.

The cognitive dissonance was also annoying to experience, as it dawned on me that I was happy, invalidating all of my previous beliefs about how painful and terrible life was. When I went to volunteer at the mental health group, I heard someone share a similar story to mine, feeling like they were describing my life.

They explained how their life had spiralled out of control after university, making impulsive decisions such as coming to Australia, breaking up with their long-term partner and becoming extremely suicidal. It was the first time I'd ever heard anybody else talk about suicide, and I felt in awe at realising I wasn't alone - the person looked relatively normal from the outside. Then they said their ex-partner had been murdered that week.

Mental Health

The experience shifted something inside of me, a core realisation that *we could all die at any moment*. I realised that I was so consumed with planning my death, but had never considered the fact that I could just drop dead at any moment, or indeed actually be murdered. I hadn't stopped to appreciate how lucky we all are to be alive and healthy, especially my own friends and family. It hit me that there was no point to this 'life' thing other than to live it, as our deaths were all inevitable. The only point was to enjoy it, like I'd done that week.

On the way home, I bumped into a lifeguard who'd saved my life a few months earlier, ironically whilst I was caught in a rip whilst mermaid swimming. I'd had no idea that the 'red flags' were literal instructions, usually ignoring them. I remembered how when I was drowning, a plastic mermaid tail enclosing my feet, I'd shouted for help, realising that I didn't want to die in that moment. After she'd saved me, I took her a thank you card with a mermaid on it, and we became close friends.

Seeing her was the final reminder I needed that I was here for a reason. I decided that it was time to get proper help, booking a flight back to the UK to get the support I truly needed. I wanted to live.

THE AUDHD LENS

Suicide rates and mental health challenges are heart-breakingly high for neurodivergent people, demonstrating the struggles of living in a world that isn't designed for your brain.

Almost 8 out of 10 autistic people have a mental health condition such as anxiety or depression, with up to 67%[58] of inpatients in mental health settings being autistic, despite

---

[58] 'Number of Autistic People in Mental Health Hospitals: February 2024'. Accessed 3 February 2025. https://www.autism.org.uk/what-we-do/news/number-of-autistic-people-in-mental-health-ho-18.

only 1% of the population said to be autistic.[59] Later research has estimated that this latter figure is actually double due to the lack of diagnosis, with over 1.2 million people being autistic.[60] More than 9 in 10 of all autistic people over the age of 50 are said to be undiagnosed.[61]

Approximately 80% of adults with ADHD present with at least one other mental health condition in their lifetime.[62] More than 60% of children with ADHD are reported to have one or more co-existing mental health conditions.[63]

If you don't know that you're neurodivergent, you can't get help for the root cause of your challenges. In 2015, autistic people made up 38% of the number of people in mental health inpatient units in England, but as of 2024, this rose to 67%.[64] The average length of stay is almost 5 years, with widely reported cases of abuse occurring in such settings.

However, autism can't be treated or 'cured', because it's simply the way someone's brain works. We might be medicated for things like anxiety in response to panic attacks and meltdowns, but the fundamental reasons for our anxiety won't be identified and supported, such as sensory overload or struggles in understanding others.

For me, this feels like the equivalent of locking people up in asylums for being 'hysterical', institutionalising people

---

[59] ibid
[60] ibid
[61] ibid
[62] Ogrodnik, Michelle, Sameena Karsan, and Jennifer J. Heisz. 'Mental Health in Adults With ADHD: Examining the Relationship With Cardiorespiratory Fitness'. *Journal of Attention Disorders* 27, no. 7 (May 2023): 698–708. https://doi.org/10.1177/10870547231158383.
[63] M.Pharm, HH Patel. 'Is ADHD Linked to Other Mental Health Conditions?' News-Medical, 4 June 2018. https://www.news-medical.net/health/Is-ADHD-Linked-to-Other-Mental-Health-Conditions.aspx.
[64] 'Number of Autistic People in Mental Health Hospitals: February 2024'. Accessed 3 February 2025. https://www.autism.org.uk/what-we-do/news/number-of-autistic-people-in-mental-health-ho-18.

who think differently to most, and hiding them away from society. Although there was a huge review of the legislation in the UK allowing this to happen, confirming these systemic problems, no change has been implemented.

This leaves AuDHD-ers extremely vulnerable, with the potential for our symptoms being misdiagnosed, unable to access support that meets our needs, and fighting for survival in a world that works against us.

Masking

Masking is a learned strategy that neurodivergent people use to appear as neurotypical and blend in with others. For AuDHD-ers, it could include anything from scripting conversations, repressing urges to 'stim' or fidget, hiding our interests, or forcing eye contact.

This is often developed within childhood, where we pick up the social cues and indicators of what we 'should' be doing. As children with ADHD are said to receive 20,000 more negative comments than their peers by age 12[65], it's unsurprising that our brain develops 'creative adjustments' to survive.

Autistic people who mask have been found to show more signs of anxiety and depression, and masking has been linked to an increase in suicidal behaviours.[66]

This is why education about masking and AuDHD is so critically important. From the outside, we may appear to

---

[65] 'Children with ADHD Avoid Failure and Punishment More Than Do Their Peers, Study Says'. Accessed 3 February 2025. https://www.additudemag.com/children-with-adhd-avoid-failure-punishment/.
[66] Cassidy, S. A., K. Gould, E. Townsend, M. Pelton, A. E. Robertson, and J. Rodgers. 'Is Camouflaging Autistic Traits Associated with Suicidal Thoughts and Behaviours? Expanding the Interpersonal Psychological Theory of Suicide in an Undergraduate Student Sample'. *Journal of Autism and Developmental Disorders* 50, no. 10 (2020): 3638–48. https://doi.org/10.1007/s10803-019-04323-3.

be fine, even believing this ourselves. However, we may not realise that it's not normal or necessary to be so stressed all of the time. Combined with alexithymia, this can mean we're unaware of our masked survival tactics until this explodes through burnout, coming as a surprise to everybody.

When I was diagnosed as autistic, I realised how I had masked in *every single area of my life* without even realising it. It was subconscious, from forcing myself to make eye contact to creating 'rules' around socialising, such as the need to be 'helpful' in return for companionship. It felt like I had been living a lie for my entire life.

Most noticeable was just how much energy this used, which I hadn't even realised before. I was utterly exhausted at seeing the effort that went into every single part of my life, the internalised ableism of fighting against myself for struggling to do things like having a shower, and the endless chastising of myself for being 'lazy'.

I experienced burnout, unable to do anything other than write this book for 10 days solid. I couldn't face seeing other people and putting this mask back on, which didn't feel like a choice I could make.

This is because masking throughout your life results in a loss of identity. You stop understanding who 'you' are, and become a shape-shifter, defined by context and circumstances. This is exacerbated by the impacted self-awareness of AuDHD, meaning that we may struggle to understand our own behaviours or traits without externalising these in others.

We might 'anchor' ourselves and our realities in other people, things, or concepts, such as a partner or a job title. When this falls away, it can feel like a bereavement, because we don't know who we are anymore.

Masking can also mean that we don't access the support we desperately need, because we may appear 'fine' externally.

Mental Health

At a medical level, diagnostic criteria is also outdated, based on presentations of autism and ADHD in little boys. Just as I was dismissed as fine by a doctor for having a law degree, people are denied a diagnosis due to factors such as being able to hold down a job, or for having friends.

This is especially so for children who may not mask in some situations, but not others, meaning that the adults in their life only see one 'version' of them. For example, they may mask at school, but explode with overwhelm at home. This can be difficult to explain to a medical professional, and the child may also mask during an assessment, possibly without even realising that they're doing it. This can understandably very distressing for parents, who I imagine may doubt themselves as a result, but who ultimately know that their child desperately needs help.

Although the diagnostic criteria is largely based on deficits causing impairments in various settings in our lives, we may use a huge amount of energy masking our symptoms, resulting in hidden impairments that others cannot see or understand, until we burn out from exhaustion. This means that people who need help may also have a difficult time convincing a medical professional that they are AuDHD, which can feel invalidating and embarrassing, as though they just 'want a label' or are taking support from those who 'really need it'. Everybody deserves support, and your struggles are valid.

Whilst everybody in our society 'masks' to some extent, such as by wearing 'professional' clothes at work, AuDHD-ers may be doing this *all of the time.* I'd liken it to being an actor in a movie, constantly rehearsing scripts, conscious of your facial expressions, and trying to predict what everyone around you will say or do next. This is unsustainable, even if we've done it for so long that it feels normal.

To help with this, it can be helpful for AuDHD-ers to journal about their experiences every day, noticing the points at which they felt slightly uncomfortable, or acted in ways that didn't feel natural. Everybody will have different ways of masking, but the ways that you do so are absolutely valid.

Finding environments and people that accept you as you are is key to creating a life where you don't have to pretend to be somebody else. This isn't as impossible as it might feel - it comes from slowly allowing authentic parts of yourself to emerge, and noticing the responses of others to this. Everybody is changing and growing all of the time, and you have the right to redefine yourself at any point.

Rejection Sensitive Dysphoria (RSD)

As explained in chapter, 'Childhood', RSD is characterised as 'extreme emotional pain triggered by real or perceived rejection, lasting for a limited period of time'. It was identified by Dr William Dodson[67], who linked this exclusively with ADHD, as opposed to any other conditions.

However, in practice, it's also commonly associated with autism.[68] This likely underlies the core features of masking and neurodivergence, in working so hard to present an 'acceptable' version or ourselves to the world that it can be extremely painful when this doesn't work.

The executive functioning challenges linked with both ADHD and autism feature difficulty in regulating our emotional responses. This can be extremely dangerous, especially

---

[67] Emotional Regulation and Rejection Sensitivity - Dr William Dodson, MD - CHADD - https://chadd.org/wp-content/uploads/2016/10/ATTN_10_16_EmotionalRegulation.pdf
[68] Verywell Mind. 'Rejection Sensitive Dysphoria and Autism: What to Know'. Accessed 3 February 2025. https://www.verywellmind.com/what-to-know-about-autism-and-rejection-sensitive-dysphoria-7097539.

when combined with symptoms such as impulsivity, seeing a 5 times higher likelihood of attempted suicide for people with ADHD.[69] 1 in 4 women with ADHD have made attempts on their life.[70] Studies have shown that up to 66% of autistic adults have thought about ending their life, and 35% have attempted suicide.[71]

Nobody likes being rejected, but what's notable about RSD is the intensity of our reactions. The intense emotional pain can be so crushing that we end relationships or quit jobs, especially when combined with our impulsivity. It can often be a response to seemingly 'small' and 'irrational' things, including our own thoughts.

This can show up in our daily lives as we attempt to anticipate the needs of everybody around us. We may use a lot of effort in monitoring our words and expressions, conscious of appearing 'too much' by saying what we're thinking, or sharing our interests. Ironically, this could lead to us worrying that we seem disengaged, or assuming that a person only likes one 'version' of us, instead of who we really are.

This can lead us to burnout, because we're simply so exhausted from dealing with the maelstrom of thoughts in our head. It can feel like we're simply a vessel to please other people, pouring out our love and kindness to others,

---

[69] Shen, Yanmei, Bella Siu Man Chan, Chunxiang Huang, Xilong Cui, Jianbo Liu, Jianping Lu, Marguerite Patel, Christopher D. Verrico, Xuerong Luo, and Xiang Yang Zhang. 'Suicidal Behaviors and Attention Deficit Hyperactivity Disorder (ADHD): A Cross-Sectional Study among Chinese Medical College Students'. *BMC Psychiatry* 21, no. 1 (18 May 2021): 258. https://doi.org/10.1186/s12888-021-03247-6.
[70] Suicide In ADHD - NHS Berkshire Healthcare - https://www.berkshirehealthcare.nhs.uk/media/109514702/suicide-in-adhd-adhd-bekrshire-healthcare.pdf
[71] Autistica. 'Suicide - Autism Research | Autistica', 23 August 2017. https://www.autistica.org.uk/our-research/research-projects/understanding-suicide-in-autism.

whilst leaving none for ourselves. It can lead us to say 'yes' to everything, resulting in one day being unable to do anything.

The one-sided nature of our relationships with RSD may be unhealthy, especially if we're being taken advantage of. As in chapter, 'Vulnerability', we may find ourselves easily controlled by others, in dynamics that ease our need for clarity in relationships, such as with those who tell us what to do. Although exhausting, or upsetting, the predictability of these relationships may feel preferable to the anxiety of a relationship were the expectations of us are unclear.

RSD can also mean that we assume that other people either don't like us, or wouldn't be there for us if we needed them. This can prevent us from sharing our own struggles, or seeking support when needed, which can be exacerbated by autistic difficulties in communication. As a result, we may neglect our need for validation, emotional support, and connection, resulting in burnout as we take all of this on by ourselves.

This kind of burnout could also be social, such as occurring after an event with other people, or reaching exhaustion point after helping so many others. We may feel bad about protecting our own energy, or saying 'no' if asked to meet up, which can see us transitioning from one engagement to the next.

Social burnout can result in us withdrawing from our relationships all together. We may struggle to even leave the house, preferring to stay in the predictability of our home environments, where we can't be judged. It could see us 'impulsively' ending relationships, seemingly out of the blue, gaslighting ourselves about whether they - or we - are abusive.

Mental Health

For me, this was one of the key reasons I believed I was autistic. When I started ADHD Works, I was simply too exhausted to engage with anybody. I felt no 'joy' from seeing other people, just exhaustion. They all seemed to require energy, and me doing something for someone else, even if they didn't ask - I would figure out how to help them and offer it without realising!

If I had my choice, I would never see anybody, simply staying at home - but I also felt unbearably lonely. My therapist couldn't understand this, which made me doubt myself, feeling like a terrible person and as though I 'hated everybody'.

Understanding RSD is extremely important for AuDHD-ers, the people in our life, and medical professionals to ensure that AuDHD isn't dismissed. It doesn't mean that a person is weak, or overly-sensitive, but simply that they may need a different form of relationship dynamics to what is considered 'normal', to ensure their needs are met as well as everybody else's!

As an AuDHD-er, knowing about this can help to ensure that you protect your energy, such as by having at least one day a week to yourself, with no social plans. Recognising the RSD spiral can help with remembering that no - nobody hates you! If anyone is upset at you, it's their responsibility to let you know.

Misdiagnosis

As a result of masking, outdated diagnostic criteria and stigma, AuDHD-ers people may experience misdiagnosis throughout their lives. This is especially so given the myriad of mental health challenges and trauma that can arise as a result of struggling so much internally.

Research shows how this can also be exacerbated by gender, with autistic women (31%) reporting perceived misdiagnosis more frequently than men (16%).[72] This is likely impacted by women and girls better able to mask their symptoms. Personality disorders were the most frequent received misdiagnosis, followed by conditions such as anxiety and chronic fatigue syndrome.

In one study, over 75% of participants received an autism diagnosis 8 years after their first mental health evaluation.[73] The same trends can be seen for ADHD, as in one study, 75% of adults with ADHD were not previously diagnosed in childhood.[74] In childhood, boys are 4 times more likely to be diagnosed than girls, but in adults, the ratio is 1:1.[75]

This is largely because autism and ADHD can't be identified with a physical test, such as by our blood, but this also applies to mental health conditions in general. It's a subjective assessment often based on wider context, including a person's history, presentation of their symptoms, other people's perceptions of them, and factors such as school reports, which may not be available.

As a result, neurodivergence can easily be missed. Not having access to the support or understanding that we may need, and the cumulative effect of masking may result in mental health conditions such as depression and anxiety

---

[72] Kentrou, Vasiliki, Lucy A. Livingston, Rachel Grove, Rosa A. Hoekstra, and Sander Begeer. 'Perceived Misdiagnosis of Psychiatric Conditions in Autistic Adults'. *eClinicalMedicine* 71 (4 April 2024): 102586. https://doi.org/10.1016/j.eclinm.2024.102586.
[73] Gesi, Camilla, Giovanni Migliarese, Sara Torriero, Martina Capellazzi, Anna Caterina Omboni, Giancarlo Cerveri, and Claudio Mencacci. 'Gender Differences in Misdiagnosis and Delayed Diagnosis among Adults with Autism Spectrum Disorder with No Language or Intellectual Disability'. *Brain Sciences* 11, no. 7 (9 July 2021): 912. https://doi.org/10.3390/brainsci11070912.
[74] Abdelnour, Elie, Madeline O. Jansen, and Jessica A. Gold. 'ADHD Diagnostic Trends: Increased Recognition or Overdiagnosis?' *Missouri Medicine* 119, no. 5 (2022): 467–73.
[75] ibid

manifesting externally. Naturally, the symptoms of these would be treated first, rather than the underlying cause.

This can be extremely dangerous. For example, AuDHD-ers may be prescribed medication that makes their symptoms worse, therapy that invalidates their experiences, and given labels of 'disorders' that they do not have. I was convinced I had multiple personality disorders when I finally unmasked to a psychiatrist, who advised me that I actually had ADHD.

This didn't seem to make any sense, or explain the symptoms I had such as extreme suicidal ideation. It was only from doing my own research and learning about 'unofficial' terms like RSD that I accepted the diagnosis, enabling me to take control of my life and manage my symptoms.

If a person is diagnosed with a condition they do not have, they can't access the right support or knowledge they need to access help.

Accessing support

It will come as no surprise that accessing any kind of medical support, let alone for autism or ADHD, is very difficult in our world today. Our global and UK national healthcare systems are simply not equipped to support people, or to keep up with the changing understanding of conditions.

These are focused on treating symptoms, as opposed to individuals. Medication for conditions such as depression and anxiety are offered in 10 minute doctor appointments, whilst assessments for neurodevelopmental conditions like ADHD and autism are gate kept behind years-long waiting lists, or the ability to find thousands of pounds.

This isn't even to mention the extreme difficulty that AuDHD-ers may have in even identifying their own struggles and asking for help. I had no idea that I was struggling so much for years, because I just thought this was normal. When I became aware that it probably wasn't normal or healthy to obsessively ruminate on how to end my life, I believed there was something deeply wrong with me.

I thought I was the only person in the world who was thinking like this, feeling a huge sense of shame and fear. I was scared of being committed to hospital, being misunderstood, and trapped.

I had always struggled with basic self-care, such as going to the doctor when I was unwell. I assumed that I wouldn't be believed, and would be taking valuable time away from those who 'really needed it'. The thought of going to a doctor to explain my shameful obsession with suicide felt near impossible, especially as I believed it was all my fault.

When I eventually sought out regular therapy, overcoming excessive shame to do so, I felt further invalidated as I'd speak non-stop for an hour before leaving feeling even worse. When I later told a therapist I believed I was autistic, I was told that this wasn't possible, as I was nothing like the autistic children they knew.

Healthcare can be highly invalidating to people at the best of times, especially women who can be written off as 'emotional' or 'hormonal'. However, to an AuDHD-er who presents with wildly conflicting symptoms, it can be very difficult to imagine asking for help, and even harder to find someone who can. ADHD and autism are typically assessed separately, and only since 2013 have been able to be diagnosed in the same person.

This can be exacerbated by the symptoms themselves. I moved country so much that I didn't even have a consistent GP, and registering with a doctor felt like an executive functioning hurdle that was too exhausting to navigate until I 'really needed to'. I found describing my emotions and inner experiences extremely difficult due to not understanding them, intensified by alexithymia.

These factors can mean that AuDHD-ers don't access the help they need until the internal pain we experience becomes visible on the outside, with masking no longer an option.

Depression, anxiety and trauma
Unsurprisingly, living in a world where we can't understand others or ourselves, or access support for this, can manifest in extreme difficulties. This could look like depression or anxiety, two conditions that I simply thought of as 'normal'.

Anxiety (72%) and depression (70%) were found by one study to be the two most common co-morbid conditions diagnosed alongside ADHD in adults.[76] Approximately 40% of autistic people experience depression at some point in their lives[77], with another study identifying that 47% of autistic people had 'severe' anxiety.[78]

Anxiety is defined as a feeling of unease, which is experienced for a prolonged period of time that has a significant impact on someone's life. Depression is characterised by a low mood or loss of pleasure or interest in activities for long periods of time.

It was a revelation to take ADHD medication and realise that feeling so utterly miserable and scared all of the time

---
[76] 'Adult ADHD and Depression, Anxiety Linked in Study'. Accessed 3 February 2025. https://www.additudemag.com/adult-adhd-depression-anxiety-study/.
[77] 'How Depression May Present Differently in Autistic People – Attwood & Garnett Events'. Accessed 3 February 2025. https://www.attwoodandgarnettevents.com/blogs/news/how-depression-may-present-differently-in-autistic-people.
[78] 'Anxiety'. Accessed 3 February 2025. https://www.autism.org.uk/advice-and-guidance/topics/mental-health/anxiety.

wasn't normal. I had no idea that other people existed without a constant radio blasting 20 channels in their head all of the time, mostly variations of reminders telling me what a terrible human being I was.

Neurodivergent people are also likely to experience trauma, given their inherent vulnerabilities and needs which are unlikely to be met consistently, if at all. Simply being at school was overwhelming for me, feeling like a prison sentence to get through, with harsh lighting, too many people, and too much noise.

Burnout

Burnout is a state of physical, mental, and emotional exhaustion, often resulting from long-term stress and constant pressure. It's often trivialised within our society as simply being 'tired', especially as it's not included in the Diagnostic and Statistical Manual of Mental Disorders (DSM) as a medical condition. However, this doesn't mean it's not real, and for me, burnout can be described as a culmination of stress that results in our brains simply shutting down for an extended period of time.

Autistic burnout is said to result from chronic life stress and a mismatch of expectations and abilities, without adequate support. It's recognised by pervasive, long-term exhaustion, loss of function, and reduced tolerance to stimulus.

Adults are often diagnosed with ADHD after experiencing burnout, having put in 500% effort than average throughout their life and assuming everybody else was working just as hard to be 'normal'. ADHD burnout has been described as a state of exhaustion resulting from trying to manage ADHD symptoms over a long period of time.

Personally, I experience 'AuDHD burnout' from having a brain that is constantly fighting against itself. The autism part of my brain is playing constant catch up, desperately trying to control the ADHD part that is determined to say 'yes' to everything and start spinning lots of new plates. Masking to this level is simply unsustainable, and we crash.

This may be why so many autistic people find themselves in mental health hospitals – their symptoms may worsen until they are deemed a danger to themselves or others. Similarly with ADHD, where our impacted ability to regulate our emotions can dangerously exacerbate other symptoms such as impulsivity and hyperactivity, seeing us walk out of jobs or finding ourselves in crisis situations.

Burnout can be debilitating, resulting in us simply being unable to do anything at all, leaving us unable to do anything for months, or even years.

Demand Avoidance

Burnout can also be related to demand avoidance, such as PDA. For me, it feels like every single demand of 'ordinary life', from showering to cooking to cleaning, getting a job to having friends and socialising, are all overwhelming. My brain struggles against them from a conceptual level, arguing about why I 'have' to do these things. This makes it very difficult to enjoy things that I 'should' be enjoying, such as going to a yoga class.

This can also result in burnout, as experiencing this sheer level of exhaustion in relation to 'normal' demands can build up over time, along with masking my symptoms. For me, these feel interlinked. Every day feels like acting in my own personal movie, where I have to learn the lines and present myself in a certain way to 'pass'. It's hardly surprising that this kind of internal pressure, for so many, ends up as an explosion we cannot control.

Suicide

As seen in this chapter, there are painfully higher suicide risks for AuDHD-ers. Autistic people are up to 7 times more likely to attempt suicide than non-autistic people.[79] People with ADHD are 5 times more likely to attempt suicide than people who do not have ADHD.[80] Combine these conditions and statistics, and the risks could be even higher.

Suicide is a topic our society tends to be extremely uncomfortable with, as seen in discussions around assisted dying. For a person who has never contemplated taking their own life, it may feel very difficult to imagine how this could happen. There is silence and shame surrounding suicide, with it being a prosecutable criminal offence in England until 1961, hence the word 'committing'.

In some countries this is still illegal, as seen by a woman who was charged in Dubai for attempting suicide after experiencing domestic violence.[81]

Feeling suicidal is awful. It's like being imprisoned in your own mind, body, and life. For many people, it might feel like a logical escape to being exposed to constant demands, stress, and exclusion. It is not a choice. People who are suicidal are not choosing to feel that way - they need help.

---

79 Autistica. 'Suicide and Autism', 7 March 2024. https://www.autistica.org.uk/what-is-autism/suicide-and-autism.
80 Suicide in ADHD - Berkshire Health Trust - https://www.berkshirehealthcare.nhs.uk/media/109514702/suicide-in-adhd-adhd-bekrshire-healthcare.pdf
81 Badshah, Nadeem. 'Irish Woman Charged with "Attempting Suicide" by Dubai Court'. *The Guardian*, 9 July 2024, sec. World news. https://www.theguardian.com/world/article/2024/jul/09/irish-woman-charged-with-attempting-suicide-by-dubai-court.

Mental Health

Tips: AuDHD-ers

- Recognise and respect your limits. This may relate to aspects such as sensory needs, workload, or social interactions. Keeping a mood journal can help with this.

- Spend some time identifying how you mask. You may not even realise the ways you mask, but trying to observe yourself in different situations can help you to create a list of your unique strategies, such as by scripting conversations or keeping yourself from speaking.

- Say no when needed. You don't need to give an explanation - no is a full sentence!

- Give yourself permission to unmask, finding safe spaces where you can fully be with yourself. This might look like certain people, or environments, or simply being by yourself.

- Identify your triggers and how these impact your mental wellbeing. If you've experienced burnout before, note down the factors that led to this. Be pro-active in checking in with yourself to ensure you can take action before things reach that point!

- Seek professional support from a neuro-affirmative therapist and/or coach. They are out there, and they will validate your experiences, supporting you to work with your brain instead of against it.

- Be nice to yourself! Simply noticing your internal narrative and how you talk to yourself can help you to understand what kind of pressures you may be putting yourself under. Remind yourself that you are doing your best.

- Take intentional 'rest', whatever that looks like to you. For example, you could block off at least one evening a week In your calendar to do the things you enjoy, or book a regular massage.

- Adjust your expectations of yourself – you are not a human doing! Consciously identify what your measures of 'success' are, and whether you're moving the goalposts.

- Allow yourself to process and feel your emotions in the ways that work for you. This might look like therapy, journalling, exercise, or anything else that helps you to sit with yourself and understand how you're feeling.

- Create a sense of autonomy, reminding yourself that you have choices and control over how and when you respond. Reduce pressure by reframing tasks as optional.

- Avoid comparison – neurotypical people have a completely different brain structure to you, and everybody is doing things at their own pace.

Mental Health

- Acknowledge your accomplishments - regularly! This might just look like going outside, or getting out of your pyjamas, and that's okay. Celebrating the wins helps you to reframe your mindset.

- Find a community and build a support network, identifying people who you can reach out to when you're not feeling great. For example, you may wish to join an online community or in person meet up for neurodivergent people, seeing that you are not alone.

- Ask for accommodations where it may be helpful. You don't need to know exactly what could help, but if you're overwhelmed at the thought of calling the doctor, for example, you could ask them for an adjustment to communicate with you over email. The worst they can say is no!

- Practice asking for help where possible. I know how incredibly overwhelming it can feel, and pointless, but the people in your life would want to be there for you. Emotional support, even just listening, can make a huge difference. Identify people who you trust and create regular check ins with them, so you can both share how you're doing.

- Acknowledge your feelings without judgement - it's okay to feel how you feel. You are not weak or broken - you are simply in pain. Emotions are signals from your body, so try to listen to them.

- Create a safety plan so you can have the steps of what to do if you're feeling bad, to hand. This is especially important if you experience suicidal ideation, as it's very important to get help as soon as possible - these are signals that something in your life needs to change, not end.

- Challenge harmful thoughts, recognising how quickly these can spiral with experiences like RSD. Question where the proof is, and challenge yourself to list the proof for alternative perspectives.

- If you're worried about the safety of yourself or others as a result of your mental health, contact the emergency services. You are meant to be here, and you are worthy, exactly as you are. You deserve support and to enjoy your life.

- Create a 'hope box', filling it with things that bring you comfort. These might include letters from loved ones, photos, sensory tools, things you want to do in life, or meaningful objects. Use it during difficult times to remind yourself of positive things.

- Remember that this too shall pass. Your experiences, including mental health challenges, do not define you. Although it might feel unimaginable to experience anything other than the pain you might be in right now, this is temporary. You have survived until now for a reason - don't give up.

Mental Health

- Notice small changes and progress. It can feel incredibly overwhelming to struggle with your mental health, especially as an AuDHD-er. However, every day is a learning opportunity. Even if it feels like you're repeating the same mistakes, look for even the tiniest of differences. It's not realistic or possible to be 'happy' all of the time, and progress is a process - it doesn't happen overnight. Be kind and patient with yourself.

- Remember that the pain you may be experiencing right now is preparing you for something greater. 'The cracks are how the light gets in' - struggling with your mental health doesn't define who you are as a person, but your ability to survive in a world that's not designed for your brain is testament to your strength, resilience, and uniqueness. It can be difficult and lonely to be different, but that doesn't mean that there's anything wrong with you. Take small steps to change your environment - not yourself.

Tips: loved ones

- Check in on the person regularly, such as by dropping by their house, or contacting them in a way that feels accessible to them. Recognise that they may not ask for help, so be proactive!

- Ask them for help for any of your own challenges - modelling how to ask for it, and letting them know that they can always do the same in return.

- Remind them that they are not a burden, and their challenges are valid.

- Avoid giving advice unless it's asked for - simply asking someone if they'd like advice or for you to listen can be a great help.

- Remind them that you can handle whatever it is that they're experiencing (and get your own support too, such as therapy).

- Be a safe space, in encouraging them to be themselves without fear of judgement, with unconditional positive regard.

- Acknowledge the effort in masking, offering compassion when they feel drained and need alone time to recharge.

- Encourage professional help, especially with people who are neuro-affirmative, such as therapists or coaches specialised in AuDHD.

- Create a safety plan together, discussing strategies for times of crisis, such as how to stay calm or grounding techniques.

- Normalise asking for help by reminding them that this is a strength, not a sign of weakness.

Mental Health

- Help navigate systems such as healthcare or benefits applications, which can be difficult for AuDHD people to access. You could offer to go to a doctor's appointment with them, for example, advocating on their behalf where needed.

- Discuss signs of burnout or struggles with mental health, and help the individual to recognise these as well.

- Offer autonomy and choices, empowering them to control the situation where possible.

- Avoid giving orders, use instead language such as, 'do you think we could..?', framing tasks as joint activities to reduce the feeling of being pressured.

- Help to build a support network, such as by connecting with friends through an online community.

- Celebrate their wins - big and small! We may forget to do this for ourselves, so offering positive recognition of their achievements pro-actively can mean a great deal.

- Be patient with emotional regulation challenges, offering reassurance and allowing them to process feelings at their own pace. Validate their experiences using their preferred language, such as RSD, without questioning it.

- If you're worried about someone, ask them about it directly. For example, asking 'are you thinking about taking your own life?' isn't going to encourage them - it will help open up the conversation. If they say yes, don't panic - just listen.

- Avoid minimising their feelings or experiences, such as by telling them to 'get over it'. Instead, showing empathy such as 'I can see that you're in a lot of pain', can be very validating.

- If you believe someone is in immediate danger, call the emergency services.

- Remind them of small changes. It can feel frustrating to experience these challenges, but every time we experience them there's something that's likely to have been different, even if it's something tiny, such as the length of time of a panic attack. Pointing out signs of progress can help us to feel hope.

7. Trauma

Despite my best efforts, when I arrived back in the UK to 'get help', things quickly fell apart again, seeing me book a trip to Bali for a month later, and forget all about seeing a psychiatrist. However, when I found myself pacing outside of an ex-boyfriend's house trying to convince myself not to book a flight to Mexico during that month, I remembered why I had come back to London in the first place.

Instead of booking flights, I booked an appointment with the first psychiatrist that came up on Google. I was so sick of the constant chaos, and just wanted to be 'normal', whatever that would take.

So, I went to the psychiatrist appointment ready to be committed to hospital, fully unmasking for the first time in front of a healthcare professional - or anyone. I presented the entirety of my messy life, including my suspected myriad of co-occurring mental health conditions, questioning how one person could have ALL of them. They interrupted me and asked a series of questions before saying, 'you don't have any of those conditions. You have ADHD.'

I burst out laughing and said I had a *real* problem, not one made up for little boys, exasperated at finally letting someone into the parts of my brain I'd kept so hidden for so long, and them disagreeing with my reality. ADHD had never even come up in my thorough daily research of mental health conditions - didn't *everyone* struggle to pay attention? Anyway, as I told the psychiatrist, I had a *law degree* and A grades in my exams, so I couldn't possibly have ADHD.

They said that I had 'really, really bad ADHD.' This seemed contradictory to the law degree point, but I did some quick mental calculations that actually, he wasn't trying to put me into hospital as I'd expected. I also reasoned that as I didn't know anything about ADHD other than the drugs were apparently 'productive', it might not be such a bad thing.

When I asked for the medication, I was told that various other bureaucratic checkboxes needed to be ticked off, including getting people who'd known me throughout my life to fill in forms and a follow up assessment. As I was going to Bali a few days later, I said I'd return in 3 weeks as planned.

I didn't return for over a year. Within a few days of my 'holiday', I experienced an attempted kidnap and a physical fight. Within a few weeks, I'd moved to another country into a stranger's home, who'd said they'd sponsor me to stay through a partner visa.

This person felt like my 'saviour' - literally and metaphorically. It felt like joining a cult for one, where I happily offered up full control of my life, mind, and future, excited to be a completely new person and start over. I forgot all about ADHD, which I was still doubtful about whether I actually had.

However, some weeks later I found myself in the same pattern of a mental health crisis, trying to leave, claiming that I was 'crazy'. This time, however, I was taught some psychological strategies to reframe my own thoughts, recognising how I was unconsciously repeating cycles of self-sabotage. When I mentioned the ADHD diagnosis, I was taught to reframe it as a 'bunch of letters that don't mean anything' - it wasn't 'real'.

So I stayed, seeing the relationship as the best thing that had ever happened to me. I couldn't believe how lucky I was to find someone who wanted to be with me, despite seeing how 'crazy' I was.

However, these 'strategies' meant that I completely lost my already very limited ability to trust myself or my experiences. Whenever I got upset, I'd simply brainwash myself into believing it was from my past 'trauma', simply repeating the steps until I found a conclusion that made it all my fault and therefore within my control, convincing myself that I could 'choose' to be happy. Things became very confused very quickly, and I lost my grasp of reality.

I was extremely isolated, having stopped clubbing or drinking alcohol, and knowing nobody except my partner, who was often travelling. I couldn't understand how to make friends, and felt unbearably lonely, often scrolling social media and comparing myself to others. After one self-brainwashing incident, I deleted all of my online accounts, determined to be 'happy'.

I was then extremely bored, with nothing to fill my days other than reading endless spiritual books. My partner got me an office job through their friend, but I only lasted a few days, experiencing a hysterical panic attack when I was asked to cold-call people and read a script to them. I couldn't understand why this was so difficult, but with the person watching me with a raised eyebrow across the desk, I could barely speak. I left in tears, quitting the job and feeling like the weakest person alive.

I'd expected to stop modelling altogether in this new remote location, but it found me - literally. By coincidence, someone I'd shot with on the job I did whilst planning to take my own life, saw me on the street and invited me to a launch party that evening for that very campaign.

When I went to the party, I had a panic attack. I'd never experienced anxiety like it, especially being in a crowd where I couldn't drink alcohol, with the harsh lights, loud music, and energy from the crowd feeling like they were searing through my skin. I felt so embarrassed, like everybody was judging me for looking absolutely nothing like the framed campaign photograph on the wall. I left quickly without speaking to anybody, feeling intense shame as I realised I couldn't escape my own brain.

However, I then started getting requests for modelling jobs through word of mouth. Before I knew it, I'd met people through work who seemed to want to hang out with me, asking me to teach them how to pose for photos. Work became blurred into my personal life, as I turned shoots into opportunities to make friends. I offered to work for everybody as part of these relationships, including co-ordinating photoshoots and running social media accounts.

Suddenly, I was back to being the social co-ordinator. However, instead of clubbing nights, I was organising photoshoots for brands, as many people I knew had large followings on social media. It was incredible to feel like I had friends, even though I was still strategising a transactional basis for them all by being as 'useful' as possible.

They felt like some of the first people I'd been friends with who didn't drink alcohol and seemed to like me as my awkwardly sober self. I felt like I finally belonged somewhere, even if I was the one organising it all and people were being paid to join.

It was also amazing to feel like for once, I had agency over my own work. I organised my own photoshoots, set my own rates, and even worked as a photographer on

Trauma

some jobs, finding that I much preferred being behind the camera helping models to feel comfortable, instead of in front of it.

It felt like I had a sense of of creativity and control, that was actually being valued, as I organised incredible experiences in beautiful places. I was constantly connecting the dots around me, setting up a blog to document it as I went. After working with a model who was struggling in confidence one day, I went to a yoga class afterwards, and had the idea of writing an A to Z blog post to help models, scribbling it down after the class.

When I got home, I started writing, and didn't stop. I realised it was far too long for a blog post, deciding to figure out how to share it as an e-book, despite having no social media accounts myself. Every word of advice I wrote for models gave me evidence that the things that had happened to me were not my fault - the industry was broken. It felt like magic, as though the words were flowing from somebody else.

However, things outside of the world of work I'd created for myself were deteriorating. When I had my palm read by a stranger who described my unhappiness and the danger I was in, to my face, I was in denial, telling them that they were wrong. They told me to take my money back if that was the case, leaving me in tears, as I realised that they were right.

I read through my diary and realised how I'd cried every single day, the pages filled with my handwriting about how unhappy I was, but of how I should just be able to think my way out of it. It was just my past that I needed to escape from. I attributed every harsh comment, argument, and emotional explosion to my past, refusing to recognise how serious things were, blaming myself. I was so shocked that I ripped up the journal and threw it away, hoping that I could start afresh by simply stopping journalling.

However, writing the modelling book became an escape from a reality that felt increasingly unsafe with my partner. If I wasn't writing at home, I felt constantly on edge, as though an argument could erupt at any second. I felt like nothing I did was right, and as though I was expected to meet rules that I didn't know, and couldn't understand.

I normalised physical assault until I had an injury that I was worried would leave a bruise, impacting my modelling jobs. I cried hysterically as my brain felt like it was imploding. I felt like if I put ice on it, I'd be making an accusation of domestic violence, the potential reaction to which terrified me even more. I was frozen, unable to move.

It was only when a friend spotted this, that I understood and accepted that I was in danger, and had to leave. They supported me through it, giving me somewhere to stay and helping me to collect my things.

It was the first time I'd ever experienced anything like it - help I didn't ask for, but was given unconditionally, with zero expectations in return. I felt unbearably guilty about this, feeling like a burden and as though I'd somehow manipulated them, but I also had no energy left to fight it, experiencing such intense grief that all I could do was cry.

I felt like I had broken and rebuilt myself so many times that my soul had splintered into pieces, with no idea of who I was, feeling hopeless about the future. All I had left was the modelling book, which I continued to throw myself into, dissociating from reality.

The AuDHD Lens
Unsurprisingly, given how difficult it can be to be neurodivergent, especially undiagnosed and unsupported,

Trauma

AuDHD-ers are likely to experience trauma throughout their lives. This is exacerbated by their vulnerability and needs not being met, such as sensory overload.

For example, the prevalence of Post Traumatic Stress Disorder (PTSD) is over 6 times higher among adults diagnosed with ADHD (10%), compared to those without it (1.6%).[82] This can become very confusing, especially as symptoms such as hyperactivity and memory challenges can occur in both PTSD and ADHD. Children with ADHD are also more likely to be victims of peer victimisation than those without.[83]

This could also be linked to the coping strategies we develop, as 84% of ADHD-ers receiving inpatient substance abuse treatment had co-occurring PTSD.[84]

The same can be seen for autism, with a significantly higher proportion of adverse childhood experiences found being experienced by autistic children compared to those who were not autistic.[85] One study found that approximately 60% of autistic people reported probable PTSD.[86]

---

[82] Adams, Zachary, Thomas Adams, Kirstin Stauffacher-Gros, Howard Mandel, and Zhewu Wang. 'The Effects of Inattentiveness and Hyperactivity on Posttraumatic Stress Symptoms: Does a Diagnosis of Posttraumatic Stress Disorder Matter?' *Journal of Attention Disorders* 24, no. 9 (July 2020): 1246–54. https://doi.org/10.1177/1087054715580846.

[83] Efron, Daryl, Michell Wijaya, Philip Hazell, and Emma Sciberras. 'Peer Victimization in Children With ADHD: A Community-Based Longitudinal Study'. *Journal of Attention Disorders* 25, no. 3 (February 2021): 291–99. https://doi.org/10.1177/1087054718796287.

[84] 'Posttraumatic Stress Disorder Is Highly Comorbid With Adult ADHD in Alcohol Use Disorder Inpatients - Hussein El Ayoubi, Paul Brunault, Servane Barrault, Damien Maugé, Grégoire Baudin, Nicolas Ballon, Wissam El-Hage, 2021'. Accessed 3 February 2025. https://journals.sagepub.com/doi/abs/10.1177/1087054720903363?journalCode=jada.

[85] Attwood & Garnett Events. 'Attwood & Garnett Events'. Accessed 3 February 2025. https://www.attwoodandgarnettevents.com/blogs/news/autism-and-trauma.

[86] https://neurodivergentinsights.com/. 'How Are Autism and Trauma Related? - Neurodivergent Insights'. Accessed 3 February 2025. https://neurodivergentinsights.com/autism-infographics/autismandtrauma/.

People with developmental disabilities have been found to be 3 times more likely to experience trauma compared to their peers without such conditions.[87]

Trauma, mental health, and neurodivergence can become highly complex to untangle and make sense of.

TRAUMA

Trauma results from an event, series of events, or circumstances that is experienced by an individual as harmful or life threatening. Whilst unique to the individual, the experience of this trauma is said to generally cause lasting adverse effects, impacting our well-being.

Personally, I'd describe trauma as anything that leaves an invisible, psychological wound on our souls - something that cuts us on the inside. For example, having been bullied as a child for having 'yellow' skin like a television character in *the Simpsons*, I will always flinch slightly at the sound of the theme tune, the memories of shame rushing back. These kinds of uncomfortable traumas can sometimes be referred to as 'little t traumas', highly distressful experiences on a personal level, but maybe not so obvious to the outside world.

In contrast, a 'big T Trauma' might be more obvious externally, which are the types of experiences we're conditioned to traditionally associate as being traumatic. For example, emergencies involving death, planes crashing into buildings, war, natural disasters, and so on. It can be acute, resulting from a single incident, or chronic, resulting from repeated and prolonged events.

---

[87] Attwood & Garnett Events. 'Attwood & Garnett Events'. Accessed 3 February 2025. https://www.attwoodandgarnettevents.com/blogs/news/autism-and-trauma.

Post Traumatic Stress Disorder (PTSD) and Complex Post Traumatic Stress Disorder (C-PTSD)

PTSD is something that can leave us in an intense state of fear whenever we're reminded of a certain traumatic experience, including through unwanted memories of the event such as nightmares or flashbacks. It can see our reactions become 'disordered', if the invisible cut is deep enough - it depends on the person, not the event itself.

For example, I once reversed a car I was driving by a millimetre when I heard a scream, but couldn't see anything in my mirror. I thought I'd killed somebody, having a meltdown on the side of the road where the cyclist who'd gone behind my car and shouted a warning had ended up comforting me. After that experience, I struggled to get back into a car without experiencing intense fear and paranoia for months on end, avoiding driving wherever possible.

C-PTSD results from exposure to varied and multiple traumatic events, often of an invasive, interpersonal nature, experienced over a long period of time. It's like having thousands of invisible paper cuts, happening every day - the trauma simply repeats itself.

As a result, C-PTSD doesn't manifest with specific triggers in specific situations, but this fear becomes constant. An individual with C-PTSD may be in 'flight or fight' mode *all of the time*. The main difference between PTSD and C-PTSD is the length and frequency of the trauma.

For example, the many toxic relationships I've been in throughout my life have seen me develop severe issues with trusting other people. C-PTSD may be seen in situations such as abusive relationships and ongoing childhood neglect, given that this kind of trauma tends to happen for a prolonged period of time. It can be insidious, happening over time through endless conversations and moments and experiences.

Despite these conditions having a debilitating impact on a person's life, PTSD has only been recognised as a discrete diagnostic category since the 1980s, with C-PTSD still not being recognised as a separate condition in the DSM. However, the International Classification of Diseases (ICD) does define C-PTSD as a distinct condition, which is generally followed in the UK.[88]

Both PTSD and C-PTSD may feature symptoms such as re-experiencing the trauma through intrusive memories, flashbacks, and nightmares, avoiding situations that are linked to the trauma, changes to mood and thinking, and feeling on edge, becoming easily irritable or scared, with difficulty concentrating and sleeping.

C-PTSD includes the diagnostic criteria for PTSD, along with 3 additional categories of symptoms, including difficulties with emotional regulation, an impaired sense of self-worth, and interpersonal problems.

Despite the various potential for crossover of symptoms and high likelihood of trauma to occur, not every AuDHD-er will necessarily experience a traumatic 'disorder'. Trauma and AuDHD may be inextricably linked, such as a child being told off for their neurodivergent traits repeatedly, which they cannot control. Masking and coping strategies such as using alcohol or drugs can also complicate the matter further.

NEUROLOGICAL FACTORS

The autonomic nervous system plays a role in AuDHD and trauma, controlling fight-or-flight responses, along with emotional regulation and sensory processing. The

---

[88] 'ICD-11 Complex Post-Traumatic Stress Disorder: Simplifying Diagnosis in Trauma Populations'. *The British Journal of Psychiatry* 216, no. 3 (March 2020): 129–31. https://doi.org/10.1192/bjp.2020.43.

prefrontal cortex, responsible for executive functioning, is also developmentally impacted by both autism and ADHD.

AuDHD brains will also have a different response to actual or potential trauma than a neurotypical brain. For example, we may have different experiences of sensations, which sees me jump half a foot in the air every time my doorbell rings. Our differences in experiencing the world around us means that we may find things traumatic that other people do not, which they may find hard to imagine, such as being repeatedly exposed to a crowded lunch room on a daily basis at school, or fluorescent lighting in an office.

Due to our brain differences, we may also experience differences in how we regulate and respond to our own emotions. RSD may emerge from a lifetime of feeling rejected and excluded, but it may also stem from having a smaller amygdala, the part of our brains responsible for processing fear and other emotions.[89] As a result, people with ADHD may experience lower emotional processing capabilities, and higher impulsivity in terms of managing emotional responses effectively.

One study identified that autistic children had larger amygdala-connected brain regions than non-autistic children at all ages, with differences growing over time and being more apparent in children with prominent social difficulties. The brain regions most impacted varied differently between boys and girls, supporting evidence that autism presents differently among sexes. Boys showed most impact in the areas responsible for anxiety and detecting appropriate social behaviour, and in girls, this was in the areas

---

[89] Tajima-Pozo, Kazuhiro, Miguel Yus, Gonzalo Ruiz-Manrique, Adrian Lewczuk, Juan Arrazola, and Francisco Montañes-Rada. 'Amygdala Abnormalities in Adults With ADHD'. *Journal of Attention Disorders* 22, no. 7 (May 2018): 671–78. https://doi.org/10.1177/1087054716629213.

responsible for anxiety disorders and social perception and communication.[90]

Having a larger than 'normal' amygdala may correlate with heightened emotional responses and a stronger perception of fear and anxiety. This is why autistic people may struggle severely with anxiety, particularly in relation to uncertainty and unpredictable situations, such as changes to their environment or routines.

It's difficult to say what this may look like in an AuDHD-er, but one thing is for certain: there's significant variability amongst neurodivergent individuals in how they process and experience emotions. This can result in experiencing the 'invisible cut' of trauma from situations others may not be able to understand, such as our own thoughts. Our brains may be wired to be constantly hyper vigilant, being more vulnerable to experiencing trauma as a result.

This is made even more complex by the potential of trauma experienced during developmental stages, including genetics, given that both autism and ADHD are neurodevelopmental conditions. Complications during pregnancy (22%) and childbirth (10%) may significantly increase the likelihood of a child developing autism, with an argued 44% higher likelihood for children exposed to complications both before and during labor.[91]

The same can be seen for ADHD, with children whose mothers consumed alcohol during pregnancy reportedly being 1.55 times more likely to develop ADHD compared to those who did not.[92] The same is seen for mothers who

---

[90] 'Altered Development of Amygdala-Connected Brain Regions in Males and Females with Autism | Journal of Neuroscience'. Accessed 3 February 2025. https://www.jneurosci.org/content/42/31/6145.
[91] 'Can Birth Injury Cause Autism? | Raynes & Lawn'. Accessed 3 February 2025. https://rayneslaw.com/can-birth-injury-cause-autism/.
[92] Han, Ji-Youn, Ho-Jang Kwon, Mina Ha, Ki-Chung Paik, Myung-Ho Lim, Sang Gyu Lee, Seung-Jin Yoo, and Eun-Jung Kim. 'The Effects of Prenatal

smoked during pregnancy, with a 1.5 times higher likelihood of ADHD.[93] Children who were born via caesarean delivery were also found to be more likely to develop ADHD.[94]

Head injuries also increase the likelihood of ADHD occurring, although ADHD itself increases the risk for head trauma, with a 2-3 times higher likelihood of children with ADHD obtaining head injuries through impulsivity.[95]

All of these experiences may influence the development of a person's brain, possibly resulting in a higher likelihood of a brain wired to react to potential danger more severely than those who have not experienced trauma. The fundamental thing to understand is that this is something that we are born with.

Adverse Childhood Experiences (ACEs)

AuDHD-ers have a much higher likelihood than neurotypical people of experiencing ACEs.[96] These could include physical, sexual, or emotional abuse, living with someone who

---

Exposure to Alcohol and Environmental Tobacco Smoke on Risk for ADHD: A Large Population-Based Study'. *Psychiatry Research* 225, no. 1 (30 January 2015): 164–68. https://doi.org/10.1016/j.psychres.2014.11.009.
93   'Maternal Smoking During Pregnancy and ADHD: Results From a Systematic Review and Meta-Analysis of Prospective Cohort Studies - Yan He, Jian Chen, Li-Hua Zhu, Ling-Ling Hua, Fang-Fang Ke, 2020'. Accessed 3 February 2025. https://journals.sagepub.com/doi/10.1177/1087054717696766.
94   Zhang, Tianyang, Anna Sidorchuk, Laura Sevilla-Cermeño, Alba Vilaplana-Pérez, Zheng Chang, Henrik Larsson, David Mataix-Cols, and Lorena Fernández de la Cruz. 'Association of Cesarean Delivery With Risk of Neurodevelopmental and Psychiatric Disorders in the Offspring: A Systematic Review and Meta-Analysis'. *JAMA Network Open* 2, no. 8 (28 August 2019): e1910236. https://doi.org/10.1001/jamanetworkopen.2019.10236.
95   Risk of Traumatic Brain Injury Among Children, Adolescents, and Young Adults With Attention-Deficit Hyperactivity Disorder in Taiwan - https://doi.org/10.1016/j.jadohealth.2018.02.012
96   Kerns, Connor Morrow, Craig J. Newschaffer, Steven Berkowitz, and Brian K. Lee. 'Examining the Association of Autism and Adverse Childhood Experiences in the National Survey of Children's Health: The Important Role of Income and Co-Occurring Mental Health Conditions'. *Journal of Autism and Developmental Disorders* 47, no. 7 (July 2017): 2275–81. https://doi.org/10.1007/s10803-017-3111-7.

abused drugs or alcohol, exposure to domestic violence, living with someone who has gone to prison or has a serious mental illness, or losing a parent through divorce, death, or abandonment.

Other examples could include emotional or physical neglect, being a young person with caring responsibilities, criminal activity, long-term unemployment, bereavement, low school attendance and isolation.

Experiencing ACEs can have a significant impact on our future health. As clinical psychologist Richard Bentall explained, 'the evidence of a link between childhood misfortune and future psychiatric disorder is as strong statistically as the link between smoking and lung cancer.[97]

The impact of ACEs can result in disrupted neurodevelopment, impairing our social, emotional and cognitive abilities, leading to health-risk behaviours, illness, and early death.

Autistic children are at a higher risk of ACEs, including a 3-4 times higher risk of being bullied than their peers.[98] Research has also shown how ADHD is linked with socioeconomic disadvantages including financial difficulties, younger material age, and single parent status.[99]

This may be linked with genetic factors in AuDHD, potentially seeing parents being undiagnosed and therefore unaware of their own neurodivergence. For example, as ADHD has only been diagnosable in UK adults since 2008, it's highly likely that thousands have been missed

---

[97] Richard Bentall, 'Mental Illness Is A Result Of Misery, Yet Still We Stigmatize It', Guardian, February 26, 2016

[98] Hoover, Daniel W, and Joan Kaufman. 'Adverse Childhood Experiences in Children with Autism Spectrum Disorder'. *Current Opinion in Psychiatry* 31, no. 2 (March 2018): 128–32. https://doi.org/10.1097/YCO.0000000000000390.

[99] Russell, Abigail Emma, Tamsin Ford, and Ginny Russell. 'Socioeconomic Associations with ADHD: Findings from a Mediation Analysis'. *PLoS ONE* 10, no. 6 (1 June 2015): e0128248. https://doi.org/10.1371/journal.pone.0128248.

and therefore unable to access support needed to help them.

Parenthood may be extremely stressful for AuDHD-ers, with a higher likelihood of women being diagnosed with post-natal depression and anxiety disorders.[100] The same is true for autistic women, who may also experience trauma during birth as a result of sensory and communication differences.[101]

If these parents are unaware that they are neurodivergent, it may be extremely difficult for them to access support, the effects of which can filter down to their children. Maltreatment occurring prior to young adulthood has been found to be more common among people with ADHD compared to those without ADHD.[102] Research has also found that women who experienced abuse as children are also more likely than women who were not abused to have an autistic child.[103]

This doesn't help the controversy and stigma of AuDHD being related to 'bad parenting'. This is definitely not the case, especially as these conditions are neurodevelopmental, and parents are likely doing the best with the resources that

---

100 'ADHD as a Risk Factor for Postpartum Depression and Anxiety - MGH Center for Women's Mental Health'. Accessed 3 February 2025. https://womensmentalhealth.org/posts/adhd-as-a-risk-factor-for-pmad/.
101 Hampton, S., C. Allison, S. Baron-Cohen, and R. Holt. 'Autistic People's Perinatal Experiences II: A Survey of Childbirth and Postnatal Experiences'. *Journal of Autism and Developmental Disorders* 53, no. 7 (2023): 2749–63. https://doi.org/10.1007/s10803-022-05484-4.
102 Stern, Adi, Jessica Agnew-Blais, Andrea Danese, Helen L. Fisher, Sara R. Jaffee, Timothy Matthews, Guilherme V. Polanczyk, and Louise Arseneault. 'Associations between Abuse/Neglect and ADHD from Childhood to Young Adulthood: A Prospective Nationally-Representative Twin Study'. *Child Abuse & Neglect* 81 (1 July 2018): 274–85. https://doi.org/10.1016/j.chiabu.2018.04.025.
103 Stern, Adi, Jessica Agnew-Blais, Andrea Danese, Helen L. Fisher, Sara R. Jaffee, Timothy Matthews, Guilherme V. Polanczyk, and Louise Arseneault. 'Associations between Abuse/Neglect and ADHD from Childhood to Young Adulthood: A Prospective Nationally-Representative Twin Study'. *Child Abuse & Neglect* 81 (1 July 2018): 274–85. https://doi.org/10.1016/j.chiabu.2018.04.025.

they have available to them. I know that if I was to become a mother right now, it would be unbearably stressful - from the change in routine, sensory aspects, sounds of crying, anxiety, and changes beyond my control. It's hard enough to look after myself, let alone anybody else!

However, there is strong evidence of AuDHD children experiencing difficult childhoods, from trying to fit in with peers, to being understood and accepted at home. Our reaction as society to this should be to provide the children and adults in their life with additional support and education.

Social factors

Research indicates that autistic people may be more likely to experience traumatic life events, especially interpersonal traumas such as bullying and physical and sexual abuse.[104] 9 out of 10 autistic women have been victims of sexual violence, compared to around 30% of women in the general population.[105] People with ADHD have been found to be more likely to be victims and perpetrators of interpersonal abuse.[106]

This may fundamentally be rooted in differences in social communication and understandings. Although autism has stereotypically been associated with a lack of empathy[107],

---

[104] Cooke, Kassandrah, Kathryn Ridgway, Laura Pecora, Elizabeth Westrupp, Darren Hedley, Merrilyn Hooley, and Mark A. Stokes. 'Individual, Social, and Life Course Risk Factors for Experiencing Interpersonal Violence among Autistic People of Varying Gender Identities: A Mixed Methods Systematic Review'. *Research in Autism Spectrum Disorders* 111 (1 March 2024): 102313. https://doi.org/10.1016/j.rasd.2023.102313.
[105] Cazalis, Fabienne, Elisabeth Reyes, Séverine Leduc, and David Gourion. 'Evidence That Nine Autistic Women Out of Ten Have Been Victims of Sexual Violence'. *Frontiers in Behavioral Neuroscience* 16 (26 April 2022): 852203. https://doi.org/10.3389/fnbeh.2022.852203.
[106] Emma. 'What Is the Evidence for ADHD as a Risk Factor for IPV and Sexual Violence?' National Elf Service, 6 November 2023. https://www.nationalelfservice.net/mental-health/adhd/adhd-risk-factor-intimate-partner-violence/.
[107] Shalev, Ido, Varun Warrier, David M. Greenberg, Paula Smith, Carrie Allison, Simon Baron-Cohen, Alal Eran, and Florina Uzefovsky.

the 'double empathy problem' suggests that this goes both ways: non-autistic people may find it equally difficult to imagine how autistic people feel.[108]

This stereotype is contradicted by a study finding that 78% of autistic participants experienced 'hyper-empathy', an emotional response so powerful that it causes distress.[109] This can mean that people feel empathy so much that they experience pain, absorbing other people's emotions. This is heightened by the tendency of autistic people to be able to identify patterns in behaviour.

For me, this makes perfect sense. I spend so much time worrying about what other people are thinking, experiencing, and needing, that I forget all about myself. My impacted executive functioning skill of self-awareness means that I experience other people's emotions more strongly than I do my own. I experience heightened anxiety around 'being perceived' by other people, especially in group settings, becoming overwhelmed by lots of different people's emotions and perceived judgements.

This may be exacerbated by alexithymia, a difficulty in identifying and feeling our own emotions, which may be commonly experienced alongside autism[110] and ADHD.[111]

'Reexamining Empathy in Autism: Empathic Disequilibrium as a Novel Predictor of Autism Diagnosis and Autistic Traits'. *Autism Research* 15, no. 10 (October 2022): 1917–28. https://doi.org/10.1002/aur.2794.
108   Cheang, Rachael Ts, Maya Skjevling, Alexandra If Blakemore, Veena Kumari, and Ignazio Puzzo. 'Do You Feel Me? Autism, Empathic Accuracy and the Double Empathy Problem'. Autism: *The International Journal of Research and Practice*, 17 May 2024, 13623613241252320. https://doi.org/10.1177/13623613241252320.
109   markhayes. 'Hyper-Empathy: The State That Many Autistic People Experience', 6 October 2023. https://www.autismeye.com/autistic-people-hyper-empathy/.
110   Kinnaird, Emma, Catherine Stewart, and Kate Tchanturia. 'Investigating Alexithymia in Autism: A Systematic Review and Meta-Analysis'. *European Psychiatry* 55 (January 2019): 80–89. https://doi.org/10.1016/j.eurpsy.2018.09.004.
111   Edel, M-A, A Rudel, C Hubert, D Scheele, M Brüne, G Juckel, and H-J

These differences can be a strength in some ways, but they can also be extremely dangerous, making us vulnerable to abuse from others, and in some cases, indeed perpetrating it through misunderstanding social norms. The result can be incredibly toxic relationships, resulting in ongoing trauma. Being misunderstood by our peers, teachers, family, colleagues, and even strangers can result in ongoing stress and low self-esteem, believing that we are 'the problem'.

INTERSECTIONALITY

Intersectionality recognises how various aspects of a person's identity, such as race, gender, culture, socio-economic status and more intersect to shape their unique experiences and challenges.

Culture

Culture plays a significant role in how AuDHD is perceived, including stigma, misconceptions, diagnostic disparities, language barriers, treatment preferences, and family dynamics. For example, as of 2024, Haiti was found to have the highest rate of ADHD, with 4590 cases per 100k population and the United Arab Emirates was found to have the lowest, with 552 cases per 100k population.[112] In China, it's estimated that over 90% of the country's childhood ADHD cases go undiagnosed, in contrast to three-quarters of children with ADHD receiving support in America.[113]

In contrast, as of 2019, the UK was found to have the highest autism rate, with 700 cases per 100k children, the lowest rates

---

Assion. 'Alexithymia, Emotion Processing and Social Anxiety in Adults with ADHD'. *European Journal of Medical Research* 15, no. 9 (24 September 2010): 403–9. https://doi.org/10.1186/2047-783X-15-9-403.

112 'ADHD Rates by Country 2024'. Accessed 3 February 2025. https://worldpopulationreview.com/country-rankings/adhd-rates-by-country.

113 How Fear and Stigma Are Hurting China's Kids With ADHD'. Accessed 3 February 2025. https://www.sixthtone.com/news/1007435.

identified as being Taiwan, with 199 cases per 100k children.[114] A 2023 study identified America as having the highest prevalence estimates of autism.[115] Obviously these statistics are influenced by a number of factors, including diagnostic criteria and reporting.

Race

The impact of race is also extremely important, stemming from distinct societal dynamics, historically rooted repression, and systemic disparities. For example, systemic discrimination is evident against people who are not white in all areas of our society, from healthcare to education. Autism prevalence is lower among white children (2.4%) than other racial and ethnic groups, such as Black children (2.9%), Hispanic children (3.2%), and Asian or Pacific Islander children (3.3%).[116]

Until recently, Black children in America were less likely to be diagnosed with autism than their white and Asian peers.[117] The same goes for ADHD, with Black children showing symptoms of ADHD at a significantly higher rate than white children, but being diagnosed much less often. One study found that Black children in America were 70% less likely to receive an ADHD diagnosis than otherwise similar white children.[118]

---

[114] 'Autism Rates by Country 2024'. Accessed 3 February 2025. https://worldpopulationreview.com/country-rankings/autism-rates-by-country.

[115] Talantseva, Oksana I., Raisa S. Romanova, Ekaterina M. Shurdova, Tatiana A. Dolgorukova, Polina S. Sologub, Olga S. Titova, Daria F. Kleeva, and Elena L. Grigorenko. 'The Global Prevalence of Autism Spectrum Disorder: A Three-Level Meta-Analysis'. *Frontiers in Psychiatry* 14 (9 February 2023): 1071181. https://doi.org/10.3389/fpsyt.2023.1071181.

[116] 'Autism Statistics and Facts | Autism Speaks'. Accessed 3 February 2025. https://www.autismspeaks.org/autism-statistics-asd.

[117] 'New U.S. Data Show Similar Autism Prevalence among Racial Groups | The Transmitter: Neuroscience News and Perspectives'. Accessed 3 February 2025. https://www.thetransmitter.org/spectrum/new-u-s-data-show-similar-autism-prevalence-among-racial-groups/.

[118] The Transmitter: Neuroscience News and Perspectives. 'Massive U.K. Study Finds Racial and Ethnic Disparities in Autism Diagnoses', 29 March

Even once diagnosed, children of colour were much less likely to take ADHD medication - 36% of Black children, and 30% of Latino children diagnosed with ADHD were taking medication, compared to 65% of white children.[119]

Gender also has a significant factor to play. As AuDHD diagnostic criteria is largely based on young, white boys, this can mean that girls and women remain undiagnosed until later in life, as evidenced by research.[120] This can be exacerbated by other factors, such as race, with Black women being particularly likely to be under-diagnosed with ADHD.[121] As of 2021, research showed that Black women made up the highest percentage of people aged over 16 to screen positive for ADHD in the UK, demonstrating how symptoms had been missed in childhood and having a significant impact on their future.[122]

Gender

Non-binary and transgender individuals also face unique challenges regarding AuDHD, symptoms of which can compound the challenges already experienced by these people, such as navigating social expectations and healthcare

---

2021. https://www.thetransmitter.org/spectrum/massive-u-k-study-finds-racial-ethnic-disparities-in-autism-diagnoses/.

119   Morgan, Paul L., Marianne M. Hillemeier, George Farkas, and Steve Maczuga. 'Racial/Ethnic Disparities in ADHD Diagnosis by Kindergarten Entry'. *Journal of Child Psychology and Psychiatry, and Allied Disciplines* 55, no. 8 (August 2014): 905–13. https://doi.org/10.1111/jcpp.12204.

120   Kathryn. 'Podcast Recommendation: Moving Forward for Women and Girls with ADHD with Dr. Ellen B. Littman'. *Center for Mindful Therapy* (blog), 6 October 2023. https://mindfulcenter.org/podcast-recommendation-moving-forward-for-women-and-girls-with-adhd-with-dr-ellen-b-littman/.

121   THE UNDERDIAGNOSIS OF ADHD IN BLACK FEMALES - Kiana Clerkley - California State University - https://scholarworks.lib.csusb.edu/cgi/viewcontent.cgi?article=2641&context=etd

122   'Attention Deficit Hyperactivity Disorder (ADHD)', 10 October 2017. https://www.ethnicity-facts-figures.service.gov.uk/health/mental-health/prevalence-of-adhd-among-adults/latest/.

disparities. They may experience additional barriers to accessing appropriate support, such as discrimination, bias, and a lack of culturally competent healthcare providers.

This is especially concerning given that people who do not identify with the sex they were assigned at birth are 3 to 6 times as likely to be autistic as cisgender people.[123] One study found that non-binary (63%) and transgender (37%) people with ADHD experienced anxiety disorders, for which they require healthcare services tailored to their specific needs.[124]

Socioeconomics

The socioeconomic class of an individual can play a significant role in their ability to access support. For example, a 'two-tier' system has developed within the UK, with NHS assessments for autism and ADHD often spanning years, if available at all. Private assessments are likely to cost thousands, only available to those who can afford it.

Even then, NHS doctors may refuse to accept shared care, as seen by recent collective action of some doctors in the UK who have stopped prescribing ADHD medication or recognising private diagnosis' due to the additional workload involved.[125]

Students who have ever been eligible for free school meals are more likely to be autistic than those who have

---

[123] The Transmitter: Neuroscience News and Perspectives. 'Largest Study to Date Confirms Overlap between Autism and Gender Diversity', 14 September 2020. https://www.thetransmitter.org/spectrum/largest-study-to-date-confirms-overlap-between-autism-and-gender-diversity/.
[124] 'Evaluation of the Relationship between ADHD and Comorbid Psychiatric Conditions: A Comprehensive Study on a Large Cohort'. Accessed 3 February 2025. https://www.scirp.org/journal/paperinformation?paperid=130631.
[125] Lind, Sofia. 'GPs Asked to Pull out of ADHD Shared-Care Agreements as Part of Collective Action'. *Pulse Today* (blog), 25 November 2024. https://www.pulsetoday.co.uk/news/clinical-areas/mental-health-pain-and-addiction/lmcs-ask-gps-to-pull-out-of-adhd-shared-care-agreements/.

not.[126] In contrast, higher monthly total household income has been strongly associated with a decreased likelihood of autism.[127] A similar trend is seen with ADHD, with children in families of low incomes are 1.8-2.2% more likely to have ADHD than their peers in high income families.[128]

This disparity places them at a substantial disadvantage in being able to access and afford healthcare, especially on an ongoing basis. Socioeconomic factors such as unstable housing and lack of access to quality education can exacerbate difficulties AuDHD-ers may experience.

Ultimately, the more intersectional factors that cross over to shape a person's experience that diverges from the stereotype of a young, white boy, the harder it likely will be for them to access support and tailored understanding of their unique circumstances. This exacerbates other forms of trauma that these people may experience, such as discrimination, racism, and existing disparities in our society.

This has a devastating impact, as without representation and support, others will be less likely to access support after them. For example, within the ADHD community, there's a distinct lack of intersectional voices. Too many times I have spoken on panels that are completely white, showing only one experience of neurodivergence, inadvertently excluding those who have had different experiences. Change needs to happen on a broad basis within our society to break the systemic cycles of trauma that unfortunately still exist today.

---

126 The Transmitter: Neuroscience News and Perspectives. 'Largest Study to Date Confirms Overlap between Autism and Gender Diversity', 14 September 2020. https://www.thetransmitter.org/spectrum/largest-study-to-date-confirms-overlap-between-autism-and-gender-diversity/
127 'The Association Between Socioeconomic Disadvantage and Attention Deficit/Hyperactivity Disorder (ADHD): A Systematic Review - PubMed'. Accessed 3 February 2025. https://pubmed.ncbi.nlm.nih.gov/26266467/.
128 ibid

Tips: AuDHD-ers

- Acknowledge the impact of trauma, taking time to understand your trauma responses as valid responses to living in a world that isn't designed for your brain.

- Be gentle with yourself. Healing from trauma is a lifelong, exhausting process, but you are doing the best you can.

- Practice self-acceptance, acknowledging your needs and experiences as valid.

- Create safe spaces for processing your trauma, setting boundaries where needed, such as limiting contact with people who exacerbate trauma reactions.

- Use grounding techniques for sensory overload, such as by counting your breaths.

- Honour your needs by planning for predictability and managing potential changes in advance to cope with feelings of uncertainty.

- Give yourself choices to foster a sense of control over your environment, such as consciously deciding what to wear that day.

- Seek out neuro-affirming, trauma-informed care and support, such as from a therapist. This can feel intimidating when we've had a lifetime of being misunderstood, but there are people out there who can help.

- Cope in the ways that you need to, such as by stimming or journalling. Some strategies may be more destructive to our wellbeing than others, such as smoking, but be kind with yourself and break changes you want to make into small steps.

- Build trauma-aware routines, such as scheduling intentional rest before and after socialising.

- Make accommodations for yourself where relevant, such as by attending a new place in advance of meeting somebody there, or taking along some notes. This is nothing to be ashamed of!

- Challenge negative beliefs about yourself, such as feeling 'broken', questioning what this really means and whether there's any proof. Trauma does not define you, and you are not alone.

- Be careful about your relationships, building trust over time. Do better than me and try to avoid moving in with strangers! Take time to process your relationships, understanding who makes you feel good about yourself - and who doesn't.

- Set boundaries around trauma processing. When we open this 'mental box' of trauma, it can feel all-encompassing and overwhelming. Setting boundaries such as scheduling the amount of time you will spend thinking about it in a given day can be very helpful to control intrusive thoughts, noting them down for later.

- Rebuild trust with yourself through taking small steps of self-compassion. By setting yourself small decisions, such as to drink a glass of water when you wake up each morning, you are reminding yourself that you can take care of yourself.

- Engage in trauma healing at your own pace. Healing isn't a straight line, and it's okay to have setbacks. Remember to celebrate your progress and move at your own pace. Things will feel easier over time.

- Acknowledge the unique layers of intersectionality and trauma, recognising that your trauma may not be easily understood by others - but you can validate your own experiences.

- Reject internalised ableism or oppression, reaffirming your worth and the value of your unique perspective.

- Find or create a trauma-aware, intersectional community. Find others with similar interesting identities to find understanding and solidarity. For example, ADHD Babes is a brilliant resource for Black women and Black non-binary people of African-Caribbean descent with ADHD.[129]

- Set firm boundaries, especially against any situations that may feel triggering. You don't need to put yourself in situations that are going to hurt you.

---

[129] https://www.adhdbabes.com/

- If you feel comfortable to do so, talk to others in your life who you trust about your experiences, needs, and preferences.

- Recognise intergenerational trauma, especially if you come from a background with historical oppression. This may feel overwhelming, but you are making a difference simply by recognising this and looking after yourself.

- Remember that everyone is doing the best that they can with what they have available to them. This might feel especially difficult with people like parents who have undiagnosed neurodivergence and are unwilling to engage in conversations about it, but understanding how they may have built up internalised resistance due to their own struggles can help with forgiveness. It doesn't mean that you have to have them in your life on their terms - this can explain, but not excuse, behaviour.

- Recognise red flags in abusive relationships, such as by making a list of potential warning signs to look out for. Equally, make a list of green flags, signs that you can trust an individual.

- Trust your intuition: you have survived this far, so it must be doing something right!

- Create exit strategies, especially for situations that you may feel nervous about, such as parties.

Trauma

- Document your own feelings and experiences, such as in a journal, to help build self-awareness and understanding.

- Create personalised safety plans, including physical and emotional safety, along with identifying your support network, triggers, and coping tools.

- Remember that you are NOT the problem. You might have experienced a huge amount of trauma throughout your life, but understanding your own vulnerabilities and needs can be extremely empowering to protect yourself going forward.

Tips: loved ones

- Understand trauma responses and how they manifest, such as heightened anxiety, hyper-vigilance, or impulsivity. Open up conversations about this with your loved one to learn about their experiences.

- Create sensory-friendly, safe spaces by learning about their sensory needs and preferences.

- Validate their feelings, even if you don't fully understand the triggers. Saying something as simple as, 'I can see that this is really difficult' can go a long way to help them feel seen and heard.

- Respect their boundaries, avoiding pushing them into situations they aren't ready for, and double check their 'yes' when you think that they may be pushing themselves too far.

- Avoid giving advice unless it's asked for - they've likely tried a lot already!

- Provide routine, stability, and predictability. For example, having a time to connect regularly set in the calendar for the same time, at the same place each month can help significantly.

- Support them to find neuro-affirming, trauma-informed care, such as an AuDHD therapist, whilst respecting their boundaries if it's not something they wish to look into due to a lack of trust. You could offer support in accessing this, such as by offering to accompany them.

- Acknowledge their coping mechanisms, such as alcohol or intense hyper-focus on certain activities to the point of dissociation. Instead of criticising these behaviours, ask how they are helping them, without judgement, offering alternatives where helpful.

- Foster trust and communication, being consistent, clear, and honest. Be willing to adapt your communication style to their needs.

- Listen actively and without judgement, reminding them that you are there for them regularly.

Trauma

- Help them to feel in control by offering choices and encouraging self-advocacy. Equally, respect and support their preferences, such as if they find it difficult to make a decision. Making 'small decisions' with their support and checking in, such as where to go for lunch, can be extremely helpful.

- Be patient with their healing journey, staying present and showing compassion. Reassurance and positive feedback is key.

- Acknowledge the complexity of intersectionality, avoiding minimising or dismissing their experiences. Educate yourself about their experiences by doing research into particular areas, for example, recognising openly that you may not be able to ever truly understand what their unique experiences are like, but would like to try.

- Respect their autonomy, asking for permission before physical touch, and let them decide how to engage in conversations.

- Be mindful of micro-aggressions and misunderstandings. If you catch yourself or others using dismissive language or stereotypes, address it.

- Recognise systemic barriers, advocating in your community for more inclusive practices that reduce these barriers.

- Offer to help them navigate support systems or connect with resources.

- If you're worried about the potential for abuse in a relationship for example, discuss this with your loved one in a sensitive and non-judgemental way, such as by asking open-ended questions about their experiences. Avoid doing anything that may alienate them, such as by telling them that you don't like the person. Simply remain a safe space for them to seek out support when needed.

8. Support

Miserably, I booked a ticket back to the UK, feeling hopeless about my future. When I returned, I stopped making an effort in my friendships there that were based on alcohol, seeing many of them fade away as a result. I holed myself up in the flat I'd found to stay in for a few months, writing my book from 6am to 12am. I decided to just finish writing the book, and *then* I could take my own life, because I wouldn't have completely wasted it.

This decision, and my experiences abroad enabled me to set boundaries around work, which for the first time ever, were for no other justification than they were what I wanted. I asked my model agency not to send me on any shoots that involved maternity clothing, recognising how triggering these were for me, and they agreed. However, when I was on a shoot with 100 outfits, 10 of them were maternity, requiring me to put a fake baby bump on, even though it was unrecognisable (so my face would be cut off).

For the first time ever, I said no on a job. I suggested they replace the 10 outfits with some of the thousands in that factory, satisfied that I had the agreement from my agency that this wasn't supposed to happen. As a result, I was shouted at by both the client and the agency, telling me to 'just do it' as it was unrecognisable, but I explained that it was the principle. I was sent home, and told I'd never be booked for that client again, but I didn't care - I had finally stood up for myself.

The modelling jobs dried up, but I didn't mind, immersed in my writing, until I woke up one day to find my motivation had disappeared. When I sat down to write, I found myself staring at the window and trying to figure out if jumping off the balcony would kill me, or just land me in hospital. I was extremely annoyed at myself, having already reached 75% of the way through the book.

It was at this point that I remembered the psychiatrist who I was supposed to return to a year earlier, to finish off the ADHD assessment. Despite extreme embarrassment, I booked an appointment, because I felt like at least I had a bigger reason than me: the book. Accessing support wasn't for me - it was for other people. The diagnosis was a means to an end - my end.

However, this also meant having to find the forms I'd been sent a year earlier, and getting people in my life to complete them. This proved very difficult, as I met refusals on the basis that 'ADHD is a condition made up by psychiatrists to get money out of people', and they 'didn't have a printer'. I was becoming increasingly angry at everybody I knew, beginning to see the reality of many of my relationships when I dared to ask for help.

Eventually, I found willing contributors, and returned to the psychiatrist. I was given a prescription for medication, and became extremely angry to learn that this would cost £300 per month, *for the rest of my life*. I asked about transferring to the NHS, but was told this wasn't possible due to the need for re-diagnosis, which could take years. I explained that I literally didn't have the money, and was advised to ask my parents for help, who also couldn't afford this ludicrous subscription.

So, I rationed the medication instead, taking it only when I 'needed' it, instead of on a daily basis as was prescribed. The first time I took it, it felt like putting on glasses; I could literally see the dust and mess that everybody else always seemed to point out, but had always been invisible to me. I was able to write again, and the thoughts of suicide disappeared.

However, irregular use of the medication led to highs and lows that severely impacted my health. I experienced side effects like loss of appetite and a dry mouth, but I thought it was worth it to finally feel in control of my life. I wasn't told about any other kind of support that existed for ADHD, believing medication was my only option.

This newfound sense of confidence saw me change model agency representation. My new, highly 'accredited' agency seemed brilliant in comparison. However, a few weeks in, I quickly understood that they were trapping me in debt I wasn't told about in advance, for things like hair appointments and photoshoots for my portfolio organised on my behalf.

I demanded transparency, only to be told that I was 'uneducated' - it apparently wasn't debt, despite coming with a high interest rate for repayments, just 'investment'. When I tried to leave, I was told that wouldn't be possible unless I signed a Non Disclosure Agreement.

Despite refusing to do so upon unofficial legal advice, I still received regular correspondence from their lawyers, pressuring me to sign it. Each email felt unbearably unfair and stressful, as I ruminated on possible worst outcomes. I had no money to pay for a lawyer, and felt trapped, overthinking the agreement as potentially able to prevent me from ever working again, or publishing the book.

I was so furious from a fairness and social justice perspective that this situation had happened, especially as I was literally writing a book about exploitation in the modelling industry. My complaints to organisations that claimed to be able to help were ignored. Eventually, I signed the agreement, having becoming extremely unwell from stress and having regular panic attacks.

My psychiatrist's response to my worsening health was to increase the dosage of my medication, which made me question their motives, as I felt it was already contributing significantly to my chaos. Unable to see any other option, I went along with their decision, still rationing my doses.

As a result, my skin went grey and I developed acne all over my face. I lost 10kg of weight and looked like a skeleton. At night my hip bones would hurt as they prodded into the bed I lay on. I'd never hated my body more, but I'd at least finally reached the measurements that the modelling industry had wanted me to be for so many years. When people I knew burst into tears upon seeing me, I realised that I was seriously unwell, and needed to stop taking the medication.

I demanded a letter from the psychiatrist for the NHS, and registered with my local GP. I assumed I'd have to wait for years to be assessed again, but at least I'd be able to afford whatever medication I was given, and know that this wasn't financially motivated. However, the GP said that could prescribe me this medication with this letter, whilst adding me to the waiting list for an NHS confirmation of my diagnosis.

I was extremely angry, feeling like I'd been lied to by the psychiatrist, although I was re-diagnosed with ADHD on the NHS within a few months. In the meantime, I chose to stop taking the medication, as it had made me so unwell.

However, all of my previous symptoms then returned, including a constant determination to end my life, especially as I'd almost finished writing the book. I joined another model agency, but the jobs were scarce and very badly

Support

paying, with clients saying they had been warned against working with me.

This was heightened after being booked on a lingerie show abroad, which I initially accepted due to being unable to pay my rent. A couple of days later, I later realised that this was the worst thing I could possibly do, given my mental state, in addition to my discomfort around jobs involving lingerie. When I tried to cancel the job with a month's notice, the agency informed me that I'd have to cover the travel costs, which exceeded what I would have made from the job itself. With no other options, I did the job.

It was degrading, and not just because I was forced into it against my will. The day before the show, I stood with other models, us all shivering in nude thongs as a stranger openly criticised our bodies, comparing us to each other.

We were given steak tartare for lunch, despite most of the models being vegan or vegetarian, with no other options. During the show itself, I had to walk down the catwalk *blindfolded*, with a layer of diamantés obscuring my vision.

Backstage, multiple photographers were openly taking photos of all of the hungry, half-naked models backstage as we got changed. I complained, emboldened by the book I was literally writing about such practices, and nothing was done.

The anger I felt poured out of me into that book, hoping to at least be able to deter others from going down this career path.

After that job, I started looking for other options, joining a catering company for fashion events. I found waitressing impossible, because it was so mind numbingly boring and involved constant interaction with strangers within a crowd. I'd assumed hours had had to have passed, only to find out it'd been 20 minutes.

I was so bored I started counting the bricks in the wall, before giving up and going to the bathroom to cry. I couldn't figure out why I was so incapable of doing such seemingly 'easy' jobs, or why my brain felt like it was exploding.

Eventually, I finished writing the book. It had been rejected from publishers multiple times, including by one who told me I should self-publish it and hand it out for free. I didn't really care about anybody else reading it, but I didn't want to be around to have to promote it!

By that point, I'd moved into a house-share with some best-selling, famous authors who explained to me that they received only 10% of their book sales, approximately £30,000 in total. I realised that I may as well do it my way, coming across a hybrid publisher who helped me turn my manuscript into what became *'the Model Manifesto'*.

That month after I handed it in was one of the worst of my life, because I was obsessed with suicide, but I still couldn't do it. I would wake up in the middle of the night wishing that someone would come in and murder me.

Part of me wanted to stay and see the book through, but the rest of me was in unbearable mental pain at all times. I felt incredibly guilty and shameful about feeling this way, as though I was betraying my own previous promises to myself.

Recognising how unwell I was, I decided to restart the ADHD medication on the lowest dose through the NHS, take it every day, and go to yoga every day at 8am, and if I still wanted to die at the end of the month, *then* I could. I felt like I owed it to everything I'd been through, and the book, which had ignited a sense of purpose in me, to at least try this support out 'properly'.

As a result, my mental health became much better. I was taking the medication consistently, no longer fearing being unable to afford it the next month. The routine of going to yoga helped me to have a purpose, as a reason to get out of bed. I learned to do a headstand, feeling more proud of myself for this than I had in writing an entire book.

THE AUDHD LENS

Support is a controversial topic - especially when it comes to AuDHD. Whilst various kinds of medication are often offered post-diagnosis to help people with ADHD manage their symptoms, none are available for autism. For both, the general consensus is a feeling of being 'diagnosed and dumped' - but there *is* a lot of support available, if you know that it exists.

'Treatment'

ADHD and autism are neurodevelopmental conditions, not mental illnesses, because they can't be 'treated' or 'cured'. They are simply the way that someone's brain works, as both conditions impact the structure of the brain. This isn't necessarily wrong, or defective in any way, but simply different.

Living in a neurotypical world, with neurotypical standards, such as the expectation for children and adults alike to sit still for hours each day and stare into screens, can be especially difficult for neurodivergent people. ADHD medication is available to help with this, as opposed to changing the individual's brain wiring.

This can be compared to animals in a zoo. Out in the wild, they can act however comes naturally to them, whether that's hunting, swimming, or climbing trees. In captivity, they are domesticated to meet human standards, such as by being 'walked' by humans with leads around their necks. In zoos, they might be drugged to ensure compliance, with nearly half of all zoos in the US giving psychoactive drugs to animals.[130]

For example, 8% of domestic horses develop 'cribbing'[131], which is essentially repetitive self-harming behaviour involving the horse bitting onto something solid, before arching their neck, swallowing and grunting.

A veterinary specialist and professor, Nicholas Dodman, found that thtis behaviour stopped when prescribing the horse with naloxone medication, an opioid-blocker normally prescribed to human beings. Nicholas said, 'no one's ever seen a horse in the wild do this. This is a condition of 'domestication', keeping the horse in unnatural situations... horses spend about 60% of their time in the wild grazing, so it's not surprising that one of the things that gives them release is a sort of fake grazing, which is what cribbing is.'[132]

In the early years of humanity, humans would have been hunting and gathering. They would have needed the ability to hyper-focus on areas of interest, such as collecting berries, and the energy to catch their food. Adaptability to new environments would have been very important, as we'd have been constantly on the move.

Sensory sensitivities would have been helpful in noticing potential dangers, and acting upon them. Innovative thinking, curiosity, and creativity would have been key to evolution - and survival.

---

130   Webber, Jemima. 'Giving Zoo Animals Psychoactive Drugs Could Soon Be Illegal In New York'. *Plant Based News* (blog), 25 July 2021. https://plantbasednews.org/culture/law-and-politics/zoo-animals-psychoactive-drugs/.
131   Cooper, Jonathan J., and Melissa J. Albentosa. 'Behavioural Adaptation in the Domestic Horse: Potential Role of Apparently Abnormal Responses Including Stereotypic Behaviour'. *Livestock Production Science*, Adaptability of sport horses to stressful conditions, 92, no. 2 (1 February 2005): 177–82. https://doi.org/10.1016/j.livprodsci.2004.11.017.
132   Stolen Focus: Why You Can't Pay Attention - as told to Johann Harri - p214

Support

However, in our modern society, these strengths could be viewed as 'deficits'. Our natural energy can be seen as 'hyperactivity', bursting out of us through fidgeting as we're expected to stay still. Our innate curiosity can be viewed as 'rude', in asking questions others may not want to answer.

Our motivation to seek variety and stimulation could be seen as problematic, as we're expected to fit into boxes and stick with certain careers throughout our lifetime. Our differences can be seen as difficult, because we're not conforming to the status quo - what our society has conditioned to be 'normal'.

When our differences are invalidated, and we don't feel as though we fit into the world around us, we can internalise this as shame. We can beat ourselves up for struggling with 'easy' tasks, like taking a shower, that seem to come naturally to everybody else. The hyperactivity can go inwards, resulting in ruminative thoughts and repetitive behaviours, just like an animal trapped in a cage.

This is why AuDHD is not an illness. ADHD medication can target specific neurotransmitters affected by ADHD to make these challenges less intense, allowing us to fit into society's expectations. It was only once I took my medication that I was able to calm down and focus for long enough to apply for jobs properly, let alone stay in one for more than a month.

It's no coincidence that only after I managed to take my ADHD medication consistently from my GP that I was able to 'settle down'. Before, I hadn't been able to stay in a home for longer than a few months, was constantly moving country, binge drinking alcohol, and quit any job I started after a few days. This wasn't something rational: it was the way my brain was reacting to the expectations of being 'normal'.

This also meant that I was able to stop feeling suicidal as a way of coping. When I stopped feeling like fitting into the world was impossible, then I could start to create a life for myself that I could actually stay in. I didn't feel suicidal because I had AuDHD - I felt suicidal because the world was not designed for a brain like mine.

Stigma

The stigma around support for AuDHD is immense, such as in relation to ADHD medication. This also seen by other forms of 'treatment', such as Applied Behaviour Analysis (ABA) for autism. ABA is focused on helping autistic people to improve their social skills and behaviour to fit in with 'normal' standards, as opposed to helping them to understand their needs and advocate for them.

This is reflected in language - from a 'disorder' to 'deficits' or 'impairments', these conditions are framed negatively, at least in the medical world. This is despite scientific research highlighting the strengths that can accompany different ways of thinking - the people whose environments support the way their brain works, aren't typically the ones who get diagnosed.

This is even reflected in studies suggesting various factors can 'cause' neurodivergence, such as premature birth (or incorrectly, vaccines). When a well intentioned person told me about the higher risk of having a neurodivergent child if the mother is diabetic, I questioned why this was a 'risk' at all - it's not a bad thing!

Life can certainly be more difficult as a neurodivergent person, especially for someone who's unable to do things like speak or work, but this doesn't mean that they are broken. Neurodivergence has stayed with us for a reason - evolution hasn't wiped out those who think differently to 'most', because we're necessary for the continuation of the human race.

ADHD Medication Myths

Before being diagnosed, the only thing I knew of ADHD was that the medication could make you 'productive'. However, as opposed to simply making someone 'productive', this medication helps to regulate dopamine levels in people with ADHD, improving focus, impulse control, and executive functioning. It affects people who don't have ADHD very differently, because of their brain chemistry.

The medication doesn't necessarily enable you to be a super-whizzy human that can write books, because 'pills don't give skills'. It enabled me to see the overwhelming mess that I was living in, but it didn't provide me with any skills to be able to handle that mess! This is why I'm so passionate about ADHD coaching - medication isn't for everybody, but understanding how your brain works is. As many as 1 in 10 people don't get any results from either of the two main types of stimulants prescribed for ADHD, because of their body chemistry.[133]

Similarly, it also doesn't enable you to be able to choose what to focus on. I've coached students who have spent hours re-writing the same paragraph of an essay after taking medication. For me, it enables me to focus more on the things I already want to focus on, but it also makes coming out of this very difficult. I can write this book all day and night, but I am still surrounded by things I need to do, like eat.

Before I took medication, I was still able to get A grades in my exams and a law degree, largely without attending much of my studies at all. This information didn't stay in my head after the exam, though!

---

133 Pagán, Camille Noe. 'What to Do If Your ADHD Meds Stop Working.' WebMD. Accessed 3 February 2025. https://www.webmd.com/add-adhd/adhd-meds-stop-working.

AuDHD: Blooming Differently

ADHD medication doesn't make you less 'you'. It doesn't make you less creative, or stifle your personality, although this could be a side effect for some people which signifies that it may not be right for them. For me, it just silences the 421874290 thought channels blasting in my head all the time. I was *amazed* that other people didn't have this constant narrative blasting at them - it certainly makes life a lot easier.

This medication is *not* addictive. I don't think anybody could call my medication addictive if I often forget whether I've taken it! It's designed to make you feel normal - not high.

ADHD medication simply helps you to regulate your own behaviour and emotions, which enables you to make better choices. Before taking it, I was constantly self-medicating with 10 cups of coffee per day, Diet Coke, and alcohol. I couldn't figure out how to stop myself from getting in situations where I'd end up turning to alcohol as a crutch, but the medication helped me to do this.

However, abusing it certainly can be addictive. After someone was late to multiple coaching sessions, we uncovered that they were struggling with medication abuse. They were prescribed instant release stimulant medication, which enabled them to stay awake all night - and were taking it before going out clubbing! This is why proper medical oversight is so important, and having a holistic support network who can help identify any issues.

The side effects can be overwhelming, but in my opinion, they are not in themselves worthy of stigma around the medication as a whole. I know this first hand, having become extremely unwell on my first attempt at taking the medication, but this was largely because I didn't take it as prescribed. I was on the wrong dose, and had to solve this by myself by finding a doctor who would take my experiences seriously.

Judgement

It can be difficult emotionally to start medication, especially if you're late diagnosed. To suddenly take a pill that will change the way you think is scary, but if you're struggling, there is no shame in it at all - and it's worth a try. You haven't failed for taking medication, not anymore than someone fails for wearing glasses if they need them to see.

You are not weak, and the things you may or may not do after taking the medication do not undermine your past. They may have happened either way, but above all, you deserve a life where your brain isn't fighting against you. The things you may achieve are *not* just because of taking medication.

However, this is easier said than believed, especially because of the stigma we see in our society. It's bizarre to take medication that is regularly blasted by the national media for being 'addictive', when this actually helped me to curb my alcohol addiction. For some reason, our society stigmatises 'stimulant' medication, but some kinds of ADHD medication aren't stimulants at all, unlike others that are freely available, such as coffee.

Other people seem to have a much bigger problem with the medication than those taking it. I once coached a child who had to have two teachers sign what can only be called a witness statement after watching them take their medication, every single morning. They were unable to travel home from boarding school with their medication alone, meaning that they couldn't take it at the weekends, causing inconsistency.

When I started taking ADHD medication, I tried to only take it when I 'needed it', which I'd strongly advise against, as it made me incredibly unwell. I commonly hear this narrative around only taking it on certain days, or when someone needs to focus, but this seems wrong. You are not 'dependent' on the medication anymore than a person with eyesight challenges is 'dependent' on their glasses. You may take this for your whole life, because ADHD is a lifelong condition - but that doesn't mean you shouldn't!

We don't only need our executive functioning skills working to their full potential when we need to study or work - we need them for *everything*. We need them to navigate relationships, self-care, travel, taking breaks, and everything else we do as human beings.

When the world changes to accommodate people who think differently, maybe medication won't be needed. Until then, it is saving lives - and should be available to those who need it. Ultimately, it's important to find a doctor who you trust and follow their instructions in related to medication as prescribed, as everybody will be different.

ACCESSING MEDICATION

Especially in light of the stigma above, ADHD medication can be exceptionally difficult to access, at least, in the UK. A General Practitioner (GP) cannot diagnose ADHD (or autism), and so cannot prescribe medication without this being first administered by a psychiatrist.

In contrast, 'qualified professionals', such as psychologists, can assess and diagnose ADHD, but cannot prescribe medication. This means that individuals may seek a private assessment with the aim of accessing medication, but only find out afterwards that this isn't enough. This may be not made explicitly clear at the outset, disadvantaging already vulnerable people - so if this applies to you, make sure you ask upfront!

After the years-long waiting lists for an assessment and being diagnosed with ADHD, individuals are often placed on another waiting list for medication, which can be just as long. At the time of writing, I have been on a list like this for a year, waiting for a medication review. This is ultimately dependent on a person's GP and circumstances, such as where they live, as every NHS Trust is different.

Titration

When an individual is initially prescribed medication, they will typically be placed on 'titration'. This usually lasts between 3-6 months, where the prescriber monitors their reactions to the medication and ensures it's safe for them to continue.

If they have been diagnosed privately, the individual will typically be expected to pay for the medication during this time, costing them hundreds of pounds. They will also likely be expected to pay to talk to their psychiatrist - I had to pay £200 *per month* for this, just to pick up my prescription. If I wanted to talk to them in the meantime, such as to flag my concerns about the side effects, I had to pay another £200.

Shared Care

After this time, the psychiatrist may refer an individual back to the NHS in what's called a 'Shared Care Agreement' (SCA). This means that care is split with the NHS, enabling the GP to prescribe medication based off this. However, a GP must agree to do this, and they are typically not compensated to do so.

Unfortunately, the increase in demand for medication that has accompanied the increase in numbers of people who've realised that they have ADHD, has put a strain on an already underfunded, struggling system. An individual's GP may refuse to recognise their SCA, meaning they are only left with the option to continue privately.

At the time of writing, some GPs in the UK have engaged in collective action[134] to stop recognising SCA's, even for patients they have already been prescribing medication to. This is incredibly dangerous, meaning a sudden stop in treatment, without any additional support being provided.

It's also obviously extremely stressful for the individual, who faces a choice between paying huge sums of money - *forever* - or going without the help they know can make a huge difference to their daily life. The loss of this medication can mean the loss of their job, or studies, for example. Organisations such as employers and schools also may be placed in a confusing position legally, as they may be expected to make reasonable adjustments to accommodate any changes in performance.

Prescriptons

As ADHD medication is typically considered a 'Controlled Drug', prescriptions are usually only issued for 30 days at a time. (This might be how I've managed to stay in the UK for so long!). There's usually a requirement for the individual to provide information on a regular basis, such as their blood pressure and weight, which can create extra work for GPs.

This is an extremely un-ADHD-friendly process. Every month, I have to remember to request a new prescription from my GP, which I can't do in the 'normal' ways they offer for other medication types, such as via an app. Post-pandemic, I can now request this via email, but previously, I had to visit *in person* every month.

---

[134] Lind, Sofia. 'GPs Asked to Pull out of ADHD Shared-Care Agreements as Part of Collective Action'. *Pulse Today* (blog), 25 November 2024. https://www.pulsetoday.co.uk/news/clinical-areas/mental-health-pain-and-addiction/lmcs-ask-gps-to-pull-out-of-adhd-shared-care-agreements/

Support

Getting a GP appointment at all can be hard enough, so doing this on a monthly basis in a way that lines up with when your medication will run out, especially for someone who struggles with executive functioning, can prove impossible!

Then the individual has to visit their pharmacy to collect their medication. Pharmacies will not deliver this by post, as is often offered for other kinds of medication, so we will again need to visit in person. There, we will usually have to show our ID, such as our passport.

This again, involves the person with executive functioning challenges such as memory and organisation, to do things that go against their inherent nature, such as remembering their ID! It feels incredibly embarrassing to have to do this every time I pick up my prescription, feeling like I'm doing something wrong in accessing it.

Shortages

This is, if the pharmacy has any in stock. In September 2023, a National Patient Safety Alert was issued by the Department of Health and Social Care, communicating a nation-wide ADHD medication shortage. This is not confined to the UK; the shortages have been worldwide, due to 'manufacturing issues'.

No prior notice was provided to people taking this medication, who simply found that they were unable to access it overnight. As you might imagine, this caused immense chaos and disruption. The suicide risk for people with ADHD are already 5x higher than in the general population, and suddenly stopping medication was extremely stressful to navigate. They are not taking it for fun - they need it.

Although the shortages were initially projected to last a few months, they are still ongoing at the time of writing, approximately 1.5 years later. My medication type is now usually in stock, but every month, I experience immense stress in not knowing whether it will be available.

During the shortages of my medication, which lasted for around 8 months, my life fell apart. Like many others, I attempted to ration my medication. I ended up binge drinking alcohol again, ending relationships out of nowhere, and within a few months, the closest I've ever been to taking my own life.

This wasn't just my experience. As an ADHD coach, I was suddenly supporting clients who were equally overwhelmed and struggling with their mental health. Some were self-harming to cope, others suicidal. They weren't provided with any follow up or interim support, such as therapy.

At the time, I led a petition calling for a Government inquiry into pre- and post-ADHD support, which gained over 11,000 signatures. The Government's response was essentially that it wasn't their problem, because regulatory guidelines were in place - even though they were often not being followed. However, shortly after, the NHS ADHD Taskforce was established. To date, over a year later, no clear action has been taken by this Taskforce.

So, it's very understandable to be cautious about ADHD medication - just not for the reasons you may have thought! Unfortunately, this is another symptom of a broken system, where neurodivergent people are being failed.

AUTISM AND ADHD MEDICATION

As ADHD and autism have only been diagnosable in the same person since 2013, there's a significant lack of research about the interaction of ADHD medication and AuDHD.

Medication is generally not prescribed for autism due to this condition affecting the structure of our brain, as

Support

opposed to specific neurotransmitters that can be targeted, as with ADHD. However, ADHD also impacts the brain structure, which is why it's not an illness that can be 'cured' with medication - it's lifelong.

Taking medication will still mean that you have ADHD, even if your symptoms no longer meet the diagnostic criteria due to this. It's frustrating to have the lifelong label of a 'disorder', despite my life not being significantly 'disordered' anymore, but I'd rather have this information than not.

The interaction between autism and ADHD medication is complex, and varies from person to person, just as the ADHD medication itself does. As 50-70% of autistic people are thought to have ADHD[135], it's likely that many will be taking ADHD medication, but the specific differences of this within AuDHD haven't been studied to provide any tangible results.

Even so, autistic people are likely to respond differently to these medications than expected of a 'pure' ADHD-er, because of differences in neurology, sensory processing, and co-occurring conditions. For example, although the ADHD medication enabled my brain to quieten, it also increased awareness of my environment, including my sensory responses.

They had always been there, but were masked by the ADHD - even to myself. The medication enabled me to stop putting myself in situations I didn't want to be in, like clubbing, but then the cause of the discomfort became clear.

I withdrew from many relationships, preferring to remain at home, rather than socialise at all. When I did force myself out, I'd have panic attacks, such as at a busy train station when I became overwhelmed by the crowds and noise.

---

[135] Hours, Camille, Christophe Recasens, and Jean-Marc Baleyte. 'ASD and ADHD Comorbidity: What Are We Talking About?' *Frontiers in Psychiatry* 13 (28 February 2022): 837424. https://doi.org/10.3389/fpsyt.2022.837424.

AuDHD: Blooming Differently

This is what helped me to understand that I'm also autistic, which to my understanding, is common for AuDHD-ers. When the ADHD symptoms have been treated, the autism can become clearer.

Although there's no specific medication available to help with managing symptoms of autism, there may be medication available targeted at certain areas. For example, when my panic attacks became more regular, I finally decided to try anti-anxiety medication, ironically battling my own internalised ableism against 'needing' medication for this.

For me, this medication was just as powerful as the ADHD medication in terms of the positive difference it made to my life. I had no idea it was possible to live without the constant sense of dread that I'd done something wrong, would be 'found out', or worrying about anything and everything. I couldn't believe it had been available all of this time, but I'd avoided taking it!

However, this won't necessarily work for everybody. Medications such as SSRI's can have different effects on neurodivergent people than those who are neurotypical, due to our brain chemistry. Anti-depressants and anti-anxiety medication can therefore be potentially dangerous to neurodivergent people, so it's very important to have this in mind when working with a healthcare professional, even if someone isn't diagnosed.

Medication may also be available for different challenges that may arise with AuDHD, such as sleep or depression. Obviously, ADHD medication has also been found to work in autistic people in terms of managing ADHD symptoms![136]

---

[136] Davis, Naomi Ornstein, and Scott H. Kollins. 'Treatment for Co-Occurring Attention Deficit/Hyperactivity Disorder and Autism Spectrum Disorder'. *Neurotherapeutics* 9, no. 3 (July 2012): 518–30. https://doi.org/10.1007/s13311-012-0126-9.

Ultimately, taking medication is a personal choice, and there's no right or wrong answers. There's only experimenting, and understanding what works for us. Above all, it's important to remember that taking medication doesn't make you weak - it makes you human.

OTHER SUPPORT

Medication is definitely not the only option to help manage challenges relating to AuDHD. Support may include:

- Coaching

When I became an ADHD coach a few years ago, there were very few of us. Now, I have personally trained over 400, all around the world! Coaching can be a confusing term, and the industry is unregulated, which can make it very dangerous for already vulnerable people.

It's also extremely important to ensure that any coach you work with understands AuDHD, and is neuro-affirmative. This doesn't necessarily mean neurodivergent, or having completed any particular courses or training (the quality varies!), but ultimately, that you trust them to understand your brain, and to be able to raise any issues that you may have.

Coaching is essentially about helping someone to 'move forwards', and to take action. It's often described as different to therapy, because it's focused on the future, instead of the past, but the past is still important for context. ADHD / AuDHD coaching can mean a number of things, but ultimately, it's about working with people who are neurodivergent.

However, the way I coach, and the way I train ADHD and AuDHD coaches is very different to 'normal' coaching. I found coaching very stressful as a client, because I was usually expected to 'bring the agenda' and to say what I wanted to

AuDHD: Blooming Differently

get out of the sessions. As an alexithymic AuDHD-er, I had no idea - I just knew I needed help!

So, I designed a coaching framework based on what I needed. This involves a series of exercises and perspectives to understand how ADHD or AuDHD shows up for an individual, helping them to learn how their brain works, and to make friends with it.

For ADHD, this is focused around executive functioning skills including self-awareness, memory, emotional regulation, and motivation. For AuDHD, the framework is based on paradoxes such as demand avoidance, as these add another layer to the coaching!

These frameworks serve as an optional 'menu' to use for coaching, and individuals are *not* expected to bring the agenda, to set actions from the sessions, or to necessarily do the ones they do set! I created them after coaching teenagers, who *refused* to mask or 'bring an agenda' for coaching.

What I do as the coach is hold accountability through an AuDHD lens. I will check in with them on what worked, what didn't, and what they want to do going forward. I prioritise creating a validating, safe space for someone to unmask as they are, whatever that means for them. I've coached people whilst they've been walking around, wearing pyjamas, or even doing DIY - there's never any judgement.

This is extremely helpful, because it's an environment without demands or expectations, providing space for someone to figure out who they are and what works for *them*, not what they think they 'should' be doing.

Every coach will be different, so it's advisable to take great caution in who you choose to support you. Recommendations are usually the safest bet![137]

---

[137] Here's a directory of coaches I've trained on our ADHD Works frameworks: https://www.adhdworks.info/coaching-directory

Support

- **Therapy**

Therapy is very important for AuDHD-ers to process the immense emotional challenges and trauma that can accompany being neurodivergent. However, just like coaching, it's extremely important to ensure that any therapist you work with is neuro-affirmative, in that they understand neurodiversity and will work with you as an individual.

I've trained numerous therapists (and already highly qualified coaches!), because they have often experienced challenges with AuDHD clients that weren't covered in their training. This is understandable - therapeutic approaches tends to avoid 'labels' and focus on the individual, but for AuDHD-ers, labels may be very important!

My own therapist that I saw for 2 years told me that I couldn't possibly be autistic, which put me off seeking an assessment for months, because I trusted her so implicitly - but she was wrong! I also struggled significantly with my autism symptoms as a result, beating myself up for believing this was autism, which as an autistic person, was very overwhelming!

Finding a therapist who understands, accepts, and embraces your own approach to neurodivergence is very important. This is important, to ensure we don't simply talk non-stop for an hour and leave, wondering why we didn't just talk to a friend!

It's also crucial to ensure your safety, as therapy can be very triggering, for lack of a better word. I've worked with extremely highly qualified and certified therapists who have caused significant damage as a result of their approaches, such as filming our sessions without my prior knowledge, and telling me off for not doing the homework! There's lots of different kinds of therapy and approaches, so it's a good idea to find out exactly what's involved before starting - they should be able to explain this in an accessible way to you.

Remember that just because a professional may be neurodivergent themselves, or have done a particular training, doesn't guarantee that they will be right for you - or indeed neuro-affirmative at all! Remember that trust is earned, not automatically granted, even within the therapy room.

- **Reasonable adjustments**

Autism and ADHD can be disabilities in law. This means that organisations such as employers and schools may have a legal duty to make reasonable adjustments to remove or reduce any significant disadvantages an AuDHD-er may experience in their environments because of their disability.

These can be anything, but could include changes such as allowing you to work or study from home, or on different hours to your peers. They may have a duty to pay for adjustments such as coaching or equipment like standing desks, depending on the size of the organisation, but this will be situational.

This is a legal test rather than medical. It's based on how much these conditions impact your ability to do normal day to day activities, meaning that no formal diagnosis is required for the law to apply. However, as you can imagine, this can be very confusing and overwhelming for organisations who are not medically or legally trained in these areas to navigate.

Unfortunately, this means that we may commonly experience discrimination as a result of a failure to make reasonable adjustments. This was seen by the number of discrimination cases relating to neurodivergent conditions in the employment tribunal rising by 40% in one year![138]

---

[138] https://www.nelsonslaw.co.uk/neurodiversity-in-the-workplace/#:~:text=Employment%20Tribunal%20claims,claims%20coming%20through%20the%20Courts.

Support

This can result in further challenges around employment and education for AuDHD-ers, who are already substantially disadvantaged. It's important to understand these issues carefully, because disclosure of a disability can have a significant effect on your life, which could be positive and/or negative, depending on your situation!

For more information on this, I recommend reading *'ADHD Works at Work'*, which I wrote to help both employers and employees navigating these issues.

An alarm clock

This isn't meant to sound patronising, but it's my number one tip for AuDHD-ers. Having an alarm clock, instead of using your phone, can be immensely helpful. If you can, charging your phone as far as possible away from your bed whilst sleeping will help you to relax and recharge.

As AuDHD-ers are more vulnerable to having our attention hacked by the *world leading behavioural psychologists that have designed our phones*, this is very important. Waking up and doing what *you* want to do, instead of immediately exposing yourself to notifications, messages, and noise from the outside world, will provide immeasurable autonomy and agency over your own life.

For more information on this, I recommend reading *'the Reality Manifesto'*, which I wrote to help people avoid exploitation on social media.

Tips: AuDHD-ers

- Learn as much as you can about AuDHD, and remember that one size doesn't fit all - you need to find what works for you.

- Take time to reflect on and process how you feel about medication - there's no wrong answer!

- Try to avoid shaming yourself for your perspective on medication, noticing if you think you 'don't need it' or 'want to try other options first'. These are completely valid, but remember that medication doesn't equate to weakness.

- Remember that you deserve support - whatever that looks like.

- Be cautious about who you choose to speak to about your experiences and thoughts, ensuring that you prioritise your own first, and recognising the stigma that surrounds these topics.

- At the same time, do ensure that you have a support network around you that you can trust. It may be helpful to seek out peer support from other AuDHD-ers, who can share their own experiences.

- Talk through your decisions with someone in your life, especially any changes such as starting or stopping medication.

- Always ensure that you see a qualified medical professional for topics around things like ADHD medication, and try to be as honest as you can with them about your experiences.

Support

- Seek out support such as therapy and/or coaching - you definitely deserve it!

- Remember that you are not broken, and do not need to be fixed - but knowing about AuDHD means that you can make life easier for yourself.

- Remember that AuDHD is just the way your brain works. It might be a label, but you get to choose what that means for you, and how much impact it has in your life.

- If you're considering an assessment, try to establish what you'd like out of it, or do afterwards. In many cases, you may be able to do this already, such as seeking out AuDHD coaching or asking for changes to be made to your workplace.

Tips: loved ones

- Try to notice your own judgements and opinions about diagnosis' and medication, without beating yourself up for any negativity.

- Although you may have concerns, try to do your own research and talk about these with the relevant professionals, instead of simply with the individual concerned. Talking to their doctor may be very reassuring, and far more productive!

- Try to be very conscious around conversations involving topics like medication. It's best to ask questions, instead of share advice or opinions, unless specifically asked, as these can be so sensitive for people to experience.

- Offer support, such as helping your loved one with routines and appointments, offering to join them or help them advocate for their needs.

- Financial support is likely to be extremely helpful if you're in a position to offer it, because this can be very expensive! If you can, try to ensure your loved one doesn't get into debt whilst seeking support.

- Let your loved one know that you'll be there for them and support them, no matter what.

- Try to avoid sharing any observations or judgements about how your loved one may be on or off medication unless asked.

- Seek out your own support, such as AuDHD / ADHD coaching and/or therapy. This can be an intense emotional experience for you too, and you deserve support! Helping yourself will help others around you.

- If your loved one seems resistant to your offers of support, seek this out for yourself instead! This is very common with parents of AuDHD children - they will get out what they put in, and so will you.

9. Employment

As modelling was no longer an option for me, ironically due to factors out of my control, I started applying for jobs again as my mental health improved. Having finished the modelling book, I had discovered a newfound passion for mental health and supporting others, which gave me a direction I'd never had before. Suddenly, the applications felt much easier.

However, when I received an invitation to an interview for a role as a mental health, disability, and immigration legal policy adviser, I had a panic attack. I was terrified of getting into trouble, and being shouted at for applying in the first place.

I felt like a complete fraud, with no relevant experience, and a complete inability to do any job, let alone one in law. I didn't think I could bear receiving this confirmation in person, and felt terrified about crying in front of the interviewers.

The alternative was even worse, in that I'd somehow managed to trick them into passing me to the next stage, where I'd feel like this constantly for weeks during multiple interview rounds until inevitably being rejected. I was so overwhelmed that I'd decided to cancel the interview, but lost the executive functioning ability to do so before it arrived. So, I ended up forcing myself to go.

The interview ended up being one of the most validating experiences I've ever had. I was reassured by the interviewers that there was no reason to be nervous, that this would be relaxed and friendly, and how impressed they were by my CV, which I couldn't believe.

I was surprised to find I could easily answer the straightforward questions, such as how I am at receiving constructive feedback - which I'd had a lot of as a model! It went so well that I asked if they were aware that I didn't have relevant legal experience, but they said I could learn on the job. When I asked about further interview stages, they chuckled and said that they wouldn't put me through that - I couldn't believe it.

I left feeling immensely grateful, realising that there were people in the 'working world' who would treat me with dignity, kindness, and respect as I was. I didn't expect to get it, but I'd at least learned which areas I was passionate about, and helped me to see a range of career options I'd previously written off as inaccessible.

A few weeks later, I received a phone call offering me the job, which was honestly one of my happiest and proudest moments of my entire life. Although I didn't start for a few months, I began studying legislation obsessively, terrified of being 'found out' when I started.

I also decided to move house to live as close as possible to my office. I was absolutely determined not to quit this job, and my ADHD diagnosis had confirmed to me that I would be at high risk of quitting if there were too many barriers involved.

Commuting on public transport was one of them - I couldn't handle the crowds, the lack of control over timings, and the constant change in temperatures. I regularly had panic attacks, especially if the bus or train paused, or if there was traffic, which had led me to quit previous positions, such as internships, entirely.

Employment

I also knew that living with other people would be impossible. I had repeated challenges in living with others, because I felt unable to relax at all. I was constantly plagued with thoughts about whether I was in my room 'too much' and what our social interactions should be like, and whether I was annoying them. I'd overthink every action, including going to the bathroom or kitchen, debating whether I was somehow walking too loudly or doing something wrong.

When I found the tiniest studio flat in the world over the road from my office, it felt like fate. It was a fixed term, 8 month rental contract, costing over half of my monthly salary. I reasoned that this was perfect, because I'd effectively be handcuffing myself to the office - I couldn't afford to quit. I thought I'd 'hacked' my ADHD, feeling pretty proud.

However, I wasn't prepared for how overwhelming I'd find working in an office. I had no idea what to wear, spending money I didn't have on suits that all seemed too formal and casual at the same time, becoming overwhelmed by the crowds, queues, and lighting in shops.

On my first day, I was overwhelmed by not knowing what I 'should' be doing, sitting at my computer, acutely aware of the harsh fluorescent lighting and conversations happening in the nearby kitchen. I felt like I was an actor in a movie, pretending to be an office worker, as though I'd been sent to prank my new colleagues.

I was hyper-aware of being 'perceived', unsure what 'should' be on the computer screen that faced out to the room. I didn't know what I was supposed to do in-between replying to emails - I was used to jobs where every minute of the day was mapped out for me as a model.

Ironically, my book, '*the Model Manifesto*', was published during the same week as I started my new job. I was in genuine shock and horror at being asked to go on *Lorraine* and having my face featured on the cover of *The Times*. I was mortified - all I wanted was to start my new life with a new identity, and to be 'normal'.

I had lots of introductory meetings with colleagues, who all naturally asked what I'd been doing before, which I was extremely embarrassed about. One exclaimed surprise, as they said they'd seen me on the cover of their newspaper during their commute. When I was asked whereabouts I lived, I was suddenly aware that it was quite weird to be living over the road from the office.

I kept having panic attacks about how stupid I'd been to publish the book, and how it had inevitably destroyed my life. Every single day, I was waiting to be fired, or at the very least, told off. Every single email, every single call, conversation, meeting - they all had the potential to destroy this life that I'd worked so hard for.

However, this didn't happen. My colleagues were incredibly kind and supportive. They reassured me that I wouldn't be fired, checked over my emails when I didn't know how to sign them off, and shared their own experiences. They became friends, inviting me for coffee, providing reassurance, and encouraging me to use my strengths. I felt a kind of acceptance that I'd honestly never experienced before, and was terrified of losing it, ironically becoming increasingly anxious.

At one public speaking workshop, we were asked to share a 5 minute talk on a topic of our choice. I inexplicably stood up and told everyone how I'd almost killed myself two years earlier, before bursting into tears and sitting back down. I couldn't believe my brain had just done that to me, and had never felt so embarrassed, but there was no judgement from my colleagues - just support.

As the days passed, this supportive environment quickly built up my confidence, which turned into creativity. I found that I could read huge amounts of information and translate it very quickly. I didn't really understand what I was reading, but that made it even easier, as I could pick out the most important bits. I replied to all emails immediately, learning everything I could, absolutely loving every single day, especially the wonderfully intelligent, kind, and talented people who I worked with.

I developed workarounds for my anxiety, such as creating agendas for 1:1 catch ups and emailing them over in advance. It was quite funny to be praised for this, as it was purely for my own anxiety. Before doing this, I'd arrive to catch ups in a state of immediate overwhelm, forgetting everything relevant that I was supposed to say, with no idea of how to structure these conversations. Creating an agenda seemed to make everything make sense.

The company also had flexible working hours, which worked brilliantly with my brain, enabling me to start at 8am and work during my most productive time. It also had one day of working from home per week for everyone, which was incredibly helpful for me to be able to recharge from the overwhelm of the office mid-week. I joined a nearby gym with a huge variety of classes, and did things like kickboxing, jiujitsu, aerial hoop and trapeze after work.

I had genuinely never felt so fulfilled or happy. I created a new routine for my weekends, teaching myself piano on a Saturday morning, and cycling to a yoga class on a Sunday morning.

However, at the same time, my anxiety was building up. I was still terrified of being fired, even more so as the days went on and I fell in love with my job. I was terrified of somehow being 'found out', or making a mistake and everything being over, especially as I was in the standard 'probation period'. Now that I'd discovered happiness, the pain of losing it would be too much to bear.

I took too much on, my enthusiasm meaning that I said yes to everything, and creativity seeing me trying to implement endless ideas, which were unsustainable. From attempting to create newsletters for volunteers I worked with, to administrative guides for the whole company, podcasts, social media accounts, charters, and setting up a mental health group - it was a lot.

My job description primarily related to responding to government consultations, not creating huge campaigns. I struggled with performance reviews, creating 15 page detailed documents of everything I'd done in the weeks prior, not understanding which information to prioritise.

I'd also massively misjudged my finances. After bills, I wasn't left with enough money to survive. Every day, lunchtime was a stress of its own. I'd try to wait and watch to see when other people left, and for how long. I knew I was contractually allowed an hour, but had no idea where to go or what to do. Usually, I'd rush out as quickly as I could to grab a sandwich to eat at my desk, which ended up being a very expensive daily habit!

My medication was on a monthly prescription, which I had to travel 45 minutes to get in person. I couldn't face the overwhelm and uncertainty of changing GP surgery, but also had intense anxiety about not being at work, as the surgery was only open from 9-5. Although I started at 8am, I was extremely anxious about leaving before everybody else did, which was usually around 5pm.

Others who arrived later wouldn't necessarily know that I'd arrived so early, and I didn't want them to think I was slacking off. I could make the time up, but I felt immensely awkward to simply walk out during the day.

Employment

Although I now had access to paid holiday days, I felt awkward about using them, feeling like it was an expectation. I'd also always struggled with the transitions around holidays - I'd rather just move somewhere new all together, or not go at all. To go away for a week to a new place felt like it would either be so good that I would feel bad about my 'real' life, or so bad that it was a waste of time.

Usually it was the latter, as the stress of changing my routine, especially to groups of people with expectations to socialise and 'relax', meant I had outbursts and arguments. When everybody took annual leave over Christmas, I found myself in the office alone, increasingly aware and self-conscious of how my way of viewing 'breaks' was different to everybody else's.

The office was also somewhat of a maze, as a historic old building, and I kept getting lost in it, which increased my anxiety, especially around potentially being late. I struggled with the social elements outside of the office significantly, not knowing what to talk about during team lunches or pub drinks that wasn't 'work chat'. During our Christmas party, I became so anxious that I ran home and took back a Scrabble set, which was ironically very popular!

This allowed me to regulate my social overwhelm, which I'd realised was becoming a serious issue. One day, I'd told someone to shut up when they spoke loudly in the kitchen, emailing them to tell them that nobody cared about their weekend. To this day, it is one of the most mortifying things I've ever done, something I didn't even consciously realise I'd done until I received a reply CC'ing in our managers and the Culture Code. I hadn't even registered how much the noise from the kitchen was stressing me out, simmering until it turned into an explosion.

A few months in, I attended a lunchtime event about neurodiversity in the office. It wasn't a term I'd ever heard before. I knew virtually nothing about ADHD other than the medication seemed to help me not to feel suicidal, and so was surprised to see it being talked about by this external speaker, who explained the impact it can have in the workplace. I couldn't believe that someone was describing my experiences so accurately, as though she could see into my brain.

Unable to handle the anxiety of travelling any longer, I finally joined a new GP surgery nearby. My new doctor told me that they could continue prescribing my medication, but if I wanted to go to a higher dose, I'd need to wait 7 years, as their waiting list for ADHD assessments was this long.

I couldn't believe it. I told them that if I'd had to wait on that list, I'd be dead. Indeed, it was only because I almost did die that I paid so much money to a psychiatrist in the first place.

These experiences spurred on a new idea, which was to write a book about ADHD. By then, I was convinced that it was the ADHD that was causing my challenges at work, and was determined not to let it ruin the job I was so happy in. So I had to understand it, and there was very little accessible information online or in books that I could relate to.

I also reasoned that at least it might be able to help other people who were stuck on that waiting list, as there were lots of things other than medication that could help, such as exercise and flexible working hours.

Writing helped significantly with my underlying, constant anxiety. Being in an open-plan office meant that I was constantly hyper-aware of what was on my screen, and how other people would interpret this. I became very stressed out if I had nothing to do, which happened often, as I'd often finish all of my work early on in the day.

As my job was responsive to changes in relevant areas of law, which weren't happening at the time, I had no idea what I was supposed to do if I had replied to all of my emails. Ironically, I was very afraid of my colleagues thinking I wasn't doing any work, when in reality, I'd done it all!

Writing the book, which became *'ADHD: an A to Z'*, gave me a project to do at work that took up these spare windows of unstructured time. As it was in a document format, it appeared like work from afar, so I felt a lot calmer, giving my brain a focus that wasn't the perceptions of other people and getting into trouble.

THE AUDHD LENS
Having a brain that works differently to 'most' makes fitting into traditional employment extremely difficult. Just as we may struggle with the structures, environments, and hierarchies in education, the same can apply to the workplace.

CHOOSING A CAREER
Having AuDHD means we may always be 'picked', rather than a 'picker'. As we can struggle with understanding our own desires, strengths, and areas of interest, we may find it very difficult to believe and trust in our own ambitions. We may look for jobs that we 'could' do, rather than those we actually want to do.

The executive functioning part of my brain struggles with making decisions and prioritising, whilst the autistic part needs to have certainty and predictability. I found it impossible to know whether I'd like something that I would presumably be signing up to a *lifetime* career in without having actually done it.

The interest based nervous system linked with AuDHD means that we may become extremely passionate about certain paths, throwing ourselves wholeheartedly into these in a haze of hyper focus. However, we may then find that once we manage to get a job, the novelty and dopamine wears off, leaving us despondent - until we find another path and repeat the cycle.

Whenever I managed to get any kind of job or experience, my ADHD impulsivity would very quickly react to this 'come down' of dopamine, determine it as not right, and quit. Experiencing time as 'now or not now' made these situations feel urgent, like I'd be trapped if I didn't leave immediately.

I flipped between being overwhelmed by choice, and feeling like I didn't fit into any career at all. This may be common for AuDHD-ers, who may struggle with sensory factors such as office environments and travel, without even realising that this is the source of their discomfort - not the job itself.

This can be very difficult to fit into the societal expectations of what a job 'should' look like. I saw a 9 to 5 job as a prison sentence, but also as a lifelong dream, that would always be out of reach. I hated modelling with a passion, but it also showed me that there were other ways of surviving financially, even if these were incredibly stressful.

If I hadn't have had this experience since childhood, I wouldn't have had the luxury of quitting everything I tried. This is the reality for many AuDHD-ers, who have no other option but to force themselves to fit into environments that aren't designed for their brains, causing immense distress every day. The pressure of masking and adapting to a job that we maybe didn't even want to do in the first place builds over time, often resulting in burnout.

Understanding that contrary to what we're told in school, career paths do not have to be restricted or linear, is extremely important for everyone. There's a great deal of shame around doing things differently, especially in a society where we're so often defined by others on what we do, instead of who we are.

Employment

AuDHD-ers tend to have squiggly career paths, which is a good thing! This makes our skills and experiences unique, valuable, and transferable. We can connect the dots and bring innovative perspectives, often being able to spot solutions that other's can't.

These range of experiences and skills can also make us great entrepreneurs, as people with ADHD are 300% more likely to start our own businesses.[139] However, although we might have brains that are constantly fizzing with business ideas, it might feel very overwhelming to become self-employed, especially given the lack of certainty. We may also experience RSD, especially if we keep changing our minds and feel like we 'fail' at first - which is all part of the process!

If you're an AuDHD-er, it can be very helpful to think of jobs as 'hills', rather than one big mountain to climb for the rest of your life. Trying an area of interest out as an experiment, instead of something you absolutely must make work forever, otherwise nobody will ever hire you again and your life will be over forever, will take the pressure off considerably. Every experience will teach you something new, and very few people stay in jobs for their entire lives.

Having a range of experiences is a strength in our fast-paced world, and many of the jobs that exist today may not even be there in a few years. This can be scary, but as an AuDHD-er, adapting is our speciality!

Applying for a job

Applying for jobs can be extremely difficult for AuDHD-ers, with no set 'process' for us to follow, just endless unwritten rules and expectations.

---

[139] 'The DaVinci Method' by Garret LoPorto, 2005

AuDHD: Blooming Differently

We may experience many barriers during job application processes, such as having to explain any gaps in our CV, or answer endless questions about how it's our dream to work in this role we've just found. The overwhelm of RSD may also mean we avoid applying at all, saving ourselves from rejection.

Similarly, we may take job descriptions very literally, feeling automatically excluded because we don't meet all of the criteria listed, even if these aren't 'essential'. Navigating complicated online systems that require us to type out our work experience in detail can also be very difficult for AuDHD-ers.

It can also feel overwhelming to know whether to 'disclose' your AuDHD during this process, especially if you don't have a formal diagnosis.[140] Some employers may offer guaranteed interviews to applicants who disclose a disability, but this can lead to imposter syndrome, and uncertainty about whether it's simply a checkbox exercise.

This also requires vulnerability in trusting that whoever reads our application isn't prejudiced against neurodivergence. If we already suffer with low self-esteem, this is likely to be stronger!

Some applications may require an online psychometric assessment as part of the process, which can be very stressful for AuDHD-ers, including myself! These can take many forms, such as verbal reasoning, which are fundamentally based on neurotypical ways of thinking.

For me, these tests are simply impossible. I can't understand how people know how to answer questions like 'what should a person do if their team member says they need help?' - surely it depends on the context!? If a job application

---

140   You should **not** be asked for any medical information, or 'proof' about your disability!

involved one of these tests, I'd often end up in tears, asking people like my housemates to help. It felt so frustrating to see how they simply knew the answer immediately, whereas my brain hyper-focused on the limitless scenarios and options.

Many job applications now provide the option to request reasonable adjustments, but very few provide any examples of what these actually are! I've coached many people who have asked for an adjustment, such as a phone call, only for this to be declined, without any reasons being provided.

However, employers have a legal duty to make adjustments for disabled applicants, and should take this seriously. If you're not sure what can help, it can be helpful to let them know about things you struggle with, and ask the employer to collaboratively work with you to make the process more accessible. It is not your fault!

Some examples of adjustments that may be helpful may include requesting an alternative to online assessments, asking for interview questions to be provided in advance, or to be able to submit your application in a different format to an online portal.

It's a personal decision on whether to disclose your AuDHD, but ultimately, if you have to mask yourself to get a job, the pressure is only going to continue. It can be extremely helpful, if scary, to find someone who already works at that company, such as on LinkedIn, and ask for their experiences. This is also likely to help your application, as they can give you an insight into the company culture. Most people will be happy to help!

Being yourself, and finding places that truly resonate with and inspire you, will help you to access your immense strengths and authenticity in applying. Your difference is what will make you stand out - if you fit in, you're the same as everybody else!

INTERVIEWING FOR A JOB

Recruitment processes can be extraordinarily stressful for AuDHD-ers. They often involve various stages, like an obstacle course of expectations we don't understand how to meet, especially as every company has a different process!

Depending on the job, there may be a range of different interview styles and processes. I once had an online interview where I was asked a question about who I'd invite to a dinner party, with a 30 second timer counting down. I froze and said the first people who popped into my head, including the HR manager at the company I was applying to. Even so, I managed to proceed to the next stage, so my answer must have stood out!

There may also be telephone or online interviews, which are common 'early stages'. These might be with someone to understand your motivations for applying, for example, essentially filtering out applicants who may not be suitable. These conversations may be stressful for AuDHD-ers, especially so due to them often being 'casual' in nature, making it unclear how we need to act. Asking for an agenda beforehand, or for a different format of conversation, can be extremely helpful.

Further interview stages may involve multiple people, feeling more intimidating. This can be incredibly stressful, especially if we're trying to fit ourselves into moulds such as by remembering and reciting answers in certain orders, such as by using a 'STAR Method'[141], which is commonly used within interviews, such as by the UK's Civil Service.

If you're anything like me, your thoughts may become all jumbled up and you may say things without even realising. It

---

141   'The STAR Method | National Careers Service'. Accessed 3 February 2025. https://nationalcareers.service.gov.uk/careers-advice/interview-advice/the-star-method.

has felt like I am too much or not enough in these kinds of interviews, often enthusiastically asking questions that may seem inappropriate, such as sharing my endless ideas, or trying to force myself to appear as though I am refined and calm.

Interviews may be judged on certain neurotypical criteria, such as our ability to make eye contact. I once developed an intense ritual of having to send personalised thank you cards to everybody I spoke to after an interview, which felt very awkward when this involved multiple people!

There may also be certain tasks or assessments, such as 'assessment days'. I have attended one, which was like being in a gold fish bowl, knowing that we were being observed externally through a mirrored wall. I poured water into a glass for myself and a person next to me, then thought I should extend this behaviour to everybody else, *going around the entire table of 15 people* like a waitress to fill up everyone's glasses.

Other tasks might include doing work, such as creating presentations for interviews. It can be especially frustrating if these don't correlate to the skills we need for the job! Asking for specific instructions can help to avoid overwhelm in situations like this.

It's important to know that not every job involves so many recruitment processes, as I believed when I was job hunting, assuming the multiple-stage legal training contract application process was 'normal'. It can feel easy to write off entire industries due to preconceptions, but remember that this isn't always the case.

However, it is likely that there will be certain time periods of uncertainty, such as when waiting for a decision. It's advisable to always ask about these timeframes where possible, so that you're not left in excruciating agony, constantly refreshing your emails!

As I now run a company, I take these processes extremely seriously, and try my best to make them somewhat enjoyable for everybody. I know the power of giving someone a good interview or application experience, how this can filter out into the rest of their lives, as happened for me. I always offer the interview questions in advance, and any other adjustments that may be useful, without expecting the person to know what these are.

I don't necessarily require or care whether they are neurodivergent - I just extend the same support to everybody! Job recruitment is a highly outdated process, where our ability to perform under pressure is often more highly valued than the holistic nature of a person and whether they are the best fit for a role. Personally, I just want to make sure the person understands what is expected of them and that they will genuinely enjoy it, because I know these are the secret ingredients to success at work.

STARTING A NEW JOB

Starting a new job can feel extremely overwhelming for an AuDHD-er. It marks a significant change to our life, especially as we spend so much of our time at work. The various processes involved, such as interviews and references and contracts, can all be extremely energy consuming by the time we actually start.

Contrary to what I believed, employers do *not* typically expect you to obsessively study or work for free before you even start a job! It's advisable to reach out to your new employer and ask for a conversation about any questions that might be making you feel anxious, such as about the dress code.

It can also be very helpful to ask for a 'buddy' or mentor when starting a new job, especially if you're an AuDHD-er.

Current employees are likely to be happy at being given such an opportunity, especially considering how they may have experienced similar fears when starting in their role.

As an employer, these may be very simple processes to establish that make a huge difference. Just having one pre-defined person to speak to can be very useful for an AuDHD-er who's likely to already be stressing out about a variety of factors as they adjust to a new environment. This includes remote working, which can feel very surreal and lonely at times.

Probation

Probation periods may cause extreme stress for AuDHD-ers. This period is often a normal part of new employment, giving both the employer and an employee an opportunity to test out whether they are right for the role. Personally, I found this very difficult, feeling like these were extended interview experiences. I struggled to comprehend what *precisely* I needed to do to pass probation, and how I could control it.

As a coach, I often work with people who are scared to tell their employers about their neurodivergence at the start of their employment, especially during a probation period. This makes sense if they fear stigma, but also can be counter-productive as they may need certain adjustments to help them to do their job, and to pass probation.

Employers could make a huge difference for AuDHD-ers by explaining the clear purpose of probation and setting out clearly what is expected of an employee to pass it. Simply having the reassurance of people not 'normally' failing probation could be a huge help. Regular feedback can also be very effective in reducing anxiety.

If you're an AuDHD-er, it's important to remember that recruitment is very expensive and time consuming! If you're

AuDHD: Blooming Differently

in the job, presume that your employer wants you there and to succeed. Training a new employee is a lot of effort, and you failing your probation means admitting that they've made a mistake.

However, it is also an opportunity for you to see if you like the job. Although it might feel impossible to leave, trying out a new role can help you to see if it's right for you, which might include everything from the culture to your daily tasks.

In terms of training and learning on the job, remember that you are not expected to be perfect overnight. It's natural to have a learning period, and understanding how you learn best can be very helpful to process lots of new information. You may not be given a lot of responsibility straight away, as you adjust to the role, but this doesn't mean that you're doing a bad job, or that things will stay that way.

There may be various courses for you to do in terms of training, or you might shadow other employees. It's always helpful if there's a crossover period with people who were doing the job previously, or to receive handover notes.

Asking for clear expectations and instructions can be very useful in terms of ensuring that you're doing what is expected of you. I struggled with knowing what was a 'normal' amount of effort, but having someone to check in with on these things who understands your neurodivergence can be extremely helpful.

Staying in a job

Sometimes, you may need to be in a job for a while to understand what kind of support may be helpful, or to decide whether to disclose AuDHD at work. For example, if you have to commute somewhere you've never been to before during rush hour, it might become apparent after a few weeks of panic attacks that an adjustment could be helpful to start work earlier or later to avoid this!

Every experience of a job will be unique, particularly so within the context of your colleagues. Some jobs may be more 'social' than others, involving open-plan office environments or team social events, which can feel stressful to navigate as an AuDHD-er. Having a list of 'topics' to hand can be helpful, as well as remembering that you don't have to say yes to social invitations!

Managers

As an AuDHD-er, your relationship with your manager is critical and fundamental to your success and wellbeing at work. Research has shown that managers have a greater impact on employee's mental health (69%) than doctors (51%) or therapists (41%).[142] If your manager is not supportive of your neurodivergence, it's advisable to ensure this is flagged with HR, to ensure you are legally protected against discrimination.

Neurodivergence can easily result in misunderstandings within the workplace, where we may be navigating RSD, intense anxiety about our performance or being fired, and attempting to build relationships with others. Both being a manager, and being managed as an AuDHD-er can feel unnatural, especially if we have struggle with authority or hierarchies, as can often be seen with AuDHD-ers.[143]

---

[142] 'Managers Impact Our Mental Health More Than Doctors, Therapists — and Same as Spouses | UKG'. Accessed 3 February 2025. https://www.ukg.co.uk/about-us/newsroom/workforce-institute-managers-impact-mental-health.
[143] Forby, Leilani, Nicola C. Anderson, Joey T. Cheng, Tom Foulsham, Bradley Karstadt, Jessica Dawson, Farid Pazhoohi, and Alan Kingstone. 'Reading the Room: Autistic Traits, Gaze Behaviour, and the Ability to Infer Social Relationships'. *PLOS ONE* 18, no. 3 (1 March 2023): e0282310. https://doi.org/10.1371/journal.pone.0282310.

This can result in various challenges. From misunderstandings instructions, to difficulty asking for help, intense fear around performance reviews, heightened sensitivity to feedback, and overall resentment - the relationship we have with our manager can define our entire experience of a role.

Having a manager who is supportive, receptive, and understanding of your unique strengths and challenges as an AuDHD-er is ideal, but not always the case in reality. Managers may feel scared to talk about things like autism or ADHD in the workplace, lacking the support or training themselves to feel confident discussing things like reasonable adjustments, fearing the potential legal consequences of making a mistake.

Support

As an AuDHD-er, you can help your manager by providing reassurance, as ironic as that might feel! Working with your manager as a team to ensure that you're both able to bring your full selves to work and adapt environments for you to thrive only benefits you both. Remaining open, flexible, and asking for help is key.

It can feel extremely difficult to ask for help at all as an AuDHD-er, but please know that this is a strength - not a weakness! As a manager myself I would always much prefer someone who asks if they're not sure about something, than makes a mistake, or hides it from me. I don't mind explaining the same thing 10 times, knowing that certain concepts can be really confusing, but the key requirement is that we have trust between us to ensure they feel comfortable enough to ask.

Equally, I don't mind mistakes at all, knowing that these are completely normal. However, it's really important to be able to identify this and take responsibility for it, instead of trying to hide it. The stress can weigh very heavily on our minds, resulting in more mistakes being made as a result. What's most important, at least to me, is trusting that the people I work with can come to me if they do make a mistake, knowing that they won't be in trouble or told off!

As a manager, a coaching approach can be very helpful with this. Pausing to reflect and observe your own emotional reactions can help with taking the most effective action, together. Identifying *how* a mistake happened is more important than who is to blame for it, as it enables you to address the issue. It's not personal - it's just work, and it's most likely not the difference between life and death. Raising concerns neutrally and early on opens up a conversation from a curious and compassionate place, rather than allowing resentment and suspicion to build.

Colleagues

It may feel overwhelming to know how to adapt to new colleagues, and the 'rules' of these relationships. Everybody is unique, and some people will be more communicative than others, but in general, most people want to get along at work!

It's also important to be aware of how our AuDHD may present at work, and how this could impact other people. For example, many of my ideas involved areas that were other people's remit, and I often struggled to 'bring everyone along on the journey' with me. Looking after our own needs helps us to respect those of other people as well, such as by going to an exercise class at lunch to burn off extra energy. This could otherwise emerge through chatting to our colleagues, who might be trying to work!

Colleague relationships can feel overwhelming to navigate, given the workplace context, but these should hopefully be collaborative and supportive. It's helpful to understand your own capacity and limits, avoiding saying 'yes' to everything that's requested of you!

Support
Different adjustments may be required at various points throughout an AuDHD-ers career, which are no reflection on their skills or abilities, but the environment in which they are working. For example, if there's a sudden change, such as a bereavement, AuDHD symptoms may become more difficult to manage, which can impact performance at work.

In such cases an employer may arrange an external assessment with an 'Occupational Health' professional to help establish potential support that they could provide. This can feel very intimidating, and create fears about being fired, but remember: your employer does genuinely want to support you!

Common adjustments that can help AuDHD-ers in the workplace include flexible working hours and locations, written instructions, agendas for meetings, coaching, and certain tools, such as dictation software. This will ultimately depend on the individual, but if you'd like to learn more, I'd suggest reading my book, *'ADHD Works at Work'*.

> **Tips: AuDHD-ers**
>
> - Access support throughout the employment process, including therapy, coaching, and any help from your friends and family. It can be very stressful!

Employment

- Try to be conscious about your applications for jobs, lining these up with your areas of interest. Quality over quantity!

- Ask for adjustments where you feel these may be helpful, such as having a chat with a current employee before applying for a role, or visiting the office prior to an interview.

- Avoid using ChatGPT for job applications - it can be very obvious from an employer's perspective!

- Be yourself. This seems simple, but by allowing your natural enthusiasm, passion, and strengths to shine through, you will stand out from the crowd of applicants in all of the right ways. Being hired on the basis of being yourself rather than a masked version of yourself means you'll feel far more relaxed in the job itself!

- Try to identify people who already work in the area you'd like to work in, asking them for an informational chat. Asking them to mentor you can be very useful, as most people will want to help!

- Remember that you don't need to stay in any situations that feel uncomfortable. Our society may have 'rules' like about the 'right' length of time to stay in a job before quitting, but you are neurodivergent!

- Equally, try to make sustainable plans and avoid changing your entire life around jobs (like I did!). Avoiding too much change at once can help with adjusting to new environments. It's important not to try to force yourself to stay in a job, such as by taking up financial commitments like rental agreements, as you're removing your own choice!

- Try to understand your own neurodivergence and create a way to explain this to others, if you'd like to. Self-awareness of yourself and your needs is extremely important to be able to thrive and to do the things you want to do, but be kind to yourself!

- Create yourself sustainable routines around work, including if you're in the 'applications' stage. Treating this like a job can help with having a routine and habits, including boundaries around things like working hours.

- Ask for a mentor or buddy when starting a new role, and check in with them regularly.

- Check out your employer's assistance programmes when starting a new role, such as therapy.

- If you're in the UK and starting a new role, apply for Access to Work. They will fast-track your application for new jobs and deal with it a few weeks. It can help with providing support above and beyond reasonable adjustments, such as coaching.

- Remember that you are enough as you are! Your brain might want to give 350%, but remember that this is a LOT in comparison to neurotypical people. Remember not to take too much on, and to regularly review your workload and capacity with your manager.

- If you can, try to talk to your manager about your neurodivergence. You could simply phrase it by explaining what kinds of environments work best for you, and you don't necessarily have to talk about AuDHD if it feels uncomfortable. However, if your manager understands your ways of working, then they can support you in the best possible ways. If you're not sure, you could speak to HR. This might seem scary, but they are there to support you!

- Identify any relevant policies, such as reasonable adjustments or neurodiversity policies, upon starting within a new role. Don't be afraid to ask questions and write things down.

- Ask for clear expectations and what your priorities should be.

- Record your achievements and 'wins' regularly. It can be very helpful to do this in a designated notebook once per week, for example, or by creating a dedicated email folder. This will be very helpful for evaluation purposes.

Tips: Loved Ones

- It can be extremely helpful to identify opportunities for AuDHD-ers to gain work experience, especially in areas of interest. For example, you could ask for any opportunities within your professional network, passing these along.

- Supporting your loved one to identify areas of interest and potential roles can be very effective, especially if they don't seem to know what these are. As a coach, I often guide them to look at their social media profiles!

- Encouraging your loved one to explore opportunities related to their areas of interest, rather than what seems 'sensible' or 'good' from a societal perspective will help enormously. They are far more likely to succeed if they're interested in something!

- Providing a lot of reassurance for your loved one when looking into employment opportunities is key, as this can be a very stressful process. Helping them with job applications and interviews, such as with role playing, can be very useful.

- You can offer support to your loved one throughout employment processes, such as attending interviews with them, or helping them to ask for reasonable adjustments if needed.

- Coaching can be extremely effective for AuDHD-ers looking for employment.

Employment

- Try to support your loved one's wishes, even if you don't agree with them, such as their decision to leave a job after a few weeks. It's better for them to listen to their needs rather than force themselves to be in stressful environments on a prolonged basis.

10. Transitions

Despite my best efforts, I couldn't control my environment. A few months into my job, the global Coronavirus pandemic hit.

I was terrified that it was the end of the world, impulsively moving in with someone I'd been dating for a few weeks, having stayed in my flat for the longest time I'd stayed anywhere in the last decade, at 8 months.

It was a very odd time. On the one hand, I suddenly became much more confident, relaxed and happy at work. Working from home for the foreseeable future due to lockdown meant no more in person meetings, which made me feel far more confident to contribute. It was amazing to be able to join meetings with my camera turned off, allowing me to be present, focused, and engaged, without obsessing over how I was being perceived by others.

However, the nature of my work had changed overnight, as it involved reviewing changes to the law, which were happening daily. I imposed intense pressure on myself to keep up with every single legal change, and the impact on vulnerable people at large.

I struggled with my own emotions about the pandemic and deaths of millions of people, including potentially every person I knew. To cope, I made a document listing out the laws made in every country, as an extremely complex and unsustainable method to try and predict what would happen next. One day I accidentally sent this to my manager, subsequently having a huge panic attack about being fired! Fortunately, they just seemed perplexed when I explained that this was a 'hobby'.

My work had also become harder because I took it so seriously within the context of the pandemic, imposing impossible standards of perfection on myself. I burned myself out, once providing 27 pages of research instead of the presumably one-pager summary that was expected of me. The stress came out in different ways, such as becoming very upset when this wasn't fully incorporated into a project, although it would have been an overwhelming task for the person responsible!

When I caught Covid, I tried to work through it, feeling scared about taking a sick day, lacking the language to know what to say and being scared about not being believed. I also figured I'd be in bed anyway, so I may as well continue my daily routine of waking up, turning on my laptop, working in bed, and going to sleep. However, the brain fog meant I was too exhausted to think properly, and I was encouraged to take time off to recover.

Having lost all interest in the *'ADHD: an A to Z'* book, which was 75% finished, and overwhelmed by my ambition to document all of the laws, I started writing a new book on the weekends. This one adapted all of the changes made by the UK Government into a fiction novel, imagining the emotional perspectives of Boris Johnson and Dominic Cummings, adding on my own elaborations. This saw me go down a deep research hole of both men, including their entire histories and relationships.

I was aware that this was an entirely weird thing to do (and it was never published!), but it felt relaxing. I immersed myself into the book as an escape from reality, and as a way to control the narrative, even if it was just for myself.

AuDHD: Blooming Differently

One day, I coincidentally connected with a friend of a friend who was working as a coach. In my head, I scoffed at how this wasn't a 'real' job, and asked them questions about it, suggesting that I could do it. They said if I was interested in being a coach, I should get a coach, recommending their friend, who was looking for clients.

I spoke to their friend out of curiosity, who explained how coaching could help us to achieve our goals, but I had the opposite problem. I couldn't stop doing things I didn't want to do, and had so many half-finished 'random' goals that they felt meaningless, but also couldn't figure out what I wanted to do longer-term in my career or life.

During one personal development meeting at work, I said that my future goals were to 'stay in this job', which was true. All I wanted was to not get fired, but as time went on, I became more restless. This made me annoyed at myself for even *considering* wanting something different, after having been so desperate to get a 'real' job for my entire life. I couldn't help myself from imagining my future 10 years on, sitting in development meetings where I'd be saying the exact same thing.

The novelty of a regular salary had also worn off, as I found myself running out of money each month. I'd also attempted to get a mortgage like a 'Real Adult With A Salary', only to find out that my salary equated to a mortgage affording me approximately half a flat in London. I felt like I'd been tricked, having been conditioned to believe that the secret to life was to get a 'stable' job, earn a salary, and buy a house, but the goal posts kept moving.

After years of a varying monthly income, it also felt restrictive to be in a job where I had the same income every month, and no opportunity to grow it, other than through drawn-out procedures of promotions or bonuses.

Transitions

The boyfriend I'd moved in with for a few months during the pandemic was a photographer, so as a carefully constructed way to get him to like me more, I reached out to a previous model agent to offer our services to clients who couldn't shoot due to the lockdown. We did a photoshoot for a national fashion brand in the living room, but I was terrified that I'd accidentally ruined my legal career by working outside of it, ruminating over whether I'd be caught. We ended up breaking up shortly after, and I moved into a new house-share.

However, earning hundreds of pounds for an idea that I'd just come up with had been an exciting high, reminding me that there could be other options outside of the '9 to 5', or even alongside it.

After I'd finished talking with this coach who clearly thought the complete opposite way to me, I burst out laughing at her £300 per hour rates, but realised my interest had been caught, especially because of my judgement. I wondered if such a thing as an ADHD coach existed, in that maybe there was someone who could help me figure out what to 'do' with my life next.

Before I knew it, I was having an introductory call with a coach who had ADHD herself - the first person I'd ever talked to who also had the condition. I bounced around the car park on the call, trying to find privacy from my housemate to hide my embarrassment of uttering the words ADHD out loud.

It was one of the most incredible conversations I'd ever had. I felt truly understood and seen for the first time in my life, and reassured that there were other people out there who had similar experiences. It made me feel so much less alone, especially because the coach had a shared legal background and had created a life she loved with the condition as a strength, instead of something to be ashamed of.

When she said the Government could help fund ADHD coaching through a grant called Access to Work, I was in shock. For years, I'd scraped together money for therapy I couldn't afford, which I'd found pretty unhelpful, as I'd just talk non-stop for an hour and leave feeling even worse.

I couldn't believe that all along, there was funding and support available. Not just any kind of support, but help that was actually relevant and useful to my brain. I was so happy to talk to this coach that I happily would have cleared out my bank account to pay for her coaching, but decided to apply for the funding first.

This meant telling my work, which caused huge anxiety. I read all of the Government guidance on the policy, making sure I knew every single thing about it, to avoid any inconvenience to my employer. A few months later, I was having ADHD Coaching, seeing my life change before my eyes.

At the end of our first session, the coach asked what goal I wanted to set for the next week. I had no idea, but presumed I needed to say something, so I said the first thing that popped into my head: finish writing the *'ADHD: an A to Z'* book, which had been untouched for months. I hoped that she might be happy with this answer.

She was surprised, and very enthusiastic, telling me she'd love to read it and give a quote. I couldn't believe it, and spent a week writing non-stop, obsessed with making it perfect.

I hadn't considered what to do next. I was very reluctant to publish it, as I had no kind of qualification or official scientific background to write such a book about ADHD. However, I had sent the half-finished manuscript to various people at points that year who had told me how much it had helped them. Also, as my coach had said she'd give a testimonial, I felt like I had to publish it.

I really regretted this, realising that this would mean 'publicly' coming out as having ADHD. I was terrified about telling my work that I'd written a book, and getting into trouble. However, I also felt like I had a public obligation to share my experiences if they could help others, recognising that I was in a very privileged position to be able to access support. I tried to focus on them, not me.

I knew that if I'd had that book at the start of my journey, I could have saved myself a whole lot of pain, money, and stress. If I could help anyone to feel how I'd felt upon talking to this coach, it would be worth it.

So, I figured out how to self-publish it on Amazon, creating a cover on Canva - a brain covered with lightbulbs and dogs. The only thing left to do was to tell my work, which coaching helped with enormously by questioning the 'worst case scenario', which was essentially that I'd just publish it under another name. Obviously, they were completely fine about it.

When I received the published copy, I impulsively decided to post a photograph of it on social media. As the likes rolled in and my heart raced, I looked a little closer at the picture. The spine of the book read '**AHD**: *an A to Z*'. I had never been so mortified, and immediately went into a spiral of how I'd ruined my life, and what an idiot I was, unsuccessfully trying to figure out how to un-publish it. I just changed the cover and deleted the post, deciding to never mention ADHD publicly again.

I was overcome with shame and cried for weeks, well into my next coaching session where my coach was excitedly wanting to celebrate me and my achievement. I also had a huge project start at work, which felt impossible to tackle.

I burned out and couldn't do anything, suddenly seeing my executive functioning abilities disappear.

At the time I'd also impulsively moved in with yet another new person I'd been dating for a few weeks. A friend pleaded with me not to, but it seemed to make perfect sense at the time. I was struggling to do anything, and felt like this person offering me a place to live was a saviour. Looking back, I can see how this was a combination of stress, overwhelm at finally accepting my diagnosis of ADHD, and burnout.

I struggled significantly upon moving in with them, becoming increasingly isolated from family and friends as I ruminated over work. My partner would leave the flat at 7am and return 12 hours later to find me in the exact same position, hardly having eaten or moved throughout the day.

I was incredibly stressed out, asking my doctor for higher levels of medication to help me focus. They refused, saying that this was a work capacity issue, not an ADHD one. My coach had worked with me on tackling my multiple projects, but they were all catching up with me, and I was becoming increasingly exhausted. I started to experience scary physical symptoms, such as temporary blindness, a non-stop twitch in my eye, and migraines.

At the same time, I kept getting messages from people about the ADHD book, despite hardly promoting it at all. When a woman messaged to say how the book had helped her to get a diagnosis, inviting me to speak at Microsoft, I thought it was a hoax. However, my ADHD coach helped me to explore the potential opportunity, recognising that I would struggle to charge for this, and enlisting a previous model agent to help.

When the agent asked how much I wanted to charge, I had no idea what to say, suggesting maybe £100. She laughed and said that she'd offer £1500, with 50 purchases of the book. I thought there was no way that anyone would pay that to hear me speak, especially as I felt like a nobody. After all, I had no official qualifications in psychology, and hardly any followers on social media - I just saw the book as my collection of embarrassing ramblings.

To my disbelief, they accepted this offer immediately. Before I knew it, I was on a Zoom call talking to the women of Microsoft on my lunch break about having ADHD, sharing things I'd never shared with anybody before out of fear of judgement - but there, all I was met with was acceptance. I had never felt so validated before, exactly as myself.

This sparked off a chain reaction within my burnout, a flicker of light within the darkness I was feeling. Working with my ADHD coach had changed my life so much that I wanted to train as one myself, but I felt terrified at the thought.

The other option I ruminated about endlessly in coaching was to qualify as a solicitor, which many people in my life advised I pursue as a 'real qualification'. When a lawyer I knew advised me that this was a terrible idea due to the inaccessibility of the industry for neurodivergent people and women, I was extremely annoyed, realising that this was the easy option of following the crowd and fitting in.

ADHD coaching was the scary option, the one that meant marking myself out as different and essentially tattooing it on my forehead. However, it was the one that if I was truly honest with myself, I wanted to do. Law was about fitting in, whereas ADHD coaching was about accepting myself as I was, and helping others to do the same.

So I eventually reached the height of my burnout, quit my job, and spent £7000 on an ADHD coaching training qualification. I couldn't tell if I was destroying my life, but for the first time in a long time, I felt free to do so on my terms.

THE AUDHD LENS

Due to impacted executive functioning associated with AuDHD, we may struggle significantly with transitions and changes to our routines. Stress can have a big impact on our 'window of tolerance', with issues in one area affecting others, sometimes without us even realising it. As a result, we may feel like everything is falling apart around us.

Transitions can be anything, and all of them can cause stress. For example, they may be 'big' ones, such as the end of a relationship or moving country, or 'small' ones, such as figuring out when to speak in conversation, or having a shower.

They may be uncontrollable, such as the seasons or periods such as Christmas (when lots of flashing, bright lights tend to erupt in the outside world!), or controllable, such as deciding what to eat for dinner. The way AuDHD-ers process information can have a significant impact on our ability to manage these transitions effectively, even if we don't realise it at the time.

Attention switching

As we may have monotropic focusing styles, it might feel painful to switch our attention from one task or environment to another. This means that we may prefer to 'deep dive' into whatever it is that we're doing, as opposed to having to constantly switch, struggling with starting or ending tasks.

With monotropism, we may experience 'attentional tunnels', which are periods of focus so deep that there's nothing left over for our surroundings. Within the tunnel, everything may be strongly interconnected in relation to that interest, which is why we might relate everything back to our interest of the moment, such in as conversions with other people. There may be hyper-awareness within the tunnel, and a hypo-awareness outside of it.[144]

This has been given a neurological basis - it's been argued that the reason for this is a malfunction in the metabolisation of the opioid peptides, which is found in a high proportion of autistic people.[145] It's also potentially linked to a difference in 'neural pruning' as we develop, in comparison to neurotypical people, meaning that we simply have more information and synapses in our brains to sift through.[146]

Ultimately, this results in difficulties with access to attention resources - how we 'grasp-to-reach' information in our brains. If we imagine a train that needs to switch track, the driver may need to pull a specific lever. In monotropic brains, the energy it takes to access the information to decide which lever to pull may be more highly impacted than polytropic brains, which can more easily switch from task to task. We're said to have an absence of 'active awareness' of context and other people, compared to others.[147]

This can provide a sense of near-constant panic, as we're subtly aware that our attention is immersed into a particular subject, and it could be pulled from us at any moment. Indeed, the ADHD part of our brain is actively triggering this non-stop, trying to distract us! Any distractions or things we

---

144 '(PDF) Attention, Monotropism and the Diagnostic Criteria for Autism'. *ResearchGate*, 22 October 2024. https://doi.org/10.1177/1362361305051398.
145   ibid
146   Columbia University Irving Medical Center. 'Children with Autism Have Extra Synapses in Brain', 21 August 2014. https://www.cuimc.columbia.edu/news/children-autism-have-extra-synapses-brain.
147   Monotropism. 'Attention Tunnelling and Autism', 6 March 2024. https://monotropism.org/dinah/attention-tunnelling-and-autism/.

need to do in the 'outside world' can feel painful, resulting in demand avoidance, like an open tab in our brain.

It could also see us 'info-dumping' at people in our lives, in the hope of sharing interesting information, but they may not respond as we expect. This is especially if the people in our lives don't share our intense passion, which can trigger RSD, and the feeling of being 'too much'. It's important for loved ones to engage with this, appreciating the safety that individual feels in the relationship to share their interest

When we're stressed out, these differences in attention switching may become more pronounced, seeing us enter a version of dissociation through immersing ourselves in our 'special interests'. This can see everything else in our life fall apart as a result, such as by ignoring messages and being too overwhelmed to reply to any of them as they build up even further.

Overall, this monotropic attention style can also bring huge benefits, such as the ability to deep-dive into knowledge and become subject-matter experts. For me, it's been a gift to learn how to access this consciously, being able to channel my monotropism into writing books like this one! Having environments that facilitate and support this are very important, such as the ability to 'block off' long periods of time in our calendars so we can engage in deep focus, uninterrupted.

Control

As monotropism means we may not bring information about the world into our brains in the same way as neurotypical people, we may find it less predictable, which can be very stressful. For me, this is fundamentally a struggle in trusting ourselves, as well as the world around us.

The impacted self-awareness that can accompany AuDHD means we may struggle with feeling as though we've concocted

Transitions

lots of different coping strategies to handle one situation, so the thought of this changing can be very stressful. For me, I think of this as spinning 100 plates at a time, and being afraid of any dropping, as they will all come crashing down.

This is why we may struggle with concepts such as going on holiday. For example, if an AuDHD-er had the coping strategy of replying to all emails immediately, maintaining a controlled and 'clean' inbox, the thought of returning a week later to endless emails may feel painful. This is why if disrupted even slightly, we may struggle with the entire routine or task that we've set ourselves.

When we're in an attention tunnel, it can be very difficult to imagine doing anything outside of that moment. We may have no idea if we'll feel that same sense of focus again in the future, and so it can be very difficult to pull ourselves out of a world in which we feel a sense of control.

The side-effect of this is subtly knowing that we've ignored everything around us, so it can feel even more overwhelming and unpredictable to face, like an 'on/off' switch in our brains. This may result in 'stimming', which seems to be very similar to the 'cribbing' experienced by horses, as we engage in repetitive, self-soothing behaviours which we can control, when forced out of our tunnels.

As a result of our AuDHD, our relationships may look different from 'normal'. For example, 'Penguin Pebbling' is a term used to describe how autistic people express affection and care through small gestures, such as by sharing information.[148] This comes from the act of penguins sharing pebbles to show that they care for one another.

We may not speak all of the time, but instead offer spontaneous interactions to as a way of connecting. This

---

148   Penguin Pebbling, An Autistic Love Language - Autistic Realms - https://autisticrealms.com/penguin-pebbling-an-autistic-love-language/

can be difficult when we beat ourselves up for being 'bad friends' because we've forgotten to reply to messages! Combined with the impulsivity of ADHD, this can also mean us unconsciously spending a lot of money on other people when we see something that reminds us of them. I am constantly sending gifts to people!

If we're familiar with an environment, and a few people within it, this may feel more predictable than a sudden change. This makes sense, especially if we're aware that 'most' people think differently to us, seeing us form small groups. It's also potentially why after discovering we're AuDHD, we might see this in everybody we know - we tend to attract each other!

This may also apply to situations such as attending meetings where our control is limited, such as those online where we're suddenly put in break out rooms to 'chat' without an agenda, with unknown people. Shifting our attention onto listening, to suddenly being a 'talker', can be very disconcerting, and we may need additional time to process this.

The same could apply in a classroom scenario, for example, where a student is asked a question by their teacher to 'check if they're listening'. They may not have processed the information in a way that they can immediately verbalise, and need time to shift 'mode'. As a result, they may be unable to answer, which a teacher could take as 'proof' of their lack of attention - when it may be very much the opposite!

To help with this, having as much control as possible over our environments is key. This is especially important during transitions, where we need to retain as much of the same habits and routines as possible, such as during moving house or changing jobs. Linked to this is the emotional dysregulation that can occur when we feel out of control and overwhelmed, which could result in the ADHD part of our brain making lots of impulsive decisions, not realising that these are linked to the discomfort of the transition.

Finding small ways we can have control in different situations is also a great way of calming our nervous system. For example, I'll often play the same 10 minute song when cleaning, giving me a set timeframe and end point. Being able to decide on and know the 'end point' is very helpful for me in all areas of my life, including when socialising with others and going to a shop. Otherwise, the thought of potentially being there forever can feel very overwhelming.

We can also create our own repetitive routines that bring us a sense of control in overwhelming situations. For example, whenever I'm experiencing a stressful time, I will re-watch all seasons of '*Gossip Girl*', which I must have seen a hundred times by now! Knowing what to expect in this show enables me to switch off, as I don't need to beat myself up if I get distracted.

To meet the needs of both autism and ADHD, we could also create blocks of time in our calendar dedicated to 'admin' or 'work' for example, keeping a list handy so we can choose what to do when that time arrives. This provides a controllable routine, with flexibility and novelty. It also helps us to avoid constant stress about when we will 'do the thing' we're avoiding.

This could apply to positive changes as well as negative ones, where we suddenly find ourselves changing our entire lives as a reaction to one change, such as breaking up with a partner after starting a new job. This is especially important to remember when navigating AuDHD, because this realisation is a huge transition in our understanding of who we are and the world around us, often sparking new 'attention tunnels' to immerse ourselves into.

I believe this is why it's often said that a diagnosis can cause people to 'make it their whole identity', because our identity has fundamentally changed! This can impact our relationships, especially as people in our life may not understand, telling us we're 'still the same person'. We are, but we are also different, and a diagnosis can affect our understanding of not only ourselves, but all of our relationships until that point. This can be overwhelming and lonely to figure out alone!

I often coach people who feel that everyone in their life is bored of hearing about ADHD, but we're often seeking validation in wanting to share our experiences and figure out a new sense of control together. As a loved one, dedicating time to doing this, and engaging with their interests collaboratively, can be extremely helpful for AuDHD-ers. Ironically, if we're stressed out, we may be even less likely to be able to focus on anything else, so this will help us to process and transition as needed.

AuDHD Inertia

As our brains are seeking predictability (autism), but also novelty at the same time (ADHD), we may find ourselves stuck in 'inertia' mode.

Autistic inertia has been described by Quinn Hansen as, 'the tendency that autistic people have to want to remain in a constant state. When we're asleep we want to stay asleep, when awake we want to stay awake, when we're working on one thing we want to keep working on it, when we're doing one thing we want to keep doing that one thing, etc.'.[149]

---

[149] Quincy. 'Task Initiation, Executive Functioning, and Autistic Inertia.' *Speaking of Autism...* (blog), 24 March 2020. https://speakingofautismcom.wordpress.com/2020/03/24/task-initiation-executive-functioning-and-autistic-inertia/.

I'd like to coin another version of this: AuDHD inertia. This is the pull from our ADHD part of the brain to be doing something else, and change state, in a need for novel stimulation. This can feel exceptionally painful, where we know what we want to do, but can't do it. It feels like painful boredom, but we can't shift gear to do something that we know will help us to get out of it.

We may find ourselves very easily trapped in environments that simultaneously offer novelty and certainty, such as scrolling on social media. We know that the content will always refresh, but we also don't know what we might see next.

It can make starting or stopping tasks very difficult, and bring challenges to all aspects of daily life. For example, I've coached people who have a 'morning routine' of hitting 'snooze' on their alarm multiple times. Every time the alarm goes off, it's like a signal to get up, but they can't - their autistic side wants to stay asleep. The ADHD side is pulling them to wake up, but the snooze function offers a predictable way of 'balancing' this. In reality, it's starting their day off by already mentally beating themselves up!

This can be exacerbated by other factors, such as executive functioning difficulties. We might struggle with 'basic' tasks, such as choosing a television show to watch. It might feel more comfortable to simply scroll every single show, instead of shifting task to actually watching one at all!

As a result, we may experience procrastination, avoidance, and immense stress. We may beat ourselves up for being 'lazy', screaming internally for us to 'just do the thing', but ironically, the task that takes 5 minutes might feel far more difficult than the one that takes 5 hours.

To help with this, it's ideal to try and keep routines and decisions as simple as possible, with key 'pillars' and room for flexibility if needed. Planning ahead for these routines to be disrupted, because this is inevitable, can help us to feel a sense of control.

Making transitions as easy as possible is also very important. For example, I'll often wear my gym clothes to sleep if I want to go to yoga in the morning, as I know this reduces the mental block of getting changed, including the sensory aspects this comes with.

Knowing about our unique monotropic focusing styles can also enable us to structure our days effectively. For example, I know that once I go on my phone, I will be sucked into it, so I try to do any tasks I'm avoiding first, like showering! Identifying which tasks drag you into an attention tunnel, and which are harder to engage with, enables you to do the harder tasks first, recognising the additional energy this may require. This is sometimes referred to as 'spoon theory', enabling us to manage our energy effectively.

Creating our own form of transitions can be helpful to avoid being overwhelmed when we come out of it. For example, we might set multiple prompts such as alarms, to warn us that time is passing when we need to leave the house, shifting the expectation around them. Setting these throughout the day at random points can also be a great reminder to check in with our bodies and needs.

Visual prompts can also be very helpful, such as by having wall calendars and clocks. Visual timers may be very effective, providing a sense of control in watching the time tick down, but meeting our need for urgency and adrenaline in getting a task done.

AuDHD inertia may intensify during periods of stress, ironically providing us with a sense of control in the 'mid-zone' of 'wasting time'. We might trick ourselves into feeling as though this is relaxing, not realising that we're

Transitions

also subconsciously angry at ourselves for spending hours scrolling through content that's spiking our emotions.

With stress, we might feel more 'dazed' than usual, as our brain seeks this comforting familiarity. I've seen this be referred to as 'rot mode' (ironically, on social media!), where we lose huge chunks of time, engaging in the bare minimum around us, such as neglecting things like washing or eating properly, if at all. This state has been suggested to be a 'functional freeze mode' by psychologists, allowing us to continue living, but in a robotic, disconnected way, feeling emotionally numb.[150]

To help with this, we can 'name it to tame it', recognising that it's our brain's mode of 'loading', instead of laziness, showing ourselves compassion instead of anger. Speaking to ourselves as we would someone we love can help us to identify tasks that may make us feel better. Breaking these down into tiny chunks as the 'only' thing we need to do that day, such as simply getting dressed in new clothes, can help us to emerge from this mode.

Sensory

Another reason that AuDHD-ers may struggle with transitions is due to our sensory processing styles. We may experience a baseline of constant discomfort due to sensory sensitivities, keeping us constantly on edge, without even realising the cause of this.

If we're in an environment that is sensorily soothing, it can be very difficult to move from this to another, which is less predictable. Without all of the information to hand, we may feel as though this is simply not worth the effort, again

---

[150] USA TODAY. 'Bed Rotting Every Night? You're Actually in a "Functional Freeze."' Accessed 4 February 2025. https://www.usatoday.com/story/life/health-wellness/2024/07/10/functional-freeze-bed-rotting/74311337007/.

AuDHD: Blooming Differently

blaming ourselves for being 'lazy'. Every time we're in a new environment, our brains are working hard to take in all of the new sensory information, possibly resulting in overwhelm.

This may also result in challenges where we have to be 'in our bodies', instead of our minds. AuDHD-ers may feel extreme pain in situations involving certain kinds of exercise or 'mindfulness', especially if we experience physical pain in our bodies that we're not always aware of. For example, dissociation has been commonly linked with autism, being a 'circuit breaker' to separate consciousness from the overwhelming outside world.[151]

This is why 'relaxing' can be so difficult for AuDHD-ers, because it involves being present in a brain that is extremely busy! Tuning into our environment can be extremely uncomfortable, such as becoming aware of the pain we may feel at a certain light being switched on, or the sound of a clock ticking. Whilst this might feel comforting to neurotypical people, it's important to remember that AuDHD brains experience the world around them differently.

For example, I struggle significantly with the sensory aspects of having a shower and drying my hair. The sound of the hairdryer feels like it's sawing into my skull, and the different sensations of being cold, wet, and dry, feels highly uncomfortable. Similarly, going outside at all can be very difficult, due to the change in environment and temperatures that might suddenly hit us all at once.

We may also be hypo-sensitive, where we're not aware of certain sensations, or seek certain ones out. For example, I am extremely hypo-sensitive with regards to smell, so I can wear the same clothes for days on end without showering or realising that I maybe don't smell great to other people!

---

[151] LMFT, Brett Novick, MS, EdD. 'Autism and Dissociation: Is There a Connection?' *Autism Parenting Magazine* (blog), 8 May 2024. https://www.autismparentingmagazine.com/autism-and-dissociation/.

This can be exacerbated by monotropism, especially if our attention is suddenly pulled away from whatever we were focusing on, known as a 'monotropic split'. This is because we may have 'shut off' our other sensations, and be suddenly hit by them all at once upon emerging into our bodies.

When we're stressed out, these sensory differences may be intensified, resulting in a meltdown or shutdown. As an AuDHD-er, it's important to understand your sensory needs and to take these seriously - they aren't 'nice to haves', they're essential. For example, having a fidget toy with me all of the time helps to ground me when I am feeling overwhelmed by my environment.

Executive Functioning
Executive functioning can significantly impact our ability to handle transitions as AuDHD-ers. Our interest based nervous system may prioritise whatever we're interested in, or scared of, providing us with zero energy for the things that are less exciting.

The ADHD part of our brain may need a constant sense of high stimulation, which we may be able to access in controllable environments, such as working in a busy cafe. This is what can make boring or repetitive tasks so difficult, because they offer less stimulation for our brains. To help with this, we could add in extra stimulation, such as by using subtitles when watching television, or playing music at the same time as doing admin.

Due to the way we can experience time as 'now or not now', we may struggle with planning or thinking ahead, which may include setting goals for our future. This means that we may be unable to imagine certain scenarios, such as going on holiday, before they happen. As a result, we may suddenly feel extremely overwhelmed immediately before, or when we arrive, unable to figure out how we've arrived in this space or how to respond to the sensory overload of new information.

The dopamine we may feel at a 'high', such as making a new friend, can lead us to experience what I call 'shiny object syndrome'. We may be extremely enthusiastic, but experience a 'come down' afterwards, as the reality of the expectations we've set ourselves sink in. This can be overwhelming to experience, leaving us experiencing RSD as we struggle to access that same level of excitement.

This can also result in procrastination, as we may think of a task as being far more intensive than it actually is, skipping to the end rather than the start. Having a brain that's always operating at level 100, instead of level 1, can make even the simplest changes feel like huge mountains of overwhelm.

This can also result in challenges with making decisions, which can complicate transitions. For example, we may struggle with deciding which gym class to go to, so simply don't go at all. We might keep unusable items, because the thought of replacing them is too overwhelming. Finding a hairdresser might feel impossible.

Every shift in environment involves having to process this again, resulting in us potentially acting out in 'fight, flight, freeze, or fawn' survival mode. When I'm stressed, these become much more obvious, as I make lots of impulsive decisions, or find myself excessively people pleasing. I've also been known to leave parties 5 minutes after turning up, because it was too overwhelming to stay!

Demand avoidance can also be relevant here, as our brain fights against itself. We might feel as though there's an 'expectation' on us to be a certain way, such as happy on holiday, which our AuDHD brain may strongly resist. These factors can combine, making things such as packing to go on a trip feel extremely difficult, especially as we can struggle to know what to prioritise.

Again, this isn't laziness - it's the way our brain is wired. Breaking tasks down into chunks can help them to feel more manageable, trying to focus on just the first step ahead of us, instead of the staircase! Auto-piloting as many decisions as you can is a great way to avoid the discomfort of transitions. For example, you could eat the same meals on a daily basis, or decide to go to a gym class at the same time every day, regardless of who's teaching.

This is harnessing the autistic side of AuDHD, in contrast to the ADHD, which may be seeking novelty and distractions. It's especially important during stressful periods that we can access a 'low demand' zone, such as being at home with a weighted blanket.

Body doubling can be hugely helpful for challenges relating to transitions in general. Dubbii[152] is a great app which has body doubling videos for *everything* - from washing our clothes to showering! Breaking down marathons into sprints is a great way to manage transitions, separating out the aspects to be mini-goals, with defined end points. Knowing that we struggle with change enables us to prepare for this, such as by blocking off time in our calendar in advance to prepare.

---

[152] Dubbii Accessed 4 February 2025. https://www.dubbii.app.

Tips: AuDHD-ers

- Remember that your brain naturally struggles with change, and that's okay! Try to prepare for any big changes in advance, such as by dedicating time to thinking about them and what these will involve.

- Identify the situations you can and cannot control. Try to release the expectation of being able to control the uncontrollable - such as making people like you!

- Try to check in with yourself regularly to identify how much capacity you have at any one point, including how overwhelmed, dysregulated, or uncomfortable you might be feeling, making any changes as needed. It can help to set alarms to do so, or have a reminder question as your phone background.

- Know that change in one area of your life may affect the rest of it. Try not to beat yourself up for this, giving yourself extra kindness and capacity as a result.

- In situations that feel uncontrollable or difficult, identify small ways you can maintain control. This could look like stimming, for example, or deciding what time you will leave in advance.

- Talk to the people around you about how you experience transitions and change, asking for their support. For example, they may be able to help remind you if you're stressed out that you also happen to have a holiday coming up, which might be the cause!

- Avoid making any 'big decisions' when a 'big' transition is coming up, whether it's positive or negative. For example, avoid any big changes for the week before and after a holiday.

- Build in transition time, instead of expecting yourself to go from one state to another immediately, such as days to re-acclimatise to your environment.

- Structure your time to support your focus styles, such as by blocking out time in your calendar to do certain activities, where you know you won't be interrupted.

- Set 'end times' for anything you're doing when you start, which can help to provide a sense of control.

- Create predictable routines, such as packing a bag the night before school or work.

- Identify your sensory needs and triggers. It can be very helpful to create a notebook where you note down each day what was comfortable or not.

- Identify the tasks that 'suck' your attention, and those that don't.

- Try to start your day with a task that you don't want to do!

- Relax in the ways that work for you. For example, if you need to check your emails on holiday, don't beat yourself up for it, but try to ring-fence this time.

- Look for ways to incorporate novelty and stimulation into boring tasks that work for you, such as by playing music or a podcast at the same time.

- Group similar kinds of tasks together and do them in one chunk, instead of trying to do 'small' tasks as they come.

- Keep routines as simple as possible, with 'pillars' that remain the same, and room for flexibility.

- Auto-pilot as many decisions as you can to be the same, such as what to eat for breakfast, or what time to wake up each day.

- Use tools such as visual timers, clocks, wall calendars, fidget toys, and alarms to help you transition from different tasks.

- Connect with like-minded communities, who share your interests.

- Seek out an AuDHD coach, who can help you to put these strategies into action sustainably.

- Remember that you are NOT LAZY! This is not intentional, and your brain is working extremely hard all of the time to adjust to environments.

Tips: Loved Ones

- Try to avoid judging your loved one for things like procrastination or disorganisation, instead seeking to support them wherever possible. Remember that they are not lazy - their brain works differently to yours!

- Know that if an AuDHD-er is stressed, this may be for a number of reasons, including potential changes that have or haven't happened in their lives. This can be anything, covering relationships to new interests. It can be helpful to discuss this with them, collaboratively identifying how to process these changes.

- Support your loved one through transitions, recognising that the shift in environment may cause significant overwhelm.

- Help to maintain as much certainty as you can, such as by having a regular meet up with your loved one automatically re-occurring in the calendar each month.

- Support your loved one to create predictable routines, such as by keeping certain household items in the same place.

- Help your loved one to recognise and understand situations in which they may feel sensory overwhelm, such as noticing if they seem uncomfortable in certain settings.

- Try to avoid giving advice to your loved one, especially about how to 'relax'. For example, if they wind down by writing, reading non-fiction books, or watching true-crime videos, this is okay!

- Support and validate your loved one as they explore their interests, especially if these relate to AuDHD. They may be verbally processing information and seeking to share it with you, so try not to dismiss them.

- Remember that 'small' or 'easy' tasks might feel much more difficult for AuDHD-ers than others, especially those that can be done quickly! This is because of our attention styles, so doing them all in one chunk, such as through body doubling with you, can be much easier than trying to do them ad hoc.

- If your loved one is feeling overwhelmed by choice, it can be very helpful to make 'small' decisions for them, if they'd like you to.

11. Paradoxes

Becoming self-employed enabled me to use my AuDHD strengths of creativity and curiosity, which had previously been stifled by processes and bureaucracy. I started working with my coach's organisation whilst training, quickly overwhelmed by the huge demand from people in desperate need of support, and struggling to keep up with administration around following up on introductory calls.

Instead, I found myself writing advocacy letters to the government, and writing on social media about the severe challenges facing people with ADHD. I was so furious on behalf of the people I was talking to, who were mostly teenagers being failed by healthcare and education systems, that I couldn't stop thinking about it. It felt like a huge responsibility to see how many people needed help, and I only had so many hours in the day.

I also felt extremely guilty about charging anybody money, which wasn't covered in my training! These were desperate people in need of support, who had often already been stretched financially in seek of a diagnosis, and there were very few ADHD coaches available to help them.

I was working all hours, often for free. At one point, I received some important advice: 'do one thing first every morning that makes you money - you need it to live.' This was a very helpful reminder of how unsustainable my approach was, as I would have run out of money in pursuit of helping the world for free, which felt far more comfortable than charging money.

I forced myself to start every day with following up on an introductory call about going ahead with coaching, which felt very uncomfortable due to my RSD. However, I suddenly had lots of clients who'd actually paid money to have coaching with me, which felt terrifying, but exciting.

This was also overwhelming, because I just said 'yes' to every request, with zero concept of working hours. Although I struggle to focus in the late afternoon, I was suddenly coaching numerous teenagers, with short 15 minute sessions booked in multiple times a week. These always ended up being an hour each!

I also found that the clients didn't respond to how I'd been trained to assume they would, especially with teenagers. They outright refused to 'bring an agenda' to the coaching session, and were more explicit about this than I was when I had the same struggles and masked to my coach! When I asked what they wanted to focus on, they said, 'I don't know'.

This was often partly because their parents had organised and were paying for their coaching, as opposed to them. Unsure of what to talk about, I brought up the contents list of my book, *'ADHD: an A to Z'*, as there were various exercises within each chapter we could do.

This seemed to work really well, and I started to spend all of my time outside of sessions creating clients their own personalised worksheets. This gave a structure to the coaching itself, but also provided enough flexibility to talk about any issues that might come up.

However, I was still struggling emotionally, especially with the situations that these teenagers were facing, such as bullying at school, social media use, and mental health

Paradoxes

challenges that fell out of my expertise as a coach. It was very difficult to avoid taking these on myself, and I started writing another book on social media, body image, and mental health in an attempt to help.

I was inundated with ideas, unable to stop myself from acting upon them, realising that I needed to create my own company. As a result, I flew the coaching nest, and ADHD Works was born.

However, running my own company meant having to charge my own rates, which suddenly felt deeply uncomfortable. The Government grant of Access to Work was only available to fund coaching for people in work, which excluded the teenagers in school I'd been working with. The waiting list for this was also very long, and I wanted to help people now, so I ended up speaking to their employers about funding coaching as a reasonable adjustment.

I also struggled with the lack of structure, especially in having to explain to potential clients like employers what ADHD coaching actually involved, or how it worked. I didn't know how many sessions I should set in a 'package' of coaching, how long they should be, or how much to price this at.

Around that time, a publisher reached out to me about acquiring *'ADHD: an A to Z'*, having heard me speak on a podcast. Although I'd be giving up a huge amount of my own commission, in making 10-13% royalties on each book sold, I agreed on the basis of the book being able to reach more people, and the removal of a clause requiring any future books to be given first refusal rights by them.

During the editing process, I was told to replace the 'E is for Exercise' chapter with 'E is for Executive Functioning'. I really didn't want to do this, because in truth, I didn't really understand it. However, due to their insistence, I forced myself to try.

AuDHD: Blooming Differently

I then realised that the executive functioning differences in people with ADHD were a far more useful way of understanding the impact it had on someone, as opposed to the diagnostic criteria. Skills such as emotional regulation, impulsivity, and motivation reflected my own experiences much more accurately than 'impulsivity, inattention and hyperactivity'.

A lightbulb went off in my brain, and I turned this into an 'Executive Functioning Framework' for ADHD coaching, creating exercises and worksheets for clients to understand their own ADHD, as an optional 'menu' if they weren't sure what to do. The first time I nervously showed it to someone, they burst into tears, saying how validating it was to see their experiences explained so well. This also made it much easier to present to employers, as the ability to strengthen executive functioning skills provided a framework and purpose for the coaching.

This structure was a lifeline, as my personal life was unravelling, as I found out that I'd been cheated on by my partner. The thought of leaving was so overwhelming that I hyper-focused on relationship books, believing this was somehow my fault. Ironically, having coaching myself helped me to see the reality, and to leave, having made a plan that worked with my brain.

I also started modelling again on the side, to help financially, with clearly set boundaries about the kind of jobs I'd do. I doubted whether anyone would book me at the grand age of 30, and having very publicly called out exploitation in the modelling industry, but I worked more than I probably had ever done before. For example, nearly every week, I was booked to shoot for the fashion brand Next with an incredibly lovely team, traveling to Doncaster.

This was helpful financially, but very stressful practically. The jobs were confirmed the night before, meaning that

I had to constantly move around coaching sessions. I felt extremely guilty about this, and struggled to know how to manage it.

Again, coaching helped with this enormously. Having always struggled to visualise my future, finding a coach who understood this enabled me to set goals in an AuDHD friendly way. I knew that I definitely *didn't* want to be doing modelling in the future, which helped me to decide what to prioritise in that moment: coaching. I set a new priority 'short term goal' in getting 10 clients, which helped me to say no to modelling jobs and prioritise this as opposed to my endless ideas, such as an ADHD fashion line and retreat.

With this new focus, I quickly reached this goal, and decided to run the first ever ADHD retreat with my best friend, who does this as her job. Together, we budgeted for costs and value, but as soon as we put the price up, I felt extremely anxious. I was worried that no one would come, and she wouldn't want to be friends anymore.

I also felt guilty about this only being available for those who could afford it, so decided to make an alternative through an ADHD course. I wanted to make a course I would actually do as an ADHD-er, so gamified it by making lessons 5 minutes per day, for 30 days, with a weekly group coaching call.

I was so anxious that I paid thousands of pounds to a course creation coach, and an ADHD sales coach, which turned out to be the best investment I could have made. The financial investment meant I *had* to finish making the course, and the sales coach helped me to use tools such as Stripe to make purchases as ADHD-friendly as possible. They convinced me to put the price much higher than I'd planned (£25), instead offering discounts or free access to anybody who wanted this.

AuDHD: Blooming Differently

I barely left my flat for months, working non-stop on the course and retreat, which easily sold out. Before I knew it, 65 people had signed up to the ADHD course, which only increased my stress levels as I realised I'd actually have to run it.

A few days into the course, someone complained by email because the videos were not precisely 5 minutes long as advertised. When I watched them back, I realised they were right, absolutely mortified. I had a meltdown, terrified of the numerous complaints that would follow, and all of the people I'd somehow tricked into doing my course, even for free. I wanted to take the whole thing down, but they had already signed up, so I felt trapped.

I did the only thing I can do in these situations: write. I wrote a newsletter post about RSD, sharing this on LinkedIn. I explained what had happened, with the tornado of shame that I felt about this, and offered anybody a refund who wanted one. Ironically, nobody else had even noticed. Others explained that the lessons were approximately 5 minutes long, especially as some days had additional exercises to do.

Most surprising of all was the outpouring of kindness on LinkedIn, of all places. Talking about RSD had broken the 'professional' code, and people seemed to resonate incredibly strongly. So I decided to make another 30 day course for the next month, on RSD.

Making this inspired me to write to the head of the World Health Organization (WHO), trying to understand whether they could adjust the ADHD diagnostic criteria to include emotions and RSD. Bizarrely, I somehow then found myself presenting to senior Directors of the WHO on ADHD and RSD, something I never thought I'd be doing!

Paradoxes

Writing on LinkedIn also led me to train gigantic, global companies I wouldn't have even dared apply for a job at just a few years ago. One of the most surreal moments was creating a whole ADHD Champions programme to deliver for hundreds of employees at a time at Disney, enabling them to provide peer support and exercises for one another. I was constantly spinning endless plates, but it was incredible to see my ideas come to life - and work.

The ADHD retreat came around, which was one of the most amazing and stressful things I'd ever done. After a weekend of ADHD workshops, ocean swimming, and non-stop coaching, I found myself having a meltdown on the road outside my house. I couldn't understand why I felt like an animal carcass that had been eaten, feeling completely hollow, when I knew I should be feeling so happy.

I felt like this was everything I'd ever wanted, so I didn't know why I felt so alone and overwhelmed. All I was doing was working, but the 'to do' list only ever seemed to grow. Working had become a full blown addiction, and I no longer knew who I was outside of ADHD Works.

These meltdowns continued to happen regularly. When construction started outside my flat, I found myself hysterically crying as I tried to find somewhere quiet to escape the noise, which went on for *months*.

At the start of one group session, a hot water bottle filled with boiling water exploded in my face, causing severe burns. Despite a meltdown and the worst pain I'd ever felt, I *tried to carry on coaching*, holding a sponge to my face and showing everyone my burns as justification for my not going on camera, attempting to put them in break out rooms. Naturally, they were all horrified, with one person taking charge and demanding that I go to A&E.

When I arrived at hospital with my face and wrists blistering away, I looked at my phone and tried to think who I should tell. It felt like a 'serious' thing to happen, and maybe I needed some kind of support. I couldn't think of anyone, despite having friends and family. I couldn't even figure out the words to say that I was in pain, let alone that I'd burned half of my face off and was sitting in A&E. I felt incredibly lonely, and sad at how 'successful' I appeared externally, but how much of a failure I felt on a personal level.

Running a business had provided an amazing portal into creating a world where I could feel a sense of certainty over my relationships, where I had a 'role' and expectations to meet. They were *literally* transactional, and it all made sense.

However, this meant that I'd stopped seeing people outside of work, or in 'real life', as much as possible. When I went to a friend's birthday party, the first time I'd seen them in months, I found myself leaving 5 minutes after arriving. When I tried to go to a family gathering a few weeks later, I had a meltdown in the train station, overwhelmed by the crowds of people and noise. I cried hysterically and found myself in a park instead of the party, trying to figure out how to end it all.

It hit me that I was clearly unwell, and I wanted to quit. However, a coach helped me to think through my options, convincing me not to close the company and to instead get some support so I could stop doing it all by myself.

I'd previously felt that hiring any other coaches wasn't an option, because the way I coached was different to how I'd been trained, largely using my Executive Functioning framework. I also felt extremely passionate about coaching being done to a high quality, recognising the specific needs

Paradoxes

of those I worked with, which wasn't taught in traditional coaching trainings.

However, this conversation made me realise that I could create my own training course, so I decided to try it out. I had nothing to lose, and didn't think anybody would even notice, let alone sign up.

By the time the course began a couple of months later, there were 25 people signed up. I couldn't believe it. We took on some of these coaches at ADHD Works, to help manage the waiting lists of hundreds of people wanting coaching, which ironically just ended up with more overwhelm.

Whilst it was great to share ADHD coaching with more clients and coaches, it was also extraordinarily stressful on the back end, meaning we had to re-do our entire systems, placing immense pressure on our team of 2 people! Being self-employed felt like I was constantly trying to clean up messes and work less, but only created more mess and things to do.

A few months later, the virtual assistant who'd worked with me since the beginning handed in their notice. I've never experienced grief like it, hysterically crying on the floor for days. I couldn't imagine the company running without this person, not least because I had no idea how they managed all of the administration and chaotic processes we'd created!

Around this, I couldn't process how to even live, let alone work without this relationship, recognising how ridiculous and unfair this was, but being unable to control the feelings. I felt depressed in having achieved literally everything I could have dreamed of, but still feeling so lonely. I became obsessed with researching the best way to kill myself, determined not to fail. I scared myself, because I had never been so serious or rational about this before - I felt like I'd contributed 'enough' to the world.

I was extremely lucky that a therapist spotted the signs of my suicidal ideation, who convinced me me to go to the doctor and try anti-anxiety medication. I'd resisted this until that point, but it was life-changing. I couldn't believe that it was possible to survive without being an anxious mess, but the thoughts had disappeared overnight.

I decided to 'relax' by booking back-to-back holidays for the summer, accepting invitations from multiple people. This was extremely stressful, involving being around other people constantly, and navigating constant travel.

The unstructured, 'free' time felt unbearable. I couldn't stop 'masking' my symptoms, feeling like I was pretending to be a completely different person. I tried my best to think of conversation topics that weren't work or ADHD related, but this was virtually impossible, and exhausting.

I felt so much shame around struggling so much, knowing that I 'should' be having a good time. When I returned from one trip, I found myself repeatedly lost in the airport, having been unable to find my gate and going through the wrong doors. I felt trapped, and began screaming, seconds from smashing the fire alarm.

I eventually managed to get out of that room, and ran to board my plane, only to accidentally go through the wrong doors again. This was too much to bear, and I simply couldn't stop screaming, shaking, and hysterically crying. I was surprised to be escorted onto the plane by a security guard, believing they were marching me to hospital.

Before I knew it, I was writing the experience out on LinkedIn. I hit publish as the plane took off, before seconds later realising that this was *a really stupid thing to do*. I couldn't understand why I did it. When we landed, I went to delete it, but it had been shared and commented on hundreds of times, so I just left it up.

Many of the comments mentioned autism, and coincidentally a post appeared on my page from an autism assessor, Harriet.[153] She was describing my experience as an autistic woman in ways I'd never seen before, and I took it as a sign, messaging her to ask for an appointment.

I had suspected I was autistic for years before then, but I didn't see the point in a formal assessment. However, at that point, I realised that things couldn't get any worse - I deserved to know one way or the other, so I could get help for whatever was happening to me.

THE AUDHD LENS

The paradoxes are so significant in AuDHD that I've made an entire coaching framework based off of it! Being autistic or ADHD alone can be hard enough, but navigating both together can be extremely hard.

This can lead us to constantly feel as though we're not 'enough', or forever chasing a feeling of peace that seems unobtainable. For me, it often feels as though the ADHD part of my brain is making a mess that the autistic part has to chase and clean up! However, every time I try to clean up a mess, it seems to only make things more complicated.

Although this can be frustrating and exhausting, they *can* work together in synchronicity. 'Twice exceptional' is a term commonly used to describe children with exceptional ability, but also disability, but I like to think of it in relation to AuDHD. We have twice the struggles, but also twice the strengths - it's just about learning how to meet in the middle.

---

[153] https://www.linkedin.com/in/harriet-richardson-0bb733163/

ALL VS NOTHING

The monotropic focus styles associated with AuDHD means that we may struggle to engage in tasks that aren't of interest, but throw ourselves in deeply to those that are. We might place unrealistic standards of perfection on ourselves, feeling as though what we're doing is pointless unless it's done 'perfectly'.

This is also related to the interest based nervous system linked with ADHD, where we may be extremely energised by novelty, before losing interest. It's very common to see this in hobbies, where we might buy lots of very expensive equipment, before the dopamine wears off!

Similarly, this can apply within the workplace. Employees may dedicate themselves entirely to a role for the first month, but find that the standards they have created for themselves are unsustainable, crashing out or quitting as a result. In self-employment, there seems to be a similar theme, where we may commonly second-guess ourselves and worry about not being as interested in something in the future.

PDA also shows up here, because whilst we may enjoy the 'deep dive' of starting something new, we may also feel very resistant to the expectation of finishing it, our brain battling against itself. The autistic side may feel a strong *need* to finish what we started, whereas the ADHD part has already moved on, a classic coping strategy to avoid the pain of RSD.

RSD can play a major part in this, which may stem from children with ADHD received 20,000 more negative comments than their peers by age 12! We may not trust our own high enthusiasm, and when the prospect of potentially failing or being criticised becomes clear, we may quickly back out, without even realising that this is the case.

Paradoxes

This can also stem from how we respond to 'achievements'. For example, when a therapist asked me how my achievements were celebrated during childhood, I automatically said that I didn't have any. The complete lack of awareness of my own achievements meant that I'd grown up without valuing myself, my efforts, or my work, which explained my low self-esteem in adulthood.

We had this conversation because I was constantly finding myself frustrated after doing something like publishing a book, feeling as though nobody cared - but I also rarely actually talked about my achievements, so they didn't know how to respond!

To balance this, we can consciously set our own expectations, instead of living by the ones that might be subconsciously programmed into our brains. Defining what 'success' means to us is extremely important for AuDHD-ers, to ensure that we're not living by neurotypical standards that aren't designed for our brains.

This comes with being honest with ourselves about the 'purpose' behind what we're doing, and setting an 'end point' that is actually achievable, like something we could tick off a list when complete. Breaking this down into short-term goals helps us to feel less overwhelmed, and not to start at level 100!

As a result, we can bring ourselves back to the 'start' of our goals, instead of attempting to start at the finish line. I see this often in coaches I train, who are extremely hard on themselves for not immediately having clients lining up to see them! The social media world we operate in now is showing us everybody else's successes, but we don't see the hard work, multiple failures, and effort that's gone into these.

Then, we can tailor our environments to help us to meet these expectations, such as by blocking out days on the calendar to enable us to 'deep focus'. A simple example is DIY. When I receive a piece of furniture I've ordered, I will often open the box immediately, and try to start building it. Around half an hour later, frustrated, I give up. This leaves bits of furniture and mess all over my flat, but I can't face looking at it anymore!

Reading the instructions first, and following these, sounds simple, but makes a drastic difference. This is ultimately a muscle we must learn to use, supported by environments that help us to remember that we do not need to do everything all at once, and celebrating our successes, instead of constantly shifting the goalposts!

PREDICTABILITY VS NOVELTY

Whilst the autistic part of our brain seeks predictability, the ADHD part craves novelty, easily becoming bored of routines, or forgetting all about them! This can see us neglect our own needs, especially in relation to self-care, which can be less intellectually stimulating than whatever we happen to be interested in at that point.

For example, we might start a habit with a food box delivery company, feeling very excited about our new routine which doesn't require the hassle of deciding what to cook every day. However, a few weeks (or days!) into this, we may find our fridge full of uneaten, gone off food. This can be extremely annoying, as we beat ourselves up as a result, ending up ordering takeout to make ourselves feel better, as we've 'failed' anyway. Frustrated, we might also decide to cancel the subscription, but forget to do so!

I regularly see this in coaching, as people start on the highs of routines, before these inevitably fall away. The most important part of AuDHD coaching is getting 'back on the horse', and realising that we are allowed to simply change the

Paradoxes

routine. We also have the benefit of additional information about what works for us, and what can disrupt a routine.

The secret to AuDHD-friendly routines is not just anticipating, but *expecting* change. This isn't a 'failure', it just keeps things interesting! Instead of beating ourselves up for becoming bored and falling into RSD infused inertia, we can simply accept that this is no longer working, and try something else.

Instead of expecting ourselves to be perfect, we can pre-plan for chaos, ironically creating a sense of certainty that feels more controllable by slowing down.

To do this, we can create structures with the information we *do* have. For example, if we want to create an exercise routine, we can identify what we do and do not like. I know that I enjoy yoga and novel forms of exercise, such as aerial hoop and trapeze, and hate running.

Then, we can look at what has worked previously - looking for the 'bright spots'. If we use my example, what has helped me to do this before is going to the same class, every morning at 7am. We then can identify what went wrong before, likely with a wealth of information we can use! What's made me fall out of this routine previously has included a teacher I liked going on holiday, going on holiday myself, and deciding to try a different class, which meant I lost the pattern.

With this information, we can then build a routine that works for us. It doesn't matter if it's the 1st or 1000th time we've tried it - we're just experimenting. The key is to break this down into the tiniest step possible, without worrying about whether we'll 'stick to it' - we won't, and that's okay! Just taking one step and trying our routine out *once* can help to start the habit, which we can then decide if we want to continue for the next day.

This sounds simple, but many AuDHD-ers will set themselves impossible routines, such as walking 20,000 steps every day. Approaching routines as experiments, and changing them up regularly, such as a 'hobby of the month', can provide us with the balance of novelty and predictability we need to stay motivated.

UNDER VS OVER-STIMULATION

AuDHD means that half of our brain is seeking peace, whilst the other half is seeking stimulation. We may crave excitement, but become easily overwhelmed, burning ourselves out. The impulsive part of our brain might makes lots of plans, whilst the autistic part is screaming at it not to.

This can mean living on an energetic rollercoaster of highs and lows, especially as we may struggle with basic self-care, such as showering and eating! This is intensified by changes outside of our control, as in chapter 'Transitions'.

It can also see us masking our symptoms to hide our distress, feeling as though we can't cancel plans we've already made, or things we've already agreed to do. As a result, we might find ourselves in a state of inertia, beating ourselves up for doing nothing, whilst feeling overwhelmed at all of the things we still need to do.

This can then result in emotional dysregulation, such as a meltdown or shutdown. The challenge is that we may easily become bored 'resting', and struggle with self-awareness, not realising how much we're taking on in the moment.

Ultimately, this requires boundaries to look after energy - which might not feel natural to AuDHD-ers! These are the invisible lines between us and other people, and the ways we teach others to treat us, including ourselves. It might involve saying 'no', which can feel very overwhelming.

However, this isn't a bad or 'selfish' thing - it enables us to only commit to doing what we actually *want* to do! Being in the best energetic state ourselves enables us to support others much more effectively.

To do this, we need to identify what make us feel drained, or pull us into an 'attention tunnel' that can be difficult to emerge from, and what makes us feel energised. This can feel uncomfortable if you've never thought about it before, but using a mood tracker app such as Daylio can be very helpful to simply observe your feelings.

Identifying what kinds of stimulation we *want* to be engaged in can help us to apply this to 'boring' tasks, such as listening to a podcast whilst cleaning. This is in contrast to scrolling on social media for hours, which can be stimulating, but not necessarily fulfilling!

We can then think of these as building blocks, ensuring we have time and structures in place to help us manage our energy. This might look like having an automatic reply on our email, for example, notifying people that we will not reply immediately. We may also wish to set boundaries around other people, such as confining time with those who are draining to a coffee, instead of having them over to our house!

As our AuDHD symptoms may change day to day, it can also be helpful to 'separate' yourself from this by consciously identifying which is more dominant on a certain day, adjusting your environment accordingly.

FEELING EVERYTHING VS NOTHING

One of the hardest parts of AuDHD can be the emotional regulation aspects, including alexithymia, meltdowns, shutdowns, and RSD. Without understanding how we feel in the moment, we may be constantly acting in 'survival mode', lashing out without meaning to.

We *do* have feelings, even if we're not consciously aware of them. For example, as I told a coach recently about my struggles with alexithymia and being unable to identify my feelings, she pointed out that I'd used the word 'feel' multiple times in conversation!

This can feel extremely bad, especially when we experience the lows, but it also allows us to feel great joy that is inaccessible to 'most'. This can feel exhausting and scary when we're not in control of it, or can't spot our warning signs.

I think of emotional regulation as learning to surf, as we can't stop the waves from coming! However, we can learn from the past, including what's triggered previous emotional dysregulation, and predict what might cause it in the future. This could involve making a tailored 'safety plan', complete with strategies to help us regulate our experiences when overwhelmed.

It can also be extremely helpful to identify how you best process emotions, as in chapter 'Learning'. For example, if you're hyperlexic like me, you might wish to write out your feelings in a journal, or turn them into a book like this one. If you're a high verbal processor, it can be very helpful to identify someone to talk through your feelings with, unmasked, such as a neuro-affirmative therapist or coach.

A friend of mine, Josephine McGrail, describes emotions as 'energy in motion'. *Doing* something with these emotions helps us to allow them to flow through us, such as exercise. It's when we're stuck in rumination mode that they can become problematic, as we're in our heads more than our bodies.

It's very important to be aware of the differences in suicidal ideation when it comes to AuDHD, as the risks are far higher. Although it can be very scary to feel this way, it's not shameful, or a sign that you're 'broken' - it's human. Your body is keeping you alive without being forced to, so she part of you must want to be here! Feeling suicidal can be a coping strategy to situations we can't escape, but this doesn't make it any less valid or dangerous to experience.

If you feel this way, please talk about it to someone you trust, and notice how much more easily these feelings disappear. Although I have felt suicidal throughout my life, a sign that I wanted help was how upset I was over feeling like this! I didn't want to die, I wanted to live, but I just felt like I didn't fit into the world.

Each and every one of us fits into the world, and we're not 'worthy' because of our job title or achievements, but simply because of who we are. Just think of a newborn baby - we don't place the same expectations of regulating their emotions on them, or judge them any less for making their suffering known! In fact, knowing about it enables us to do something about it.

If you're a loved one of an AuDHD-er, being aware of this is crucial, so you can spot any signs that they may be struggling, and help. It's important to try and regulate your own emotions, avoiding making it about 'you', but simply to listen, offer support, and be there for the person. It's also advisable to seek our neuro-affirmative support yourself, such as therapy or coaching, as this can help with the understandable worry that you may feel.

IDEAS OVERWHELM VS EXECUTION

Having AuDHD may mean we have a wonderful, ideas filled brain, but struggle to put these into action. This is largely because of the struggles in executive functioning, and our brain working very quickly, causing the people around us to find it difficult to keep up!

I think of this as having lots of different tabs in my brain, all of equal importance. Having a brain that makes connections and thinks in an innovative way can be extremely helpful, but also very overwhelming, especially for our autistic part that needs certainty.

This can be very frustrating for AuDHD-ers to experience, in feeling as though we're unable to 'reach our potential'. Being able to visualise ideas so well, and energised by this, means that we may struggle with the reality of putting them into action.

Our brains may work so quickly that we struggle to get started, constantly pulling us in new directions. Simultaneously, the autistic part of our brain may be struggling with the lack of completing what we've started previously.

We may thrive in situations where we're able to harness this creativity, but could have a tendency to overuse our strengths, burning out as a result. Ultimately, ideas aren't worth anything if they only live in our minds.

Bringing any idea to life will also inevitably involve 'boring' bits, such as administration, or setting up a website, which can drag our attention away. I once coached someone who showed me a presentation they'd made of an *'ADHD: an A to Z'* book, only to get distracted by creating an Instagram account for it. I can't imagine how frustrating it would have been to see my self-published version come out - but it doesn't mean that this version is invalid.

To overcome this, we need to strengthen our self-awareness skills. Firstly, recognising the unique strengths that you have as an individual is very important to help with confidence in executing your ideas. These are in your differences, not how well you can fit in and follow the rules! Your strengths are in all of your experiences until now, making you impossible to copy or replace, because nobody is you. Ironically, the only thing that is 'perfect' is you, because there's only one version of you in billions of people!

Then we need to connect with our weaknesses, such as the tasks or areas in life that we find most difficult or painful. Before I had a virtual assistant, I was constantly overwhelmed from trying to set up Zoom calls and manage invoices. Delegating can be very difficult for AuDHD-ers, because it requires us to break down the steps involved in a task, communicate clear instructions, and trust that it will be done.

Seeing something done in a way we wouldn't have done it can feel distressing, and the impulsivity part of our brain might redo it - or do it before we've even given the other person a chance! To avoid this, it's sensible to work with an AuDHD coach when starting to work with somebody new, who can help you to set up sustainable processes and structures, allowing them to take all of the work you don't like away.

Finally, we need to connect with our values. This can be confusing for AuDHD-ers, especially due to alexithymia and a struggle in our self-identity. However, knowing what we care about (just look at your interests!) and why, can lead us to identify what we stand for. I believe this is our 'purpose', as opposed to one particular path - it's the qualities that make us authentically us.

Our values can help us to prioritise and execute ideas with an objective lens. For example, when coaching entrepreneurs, I often remind them to start with the idea that is easiest, that people actually want, and that can make them money.

Although we all seem to have a common desire to help everybody for free, we all need money to live, and your work has value. Money is essentially an exchange in energy, and the more you have available, the more you can do things outside of this to help others. For example, setting up the coaching training enabled me to stop trying to support everybody myself, and the time to write this book!

To decide between your ideas instead of trying to act on them all immediately (and buying website URLs!), it can be helpful to write them down in an 'ideas bank'. ADHD Works' employee, Charlie Champion, actually created me one of these when she saw how many ideas I was trying to implement on a daily basis! We now have time in the calendar every month to review them, and ironically, I usually don't actually want to do the ones I've written down.

This is why it's important to identify where the ideas have come from. As a hyper-empathetic person, I'll often have emotionally charged ideas, such as offering to speak in schools for free, but struggle with the reality of this. For example, we instantly received hundreds of requests, but didn't have the resources to handle these! We may also have ideas as a result of people pleasing, or from seeing something on social media.

Picking *one* idea at a time, with a clearly defined end point, and focusing your energy on this before any others is how to execute them. Setting yourself a time limit to focus *only on this* before starting any new ideas is extraordinarily effective - though you may wish to put a reminder on your wall!

LONELINESS VS ISOLATION

AuDHD can feel like existing in a bubble that nobody else can see. It's very lonely and difficult to struggle to communicate our thoughts, or to be able to engage in the ways that other people seem to be able to. Ultimately, human connection is a core need for all of us.

The ADHD part of our brain may enjoy the stimulation of being with others, but the autistic part may be feel extremely socially awkward, resulting in exhaustion. My ADHD part says 'yes' to every invitation, wanting to be friends with everybody, and my autistic part wants to avoid the uncertainty that comes with socialising and knowing what to say.

As a result, I will often isolate myself. This is exacerbated by my monotropism, where staying at home and working feels much more satisfying than seeing friends. This can also result in workaholism, as 33% of workaholics are said to have ADHD! My tendency to people please means that the thought of social interactions is exhausting, especially when I'm so immersed in work, and struggle to think of anything else. I commonly hear from clients about the shame of seeing socialising as 'unproductive'.

This is nothing to be ashamed of, because our brains are wired to seek dopamine, which is very easily accessible through communicating via social media, allowing us to continue catching up with the inevitably long 'to do' list we may have. Staying on top of surviving can be hard enough, without allowing ourselves the luxury of having 'fun'!

In contrast, arranging to meet up at all, scheduling a time that works for everyone, choosing what to wear, leaving the house, travelling, and handling a new, unpredictable environment, can be exhausting just to think about. However, this is a million times more fulfilling than 'liking' someone's post online - it is worth it.

The difficulty is intensified with RSD, convincing us that everybody hates us and doesn't want to meet up anyway. My AuDHD means that I honestly *never* think to suggest meeting up with anybody proactively, assuming they feel the same general overwhelm at life as I do.

However, living like this is unbearably lonely. Social media presents all of the ways everyone in the world is socialising on a weekend, except us. When I lived outside a park, I felt intense sadness every time I walked by people sitting in groups, laughing together. It seemed like all I did was work.

Human connection is ultimately what makes life worth living. I once coached someone who told me about how they spoke to their 4 adult children every day, whilst beating themselves up for not being 'successful' enough at work. I explained that it's very rare for me to hear of adult-parent relationships like this, and that what they have achieved is the 'success' that everybody is ultimately working for: love.

Having known extremely rich and famous people, I can confirm that this sense of loneliness only grows with 'success'. Although it might feel exhausting, identifying a few people who make you feel good, whose company you enjoy, and setting up regularly co-occurring meetings in your calendar will be the most 'productive' thing you can ever do.

If you want to apply any of this in practice, I strongly recommend seeking out an AuDHD coach from ADHD Works, who will have been trained on supporting people to implement the AuDHD Coaching Paradox Framework. At the time of writing, it's the only AuDHD coaching course in the world!

Tips: AuDHD-ers

- Before starting something new, decide a specific 'end' point.

- Try to notice whether you're at 'level 100' or 'level 1', bringing yourself back to basics.

- Treat 'routines' as experiments, with room for novelty and flexibility, planning for these to be disrupted.

- Look back at your life and the things that have worked for you, and what's got in the way of doing the things you want to do.

- Set some core boundaries about how you spend your time and how you want to be treated, writing these out and putting them somewhere you'll see them!

- Make boring tasks fun by incorporating stimulation, such as listening to a podcast whilst cleaning.

- Observe in yourself whether ADHD or autism is more dominant on a certain day, making accommodations as needed.

- Find a way to express your feelings that works for you, such as journalling, noticing what impacts this.

- Identify the things you struggle with, and ask for help in breaking these down to be able to be done by somebody else. The people around you will be very happy to help!

- Write your ideas down before acting on them, keeping them in an 'ideas bank', with regular time for review.

- Schedule automatically re-occurring meetings in your calendar with friends.

- Take the time to identify your values, and purpose behind the busyness.

AuDHD: Blooming Differently

- If you're struggling with your mental health, speak to the people in your life about this, and your doctor.

- Seek out AuDHD coaching to help you to put this into practice.

Tips: Loved ones

- Accept that there may be some things your loved one can do very well, but in other areas, they may struggle significantly, avoiding judgement.

- Learn about how your loved one experiences AuDHD by asking them questions in a non-judgemental way.

- Make socialising as easy as possible by learning about your love one's preferences, such as doing an activity together, and planning ahead.

- Remember that if your loved one doesn't reach out to you often or reply to your messages, this isn't because they don't care - they're probably thinking about you all of the time! Providing reassurance about this, without the pressure to respond, can be very helpful.

- Helping your loved one to think about the future when talking about plans, such as checking your calendars together, can be very helpful, encouraging them to say 'no' if needed.

- Support your loved one to access support such as coaching, therapy, or medical help if they are struggling.

- Open up conversations about values with your loved one, collaboratively identifying what drives you both to do the things you do.

- Offer support where possible, such as with tasks that they may find difficult, like food shopping.

- Support your loved one with new routines or interests, avoiding shaming them if they change their mind, but validating their experiences as they are.

12. Diagnosis

I felt like an imposter when seeking an autism assessment, as though I was 'making it up'. However, I also knew that I was struggling so significantly that if nothing else, at least this would give me a clearer direction to access the help I needed.

Knowing that the waiting lists were years long on the NHS, and feeling too scared to talk to my doctor about my suspicions, I decided to self-fund this, which is a luxury that many people do not have. This was because all I did was work, but it was the best money I've ever spent.

The assessor I contacted, Harriet, explained that an assessment would take a few months, involving an initial pre-assessment screening call. This seemed too long: I wanted answers in that moment. Once that I'd allowed myself to consider a potential diagnosis, I couldn't handle the uncertainty of possibly being wrong. When someone told me about their ADHD assessor who also did Autism assessments, which costed hundreds instead of thousands of pounds, with availability that week, I decided to book it.

When I received the pre-assessment forms, I became very frustrated at the questions, such as those asking 'do you struggle with your nerves?', asked in 3 different ways. When someone who I'd asked to fill in one of the forms agreed with their irrationality, and asked me why I was going with this cheaper option when this was so important, I realised

Diagnosis

that I needed to invest in this properly, even though it'd be longer. Fortunately, this provider was extremely kind and gave me a refund!

Harriet worked at Autistic Girls[154], which is run by Dr Becky Quicke. Ironically, given her last name, I'd seen a LinkedIn post earlier that week from Becky saying that if someone wanted a quick 'in and out' assessment then they weren't the service for them. They provided detailed, holistic assessments, with specialist knowledge of ADHD and Autism in girls and women.

I booked in a free screening call, unprepared for how validating of an experience that conversation alone would be. Becky asked questions such as what had led up to the call (almost ending my own life), what it's like when I'm really interested in something (the world ceases to exist), and how my social relationships were (bad).

She advised to proceed with the assessment, and sent me some forms, questions, and online tests to complete, relating to areas like masking[155] and monotropism[156]. I scored top marks in every test, and emailed back a grand total of 39 pages back for my poor assessor, Harriet, to read through, in addition to an optional form completed by a parent.

Whilst waiting for the assessment, I became very anxious. To be told that all of these traits I'd finally accepted enough to seek help for weren't actually autism and sent away felt overwhelming. This was intensified by the reactions of people I'd known for years, which mostly included telling me I wasn't autistic, questioning why I needed a 'label', and telling me there was nothing 'wrong' with me. They told

---

154   https://autisticgirls.co.uk/
155   https://embrace-autism.com/cat-q/
156   https://dlcincluded.github.io/MQ/

me all about how there was no treatment, so what was the point, arguments I'd already had with myself countless times in my head.

I tried to explain why I was getting the assessment, but this only seemed to make things worse. I ended up telling them that I was suicidal a few months previously, and they reacted in all of the ways I'd been afraid of. This ranged from being angry that I hadn't told them at the time, to telling me that I should 'think of what it would do to them' if I felt like that again, to simply ignoring it all together. I couldn't tell which was worse, becoming mute and unable to speak.

It was confusing to know whether and how to prepare. I only had my experiences of ADHD assessments to compare the upcoming autism assessment to, which had been thoroughly rigid and uncomfortable experiences, dragging up all the ways I have failed in life until this point.

I didn't want to deep dive into other people's experiences, because I didn't want to accidentally somehow cheat by saying what I thought they wanted to hear. I had already read pretty much every book published on autism, many of which detailed the processes involved, such as showing the assessor how a person brushes their teeth.

I didn't need to worry. Harriet made me feel comfortable even before the assessment happened, sending a rough outline of how it would run. When we met, I was taken aback by how kind she was. It felt like a conversation with a friend.

Harriet started off by introducing herself and setting out the format again, explaining that we'd look at my developmental history first, followed by my present day. She assured me that however I needed to do this was fine, such as by taking breaks or moving around. She explained that she also

Diagnosis

assessed for ADHD, and that I'd been through a lot of trauma, which would all need to be carefully considered to establish autism versus anything else.

I felt like I trusted her implicitly, assuring her that if she didn't diagnose me as autistic, that was completely fine.

I told her about my home life and upbringing, and my family history, including in relation to autism. She asked about my daily life and how that looked when I was younger, covering all elements areas, from school to home. We talked about developmental milestones, like the speech and language therapy I attended as a child, and health history, such as how a build up of earwax was assumed to be the cause of my repeated walking into objects like tables.

The questions resonated with everything I'd experienced throughout my life without even realising. I explained about my lifelong approach to relationships, surprising myself by realising how hard I'd been working without even noticing. As a child, if I was injured, I didn't think to tell anyone - I didn't see the point, but I'd never thought about this before. When I was asked about my pain threshold, I realised that I had a very high one, hardly feeling physical pain, despite being extremely clumsy. These traits had continued throughout my life, where I rarely thought to go to the doctor or seek help if I was hurt - it just didn't make sense.

It was like someone could see into my brain, with questions about things like how I knew if I was hungry or needed to go to the bathroom. I have no idea. These days I try to remember to eat three meals a day at the times we're 'supposed to'. I explained how I'd eat things constantly as a child that weren't food such as paper, but at other times was obsessed with what we'd be having for dinner.

I remembered how I rocked on my chair constantly and would make up songs whilst sitting in my wardrobe.

Memories came back of experiences that had only existed in my head, things I'd never told anybody before, such as how I'd seek out a particular staircase in school, because I liked the way it smelled.

When we came to my current day to day experiences, it was pretty illuminating. I realised how all of these different strands linked up together, from the 'different voices' my therapist had pointed out that I used without being able to control during conversations, to my preference in staying home all of the time.

I explained that being around people was exhausting, including even getting dressed and leaving the house, to being hyper-aware of myself and their needs. I didn't realise how much energy it used, confessing that if no one ever messaged me asking to meet up, I'd never see anyone - it didn't feel worth the stress. I was also highly aware that this caused me to feel very lonely and isolated, which was a difficult contradiction to manage.

We talked about how I respond to others' distress, which I find very contextual. I can either be great and hold the space, such as being absolutely fine with people crying during coaching, or I can find it so unbearable that it feels like my skin is burning off, usually in scenarios outside of contracted work. This is especially if I feel somehow responsible for their emotions - I will happily give them whatever they want in that moment.

When I started coaching, I'd spend hours supporting people who were experiencing difficulties, replying to every single message and request without question. I explained my complicated construct of boundaries I've now put in place to avoid this, including ignoring messages from people if they're asking me directly for something, because I can't say no. ChatGPT is a great help, but even the kindly worded boundaries it gives me to share, feel impossible to send.

Questions around relationships sparked my asking questions in return that I'd been ruminating over for years. What *is* a friendship? Aren't all relationships transactional in some way? What *does* make someone want to hang out with someone else? Why *do* people enjoy hanging out in the pub? What *is* the difference between romantic and platonic love?

These were the questions that other people, like therapists, had responded to with confusion. They couldn't understand what I was asking, instead asking me to categorise my relationships into 'acquaintances' and 'close friends'. I found it impossible to differentiate between them - that was the point. Harriet was the first person I'd met who held a non-judgemental, validating space for these discussions. Being autistic herself, she understood exactly what I meant.

We talked about routines and how I respond to changes that I can't control, which is very bad: I just shut down. It's all or nothing. Routines are very important for me, but I can't stick to them if something changes ever so slightly, such as a teacher missing a yoga class and sending a substitute. If that happens, I'll be completely out of the routine, and won't go at all.

I realised how my entire life was a reaction to demands and expectations, using up an intense amount of energy fighting against them. The entire company I'd made was a reaction to being diagnosed with a 'Disorder' and wanting to show that ADHD did indeed work - it wasn't a bad thing.

I'd always thought that I wasn't a very sensorily reactive person, but this conversation showed me that I was the opposite in some ways - which also wasn't 'normal'. I am highly sensitive to noise and people around me, but have zero interest in fashion, and would happily live in pyjamas all of the time. Everything I own at home is in 'teddy' material, such as bedsheets, which previous partners had hated, calling it cheap and tacky, but I couldn't stand the textures of anything else.

This conversation taught me that the experiences I'd had where I'd lost the ability to speak completely were actually a result of 'selective mutism'. It feels like there are no thoughts to say - my mind is just blank, and I can't form any words. This is pretty ironic given that I usually talk non-stop in social situations to avoid the awkwardness of silence. I had no idea how difficult and exhausting I found speaking in general until someone asked me the question - I'd always prefer to write than talk, if possible.

We talked about interests, especially around how I feel about things being left incomplete. I questioned what 'complete' means. I *cannot* leave things that have a pre-defined end point incomplete if I care about them. I try not to watch television and don't have one, because if I like a show, I will have to watch the *entire thing*, even if that means staying up all night.

It was really beautiful to end the conversation about strengths. I wish every single assessment did this, as I believe our greatest strengths are also our greatest weaknesses. For me, so many traits we'd talked about also showed my strengths, such as being able to share my own experiences in my own way that helps others to feel seen and validated. My determination to help others, even if it's at my own expense, is a sign of the kindness that permeates through my being, and this is something I value.

My sheer inability to lie is also a sign of great honesty, authenticity and integrity. I always try to do the right thing, and will quickly admit if I'm wrong, taking personal

Diagnosis

responsibility. I can take complicated structures that don't work, and turn them into something that makes sense - at least, to me. The books I've written over the years seem to make sense to other people too, many of them becoming best-sellers.

Overall, it was one of the most deeply validating, interesting, and affirming experiences I had ever had. I was expecting the complete opposite, if only because of how the diagnostic criteria is set out, but this assessment proved that things can and are done differently. It's just about finding the right people.

Afterwards, I was expecting to feel overwhelmed and upset by talking about how unlikeable and odd I was throughout my life, but I didn't. I felt fine, and more upset about the group weekend away I was about to go on.

I'd have to wait for a few weeks for the outcome of the assessment, which I'd asked to be sent by email before the scheduled follow up call. It arrived after I went to a yoga class, whilst drying my hair, reading, 'we have concluded that you do meet the criteria for autism, so we can confirm that you are autistic.'

I read it and looked at myself in the mirror. I had no idea how I was supposed to react. On the one hand, it just confirmed what I already knew. On the other, I was immensely relieved that I wouldn't have to publicly backtrack and confess that I wasn't actually autistic, having been open about my self-identification. I wasn't sure how to feel beyond that, but recognised that I would be walking out of the gym a different person to the one who walked in.

When I emerged from the changing room, I sat down on a chair in the reception area, too overwhelmed to move. Then, a man came up to me and asked if my name was Leanne. He confirmed that we hadn't met before, but he recognised me as he also worked in the neurodiversity space. When he said he was autistic too, I immediately felt a huge sense of relief and connection. It was the reminder I needed that I wasn't alone.

From that point onwards, I started recognising and honouring my own needs, experiencing burnout from having so many lightbulb realisations. For the first time in my life, I said 'no' to all invitations, writing out this book non-stop. I couldn't stop the thoughts and memories from overwhelming my brain, even whilst asleep, and the only thing that calmed it down was to write.

When I had a follow up call with Autistic Girls to discuss the outcome, I was told repeatedly that I was extremely vulnerable, and needed to make sure I had support in place. I was signposted to an excellent therapist and her support group for late diagnosed autistic women.[157]

Aspects of my autism were explained in full, such as the monotropism, helping me to unravel even more understanding of this part of me it had taken 31 years to meet. It was very helpful and validating to have the context of ADHD also explained to me, in being able to understand how the two conditions interlinked. After the call, I was sent my diagnostic report, which spanned over 80 pages, each diagnostic criteria laid out with mountains of evidence.

After the call, I didn't know what to do. I'd seen people celebrate their diagnosis with cakes online, and given that I had no food in my fridge, ordered myself one along with a meal to eat for dinner. Ironically, the cake didn't arrive - they forgot to send it!

I had no idea who to call, or what to do, and I found it too difficult to pick this book back up - the obsession had simply

---
157   https://www.catherineasta.com/

disappeared. Instead, I wrote an article for *The Telegraph* - one of the more unusual ways of processing my immediate post-diagnostic feelings!

THE AUDHD LENS

Deciding to pro-actively seek out any kind of medical support is an extremely brave, vulnerable, and scary thing to do, especially if it's a decision you've come to by yourself.

This is intensified even further when it comes to autism and/or ADHD, because it most likely means that we've lived for at least some period of time without knowing what these conditions are and how they were affecting us.

For parents and loved ones of AuDHD-ers, who face their own emotional rollercoaster in admitting that someone they care about is struggling, and who may need help they may be unable to provide. From the parents I've coached and trained, I understand that this is an incredibly complex decision, often following lots of self-blame and shame around the 'reasons' for their child's struggles.

Presumably, it feels very overwhelming to be in such a significant position of responsibility. Deciding to seek an assessment or not can be the difference between a child growing up understanding their own brain, or in contrast, feeling 'labelled'. For parents, there's often a huge amount of stigma involved in this process, including having their parenting skills brought into question. It can be very upsetting to realise that your child has been struggling without you even knowing about this, but it's nobody's fault.

Autism and/or ADHD?

As the conditions have separate diagnostic pathways (there is no 'AuDHD' diagnosis), they will usually require separate assessment processes (and waiting lists!).

It can be very stressful to try and dissect your brain into 'and/or' traits of autism and/or ADHD. Someone may experience their symptoms as primarily one or the other condition, but this may also vary between situations such as work and home, and life stages. If you've met one person with AuDHD, you've met one person with AuDHD!

If we're trying to unpick this by ourselves, it can be very overwhelming. We may feel like we don't entirely fit into ADHD or autism entirely, uncertain whether we'd meet the formal diagnostic criteria for either, but experiencing traits of both. This can impact our sense of identity and understanding of an existing diagnosis, causing us to question everything.

Ultimately, this is a personal decision. Personally, I am relieved that I waited until I found an autism assessment provider that was so neuro-affirmative, validating, and thorough, especially as I've heard many negative experiences from others of their autism assessments. It can be very helpful to speak to your doctor about this as a first step, to understand your options.

Self-diagnosis

Seeing a post on social media that describes the experiences you've had but never understood, and have never told anybody about, can feel both validating and vulnerable. I've met countless people who found out they have ADHD from TikTok, which makes sense - these apps understand our brains better than we do.

However, social media algorithms are not the same as a thorough medical assessment. Researching about neurodivergence may feel far more comforting than an assessment, for a number of reasons. Firstly, it's free, in comparison to waiting for years on an NHS waiting list, or paying thousands for a private assessment.

Secondly, social media presents to us our own tailored version of validation around neurodivergence. These platforms are individual echo chambers, where we might be able to learn about things like RSD and PDA, which are common AuDHD experiences, but definitely not in the formal diagnostic criteria!

The explosion in conversations around neurodivergence on social media have elevated the power of lived experience. Individuals sharing their experiences with others helps them to feel as though they're not alone, which leads to further dots being connected, creating a sense of both validation and community.

In contrast, the diagnostic processes are often considered to be lonely, invalidating, and overwhelming. It's well established that criteria for both autism and ADHD is outdated, based on young boys, and as it's based on deficits, individuals may question whether they would fully meet this criteria due to masking.

This is exacerbated by a lifetime of not being believed, especially if we've developed strategies to excel in certain areas. Many extremely successful people in our society are neurodivergent, such as various celebrities, but their struggles aren't presented as part of their shiny external image. To admit that we've been struggling, even to ourselves, is a very difficult thing to do - let alone to strangers who we don't know.

Next, social media provides a far more accessible and constant source of literally limitless information about neurodivergence. This is in contrast to the assessment processes, which is confined to a few conversations with one person, with limited information provided afterwards. It's common to hear of people feeling 'diagnosed and dumped' after their assessment, with very little follow up information or guidance provided.

Finally, social media can feel much safer than a 'formal' assessment, because we can stay in the safety of not knowing. Despite the outdated diagnostic criteria and obvious flaws in the medical system, a formal diagnosis can arguably still feel more validating than reaching this conclusion ourselves - but there's a chance that we might be wrong. To expose our entire lives, including our most embarrassing and vulnerable thoughts, to a stranger who is working on outdated diagnostic criteria, is extremely scary, because *what if we're wrong?*

Even with a formal diagnosis, we may still question this. Instead of questioning whether we are AuDHD, we might be questioning whether we were masking in the assessment, or somehow cheated. We might see the news articles dismissing neurodivergence as a trend, and question whether we simply paid for a diagnosis.

This can be extremely overwhelming, causing people who are already prone to rumination to feel trapped in a vortex of uncertainty, with the goal posts constantly shifting. Unfortunately, this also makes us very vulnerable, especially on the internet where we're at the mercy of algorithms, advertisers, and misinformation.

Ultimately, self-diagnosis is valid. A stranger's opinion about whether you meet their interpretation of certain criteria is just that: one person's opinion. They may have a different opinion to other professionals using the same criteria. The most important person's opinion to trust is your own - if you resonate with autism, ADHD, or anything else, that is valid enough. This is important, because if you can accept this, then you can do something about it.

If you do decide that you want to have an assessment, this is equally valid. Although it can feel extremely scary, and be incredibly expensive, it's also likely to change your life. Although I openly self-identified with autism for several years, having a formal assessment made me feel far more confident in advocating for and meeting my needs - but that is just my experience.

DECIDING TO GET AN ASSESSMENT

As an individual considering seeking an assessment, it's easy to gaslight yourself into thinking that you've made it up, or aren't actually AuDHD.

If you are considering a formal assessment for autism and/or ADHD it can be helpful to consider factors such as:
- How long you have felt like this
- What you'd like to happen or change as a result of the outcome
- What's made you think you are AuDHD, including signs across your lifetime
- What kind of support you might like to access, if you were formally diagnosed (e.g medication)
- What kind of assessment you'd feel most comfortable with (e.g in person / remote)
- Any factors that may be important to you personally (e.g cultural background, gender)
- How much money you have (!) and how long you'd be happy to wait for an assessment
- What changes you can make to your life now (e.g talking to employers to ask for adjustments)
- What support is available now (e.g applying to Access to Work to access funding for coaching)
- Whether you have a diagnosis of any conditions already, and what difference this made to your life
- What fears or concerns you might have around the assessment process, or afterwards

- How you will process the outcome, whether it's autism / ADHD or not
- Whether you know anyone who has also been through an assessment, who could share their experiences and recommendations
- Whether autism or ADHD seems to have a more significant impact on your life (which can help with deciding which diagnosis to seek first, unless you can access both at the same time)
- How your symptoms may manifest across different situations (e.g work vs home)
- Anybody who can support you through this process (e.g family, friends, doctor)
- Areas of your life that may be impacted by a diagnosis (e.g talking to your employer)
- The best and worst case scenarios

If you're considering this for somebody else, you can also apply this to them, talking it through to reach a decision together.

If done correctly, this can be one of the most important decisions you will ever make, so it's worth considering carefully. For AuDHD-ers, who seek predictability and are prone to procrastination, this might take a long time, but there's no rush - you've survived until now, after all!

If you're the parent of a child you suspect has AuDHD, then this can feel equally difficult and overwhelming. It's very understandable to feel anxiety around the prospect of 'labelling' your child, but knowing what conditions they do or do not have can only help you to support them, providing you with information.

This is particularly relevant if someone else has recommended an assessment, such as a teacher, as they may be able to spot symptoms that only manifest in certain environments, such as school. Although it can feel a very vulnerable and stigmatising process, this is about ensuring your child has the best support possible to equip them going forwards.

ACCESSING AN ASSESSMENT

Unfortunately, ADHD and autism assessments are in high demand, with NHS waiting lists spanning several years. As only 'qualified professionals' can make these assessments, a GP referral is usually required.

This may be the first hurdle, depending on your GP, who may make a first decision about whether they feel that you meet the criteria. Unfortunately, there is little oversight of this, and I often hear examples of cases where people have been denied a referral. It can be helpful to take written documentation of your reasons for seeking a diagnosis, including how your symptoms manifest with the official diagnostic criteria of ADHD, autism, or both. They may be able to refer you for NHS assessments for both autism and ADHD, if they agree.

If your GP refuses to make a referral, it may be worth making a complaint and considering a new practice, if you disagree with their decision.

If you're in the UK and your GP does agree to make a referral, you can likely bypass your local waiting time by using your legal 'Right to Choose' the assessor you'd like to work with, if they are contracted to do this through the NHS. For example, ADHD 360 and Psychiatry UK are currently providers of Right to Choose assessments, and as they operate online, their waiting lists are likely to be much shorter than the automatic NHS list your GP may refer you to.

AuDHD: Blooming Differently

Private options

It can be very overwhelming to find a private assessor, with endless options available on Google. Although it might feel tempting to go for the cheapest or fastest option, it's most important to trust the provider as much as possible. If you believe you're AuDHD, finding a neuro-affirmative assessor provider who offers both ADHD and autism assessments is ideal.

For example, Autistic Girls provided me with a free screening call, which in itself was enormously helpful and validating, even if I hadn't have gone ahead with the assessment. Although it can feel painful for an AuDHD brain to break down this process into more stages, with additional opportunities for us to back out and change our minds, I do believe this is a great way to establish whether it's right for you.

In these screening calls, you will typically be asked a series of questions about your reasons for considering an assessment, and told whether the provider recommends that you proceed. This is important, because they may be able to make a quick judgement based on whether they think you have a likelihood of meeting diagnostic criteria or not. This isn't the same as a formal diagnosis, and you may still not meet the criteria through the formal assessment process, but it's at least an opportunity to get to know the provider and understand your options.

I know some people who have had these kinds of calls with providers, which were enough in themselves to accept their own self-diagnosis suspicions. You shouldn't be 'sold' to or pressured to go ahead, especially if you're not comfortable.

This is also a good opportunity to ask questions, such as their ability to prescribe ADHD medication, or what kind of support is available after the decision is made. I was reassured by the conversation I had with Autistic Girls that the process would be worth it even if I wasn't autistic, as Becky, who I spoke to, explained how I would be provided with a full report, linking up their decision with the formal diagnostic criteria. This was really reassuring for me as an autistic person, because I had 'proof' past a simple confirmation.

Pre-assessment

When you book an autism or ADHD assessment, you will typically be sent forms to complete before the assessment itself. These may vary, as there is no 'typical' assessment process, although the NICE Guidelines do make recommendations.

Some providers may use tools such as online quizzes, whereas others may include technical assessments, such as measuring a person's ability to focus whilst playing a computer game. Others may place more emphasis on talking to other people in an individual's life, such as their friends or family. Some may request that people who've known you throughout your life complete some forms to share observations, whereas others be satisfied with a first-person review.

Further evidence such as school reports may be requested, and if you're AuDHD, you may have no idea where these are!

WHAT TO EXPECT FROM AN ASSESSMENT

Although the diagnostic criteria for both ADHD and autism is generally universal, the interpretations and applications of this during an assessment is not. When I sought out my autism assessment, I had already had 3 different ADHD diagnoses, which were all very different.

Before the first assessment, I had no idea that I even had ADHD - I just went to the first psychiatrist I found on Google. This was extortionately expensive, as I had no idea that further conversations would be required, or that I'd have to pay to access medication. I had forms for my friends and family to complete, and I was only provided with written confirmation of my diagnosis after I requested this outright. This consisted of a pretty harrowing letter to my GP, describing my symptoms.

The second was through the NHS, and literally consisted of being asked a checklist of questions by a psychiatrist in person. Within 20 minutes, they confirmed that I had ADHD, and I left.

I didn't even realise that I was being assessed for ADHD the third time around. This was as part of the medication review I'd requested, where I'd been able to avoid my GP's 7 year waiting list by using my Right to Choose. Within a few months, I had a conversation with a psychiatrist at 9pm on a Friday night, on Zoom, which I assumed was a medication review appointment.

I only realised this after being asked extended questions about my childhood and symptoms of ADHD that this didn't feel right, as the medication hadn't even been mentioned. I asked if I was being assessed for ADHD, and was told that this was a mandatory part of the review! I was quite shocked, suddenly questioning whether I would be 'undiagnosed' with ADHD, and have my medication removed. I was told that no decision could be provided until the end, so continued answering the questions, my brain on fire.

Within an hour, it was confirmed that I do indeed have ADHD, and very, very strongly. I was told I'd receive a written report, which came around 2 months later, detailing my symptoms. At the time of writing, I am still on the waiting list for my actual medication review, which has been almost

Diagnosis

10 months in total. Fortunately, I am still able to access my current dose of medication until that point.

So, it's difficult to know what to expect, as your experience will depend on the route and provider that you choose to take. However, it may be helpful to look at the NICE Guidelines for ADHD[158] and autism assessments, which are available for children[159] and adults[160], which set out guidance for medical professionals around diagnosis.

Broadly speaking, both ADHD and autism assessments should involve a qualified medical professional, such as a psychologist or psychiatrist, and a conversation about your history and symptoms. Follow up support will vary between provider, such as a psychiatrist who could prescribe ADHD medication, versus an autism assessor who may be able to signpost to additional support, such as therapy.

Some assessors may provide a decision immediately during the call, whereas others may require further review from colleagues. Ultimately, any assessment should hopefully be person-centred, focusing on you as an individual, instead of the rigid application of diagnostic criteria.

WHAT HAPPENS AFTER AN ASSESSMENT

After an assessment, you will generally be provided with confirmation of whether you do or do not meet the relevant diagnostic criteria. This can be a very overwhelming process, especially because it is ultimately out of our control.

If you are not diagnosed with a condition like ADHD or autism after an assessment, this doesn't necessarily mean

---

[158] Attention deficit hyperactivity disorder: diagnosis and management - NICE Guideline [NG87] - https://www.nice.org.uk/guidance/ng87
[159] Autism spectrum disorder in under 19s: recognition, referral and diagnosis - NICE - Clinical Guideline [CG128] https://www.nice.org.uk/guidance/cg128
[160] Autism spectrum disorder in adults: diagnosis and management - NICE - Clinical Guideline [CG142] https://www.nice.org.uk/guidance/cg142

you don't 'have' it - it just means that this individual doesn't believe that you meet the criteria. You may have traits, but they don't reach this threshold, which doesn't invalidate your experiences (although it might feel that way!).

This can be a stressful experience, especially if you weren't happy with the assessment process. For example, I've often heard from AuDHD-ers that they felt uncomfortable with being asked to do tasks that were obviously designed for children, such as lining up toys. You can always seek a second opinion.

Alternatively, you may be diagnosed with the relevant condition(s) you've been assessed for, which can be very overwhelming. Although it's ideal for practitioners to explain this in detail, allowing space for questions and signposting to support services, this often doesn't happen in practice.

At the very least, a report should be provided, which you can send to your GP to add to your medical records. I recommend arranging an appointment to talk about this with them, and to understand what additional support may be helpful that they could provide, such as therapy.

Regardless of outcome, it's important to have support around you, such as from family, friends, or a professional such as a coach or therapist, who can help you to process it. This is especially important considering the differences in how AuDHD-ers may process emotions.

Although it might feel like just having your suspicions confirmed, being formally diagnosed with a neurodevelopmental condition can feel very overwhelming. Fundamentally, a stranger is providing you with a label. This might feel validating, but also upsetting, because after all, this label does contain the word 'Disorder' - but you are not 'disordered'.

As these conditions are lifelong, you have the rest of your life to process it and decide what to do next. You do *not* need to make any big decisions immediately, such as telling the people you know, announcing it online, or quitting your job! It can be helpful to find a way to process your feelings and thoughts about this in your own way, such as through reading books like this one.

It's very common to feel a range of emotions afterwards, such as grief, loneliness, anger, frustration, and joy. It's equally common to feel overwhelmed at what to do with this information.

If you're diagnosed with ADHD and wish to take medication, then you may be added to another waiting list, or referred to another assessor, for this to be done separately, or it may be issued immediately. You'll then typically enter a period called 'tritiation', where your psychiatrist will maintain oversight for a few months of how you react to the medication, adjusting dosages or types as necessary.

If your GP agrees, you may then be able to transfer to the NHS. It's advisable to check with your GP on their requirements around this before paying any money for an assessment - and to get this in writing, if possible!

Parents

If you have a child who is diagnosed with autism, ADHD, or both, this may understandably trigger feelings of shame and fear. A very common experience I see as a coach is parents who have realised that they are neurodivergent, after seeking support for their children.

This can be confusing, especially if this possibility has never occurred to you before. As there are strong genetic components to AuDHD, it's understandable if you saw your child's behaviour as simply normal, because it might have reflected your own experiences.

At the same time, you may feel overwhelm in knowing how to best support your child. I speak to countless parents who have read my book '*ADHD: an A to Z*', and recommended it to their children, who may not be as interested! If you can, try your best to separate your feelings and experiences from theirs.

Although you may be feeling very worried about their future, please try to remember that this information can only help them. They will have their own experience of processing and navigating neurodivergence, and may not be particularly interested in it at first, which is fine - they have a whole lifetime ahead of them!

Seeking support for yourself as a parent is critical. I have met so many wonderful parents who are desperate for support for their children, but you deserve this support just as much. Having AuDHD coaching yourself can help you to understand how these traits may show up for you, and enable to understand your child.

I tend to tell every parent I speak to the same thing: you **are** a 'good parent'. The fact that you care enough to read this, or even allow the possibility of your child being neurodivergent, is proof alone. It takes a lot of vulnerability to accept that we may need help, but even more so to recognise that someone we love needs help that we may not be able to provide. This isn't your fault, and you have always done the best you could, with the capacity you had available to you at the time.

If your child has been diagnosed as an adult independently, it may feel equally uncomfortable. The same applies: you deserve help as well. It's completely fine to not know what to say or do in response to this, but if you can, simply listening and learning about your child will be enormously helpful. Asking questions, instead of sharing opinions, can open up extremely validating conversations.

Diagnosis

This isn't about you - it's about your loved one. A diagnosis is not a reflection on your parenting abilities, or someone's childhood. It may feel deeply upsetting to learn about difficulties you may not have known about before, but this is not your fault.

Ultimately, an assessment for autism and/or ADHD is an opportunity to learn and grow, not a threat or accusation.

Tips: AuDHD-ers

- If you're considering an autism and/or ADHD assessment, try to establish what you'd like to happen next. Just wanting to know is valid enough!

- Try to notice your own narratives around AuDHD, and your struggles. Instead of blaming yourself, try to treat yourself as you would a child. Self-compassion is far more productive than self-blame!

- Create a document detailing ADHD and/or autism symptoms you recognise in yourself. This can be very helpful if you decide to seek an assessment in the future.

- Remember that medical professionals may not have had specific neurodiversity training, so try to seek out those who use neuro-affirmative language.

- Look for a provider who offers both ADHD and autism assessments. If you have one condition already diagnosed, check with them whether you'd need to have a re-assessment of this to have the other.

- Ask for help from those around you that you trust. Although this can be scary, the people in your life will want to support you as best they can.

- Remember that self-diagnosis is valid, and you absolutely do not have to have a formal assessment. You know your brain better than anybody else.

- Online tests[161] can be extremely helpful to learn more about how your specific traits present, but be careful about who is providing them, especially if you have to pay for any kinds of reports.

- Remember that if you don't fit 'perfectly' with either ADHD or autism, this doesn't necessarily mean that you're not AuDHD. Not every aspect has to resonate with your experience for you to meet the diagnostic criteria.

- If you're concerned about anything involved in the assessment, such as whether you have to ask your family to complete forms, who may remember your experiences differently to you, or provide school reports that you may not have, check with the assessor. They will all have different requirements, and this decision is ultimately up to you.

- The assessment process can be very un-AuDHD-friendly, involving various stages and administration, such as having to complete forms. If you're not sure about anything, ask for help! Having a coach to help you to fill these in can be very helpful.

---

161   https://embrace-autism.com/

- Ask different assessors for more information to learn about their processes. This might be through a call, or email, if that feels more comfortable.

- Try to notice any anxieties, and explain these to the assessor, if possible. They are there to support you, and should be able to make adjustments, such as providing an agenda upfront.

- To prepare for an assessment, try to have support around you, such as a therapist.

- Remember that anybody who assesses you for autism or ADHD who has experience is a medical professional who you can't 'trick' - so don't worry about practicing or masking within the session. They should be able to see through any masks!

- Notice any narratives or fears that you have about autism and/or ADHD, challenging these. It's very normal to feel more positive about one condition than the other, which is largely a reflection of your experiences so far in relation to them, such as your parent's beliefs. Try to make your own judgements.

- Remember that everybody has their own version of this, including the people in your life. If they react negatively to you seeking support, this is a reflection of them - not you.

- If you don't agree with the decision after an assessment, explain your reasoning and ask for more information. If you're still unsure, seek out another opinion, as exhausting as this might be.

- Be as kind to yourself as possible, and remember that you deserve this support. It is not an excuse - it's just an explanation.

Tips: loved ones

- If you suspect your loved one has AuDHD, tread carefully. They will have their own interpretations of what this means to them, and may not react well to conversations about this! You could instead tell them about what you've learned, asking if this resonates with them.

- Model vulnerability and asking for help to your loved one. This could involve seeking an assessment yourself, or talking to them about your own experiences or struggles.

- Notice your own thoughts about AuDHD, and what you think about these conditions. Try to see this from the perspective of your loved one before sharing them!

- Try your best not to make any judgements to your loved one, especially if they tell you that they're seeking an assessment for autism and/or ADHD. Instead, ask them how you can be there for them.

Diagnosis

- If your loved one tells you they think they may be neurodivergent, ask them how you can help, or what they'd like to do next.

- Remember that a diagnosis will impact you too, because it will impact your loved one. Seeking out support for yourself is not selfish, and your feelings are valid.

- Try to notice where your opinions have come from, especially if you have strong emotions about neurodiversity. This may be a reflection of some inner challenges that deserve your attention, such as struggles you've experienced as 'normal'.

- Try to separate your own experiences and thoughts from those of your loved one. Support them to process this in their own way, without expectations.

- Try to avoid labelling neurodiversity as 'good' or 'bad'. Neurodivergence is neutral - we attach the meaning to it, and this will mean something different to everybody.

- Be aware of how you speak about AuDHD or mental health in general, especially around your loved one. Flippant comments or well intentioned advice may be interpreted differently to how they are meant.

- Remember that if your loved one is diagnosed with AuDHD, it is not your fault. You have always done the best you could with the capacity you had available to you at the time.

- Try to remain open and neutral to speaking about past experiences with your loved one. They may have a very different recollection to yours about certain experiences, and it's important not to dismiss this.

- Recognise the bravery and strength it takes for a loved one to consider seeking out an assessment - this is a good thing!

- Offer support in the ways that you are able to. Financially, this will always likely be helpful, given the cost of private assessments, but you can also offer help with paperwork and deadlines.

- If your loved one asks you to complete a form, please don't refuse! Treat this with the seriousness that it deserves, taking your time to answer honestly. You may wish to talk to your loved one about their experiences before completing it, to understand what they need or expect from you. This is likely to be very difficult for them to do.

- Remember that the best thing you can do for your loved one is to be there for them, validating their experiences and accepting them exactly as they are - neurodivergence or not.

13. Acceptance

There is no 'fix' for AuDHD, because you are not broken. This is yet another paradox - all of the work that goes into determining whether you are or are not neurodivergent can feel anti-climatic.

I liken this to when the fish escape the tank at the end of the movie *'Finding Nemo'*. They find themselves in an ocean, in individual plastic bags, asking 'what now?'. This reflects my own experience, but in reality, we are not fictional fishes in a plastic bags, we are human beings.

This means that there's a lifelong journey of acceptance ahead of us. There's no magic moment when we discover that all of our challenges have disappeared. There's no pot of gold at the end of the rainbow, just more rainbow.

This can make the entire process of discovery feel quite pointless, especially to a dopamine seeking brain wanting a 'solution'. However, knowing that your brain works differently means that you can accept yourself as you are, which will make your life a million times better.

ACCEPTING YOUR STRUGGLES

Discovering that you're AuDHD can be very difficult, because it brings into light the challenges that you may have experienced throughout your life. This can be especially complicated if we've already gone through the process for one condition, and having to layer another on top of this can feel invalidating and confusing.

It's important to remember that you are still you. We are all constantly growing and changing - even the cells in our body are replicating themselves as you read these very words. You are not the same person you were 10 years ago, and that's the beautiful thing about life.

However you feel is completely valid, whether you see AuDHD as a positive, negative, or neutral. It's simply part of what makes you who you are. Although it can feel like your entire reality has shifted overnight, you have the rest of your life to figure this out. You will likely find out new information about yourself in the years to come, which is what keeps life interesting, although this can feel very stressful to an AuDHD-er who already struggles with their identity!

It's normal to see AuDHD symptoms become 'worse' after a diagnosis or realisation. This is because we may be more aware of how we've been masking, even to ourselves, often without realising. We may experience burnout and sheer exhaustion from the adrenaline of an assessment process, and processing this. It's important to be kind to yourself and recognise that even if a diagnosis is just confirming what you already know, it will still have an impact on you.

This is especially so if you've been on a waiting list for years! By this point, you probably know a lot about AuDHD, and so it can feel like a 'crash' to finally receive this confirmation.

It can also be very stressful to comprehend your entire life so far, and to try and figure out what this means for you going forward. You do not have to have it all figured out. AuDHD is just an extra piece of the puzzle that makes you who you are, but there will always be good and bad times in life.

Acceptance

I've coached many people who feel hopeless after a diagnosis of autism and/or ADHD. One person described it to me as feeling like a 'prison sentence'. It's normal to struggle with conceptualising the reality of what you may or may not have already known about yourself, especially as we struggle with change!

However, it's important to remember that this is not forever. This is just your experience right now, and it will pass. AuDHD offers you new information about the way your brain works, and there's still so much all of us have to learn about what this means.

You may also discover that you are more 'disabled' than you thought you were. This was certainly the case for me with both ADHD and autism, as I realised that the things I'd taken as 'normal' were actually extremely stressful. I felt a lot of grief about how hard I'd had to work throughout my life, just to survive, and anger that I'd had to figure out why by myself.

The awareness I had of both conditions meant that I was also constantly questioning myself and my experiences. For example, I couldn't tell if I'd always struggled with certain textures and sounds, or whether this was a new thing that I was 'inventing' because of my diagnosis.

Very soon after my autism diagnosis, there were several birthday parties that I was supposed to go to. I found myself simply unable to mask any longer, or to even leave the house. For the very first time in my life, I listened to my body, and didn't go. This felt shameful and embarrassing, as I cried at home by myself for how difficult I'd always found these environments. I was scared that I'd never be able to go to a social gathering again!

However, this also passes. Becoming more aware of our struggles can be confronting and upsetting, but it also gives us more information about our needs. To start accepting these as valid, instead of dismissing them as we may have done previously, is not selfish or mean. It's not selfish to look after yourself - it's kind.

Once we understand what we struggle with, we may give ourselves permission to ask for help. This is likely to be imperfect, especially if we're not used to doing so, but it's simply a skill that we can learn. Trying to tune into discomfort and acting upon this is how we start to build these. Whether you're 17 or 70, nobody is too young or too old to learn how to look after themselves in the ways they have always deserved.

ACCEPTING YOUR STRENGTHS

It may feel just as uncomfortable to accept the strengths of our AuDHD, but this is how we go from surviving, to thriving. Recognising that you cared enough to learn this information about yourself, even if just from this book, is a great start to identifying what to do next.

Trying to notice what you enjoy doing, and what you enjoy, is key to accepting and embracing your strengths. Identifying our values and what we care about as valid 'interests' and 'skills' unlocks our ability to use these to our benefit, instead of hiding them away.

Trusting ourselves is the key to accepting our strengths. When I won the National Specialist Coach of the Year award in January 2025, I stood on a stage and told the crowd how I'd spend the entire day convinced that everybody hated me, with an hour crying in a stairwell, having a meltdown. I recognised that my strengths lie in my vulnerability to admit this, and have never felt so accepted by strangers as I did afterwards.

Instead of shaming yourself for being 'too much', 'not enough', or 'weird', you can start to accept these things as the strengths that make you who you are. Our strengths lie in our differences, not in the way we can fit into the crowd.

There is no magic formula to using your strengths - it's a daily practice of being kind to yourself. It's allowing yourself to try new things, to fail, and to try again. It's about recognising that 'balance' does not exist, because we're just human beings, trying to figure out what we're supposed to be doing with our time here.

It's important to remember that you are not, and never have been, the problem. Your environment is everything - if your surroundings don't support you, then identify what needs to change. Simply accepting that not everything is your fault enables you to take personal responsibility for changing the environment.

Ultimately, accepting your AuDHD strengths comes with defining success on your own terms, instead of what society has conditioned you to believe. It doesn't require you to win awards or publish books, but to simply accept the things that you maybe once hated about yourself as positive, instead of negative.

For me, how I know I've 'arrived' to this place is realising that I don't need to be 'normal'. I don't need to have what society deems to be 'good. I don't need to settle for a life where I don't feel liked as I am, in my full blown AuDHD. This has meant saying goodbye to jobs, relationships, and situations that didn't serve me. It may have taken me 32 years to figure out how to do this, and I'll certainly never be perfect, but I think I'm beginning to trust myself.

ACCEPTING AUDHD

You may have read this book wanting to know how to 'solve' AuDHD, and ultimately, this is about accepting yourself as you are. It's about accepting that your brain will always seek stimulation and chaos, whilst striving for routine and stability.

It's about accepting that there are things that you may find really difficult in life, and that's okay. Your life doesn't need to look like everybody else's. You are allowed to create one that works for you.

The biggest difference that came for me from this entire process was reframing the narrative in my head. Instead of constantly criticising and beating myself up for being me, I started to accept that the things I struggled with weren't my fault - they were simply how my brain was wired.

This didn't mean making excuses not to do anything difficult in life, but accepting my weaknesses along with my strengths to get the right kind of support. One of my biggest 'successes' this year has been to finally overcome the shame of my chaotic, messy flat to hire a regular cleaner.

When we accept AuDHD as an explanation for how we are, instead of an excuse to beat ourselves up, we can start making the changes we need to make to live life on our terms. Just as we can accept the flawed imperfections of the people we love, we can accept our own perfectly imperfect brains. There's certainly never a boring day!

ACCEPTING OTHERS

I couldn't finish this book without recognising the importance of accepting other people as they are. In recent years, there's been a consistent narrative against neurodivergence in our society and media, as the failings of our broken healthcare system have become more apparent.

This has largely involved dismissing neurodivergence as a 'trend', and as people wanting a 'label'. This narratives blames the people seeking support, instead of the systems that have failed them for years. Misinformation about

Acceptance

private assessors of ADHD have resulted in people having their access to medication revoked, which they accessed in line with how they were 'supposed' to.

Articles about disability benefit payments dominate our headlines, without questioning why these people need help. It can feel easier to judge others, rather than recognise the inherent failures in the systems that govern our society. To acknowledge individual's struggles requires us to acknowledge our own, or that we are equally deserving of support.

When I wrote an article for *The Telegraph* about AuDHD, I was perplexed by the stream of negative comments, so I wrote one myself. I asked why these people cared so much, to the extent that they could be bothered to write negative comments on an article about a woman they don't know.

The responses largely indicated that there was a sense of injustice. A feeling of 'us vs them', of 'weak' people who were 'entitled', 'scrounging taxpayer money'. A feeling of neurodivergent children being given an unfair advantage in exams with extra time, as opposed to their children who needed the support too.

This is completely valid, but the anger is aimed at the wrong people, making it pretty pointless. I once spoke to a journalist who told me how her daughter questioned why her friends with ADHD were allowed movement breaks in class, but she wasn't. The woman had to explain that this was because they had ADHD, but the solution is obvious. If something helps one person, then *why not* give it to everybody?

Instead of marking out individuals as needing 'adjustments' to be able to survive in work and school environments, why not change the environment?

Accepting others is absolutely key to accepting ourselves, regardless of how your brain works. When I ran a neuro-affirmative course, the participants all enthusiastically confirmed their confidence in being accepting and inclusive. When I questioned how accepting they were of people who don't agree with them, or of those who are writing these kinds of negative comments in the media, they were less sure.

I believe that this is the only way our society can move forward, especially as it becomes increasingly polarised and divisive. Instead of seeing other people as threats, we can remind ourselves that their perceptions are reflections of themselves. This means accepting that other people will not see the world the same way as we do, and that's okay - we can still co-exist.

Ultimately, we are all neurodiverse. We all think differently from one another, with a different definition of 'normal' shaped by our upbringings, cultures, and socioeconomic factors. People are not 'bad' or 'good', just as neurodivergence is neither a 'disability' nor 'superpower' - we just are who we are.

As an AuDHD-er, it's important to try to practice this acceptance towards others, just as much as towards yourself. Your feelings of anger and frustration are completely justified, but remember that the people, especially those in your life, are simply doing the best they can with the information they have available to them.

It's very normal that accepting yourself, including your own AuDHD will result in discomfort from other people in your life. This is because to prioritise your own wellbeing and knowledge of yourself is uncomfortable, because what does that mean for them?

From my experience, the majority of 'negative' reactions to your own journey of neurodivergence are fear based. It might sound ironic to think about reassuring the people

Acceptance

in your life as an AuDHD-er, but they are likely scared of what this means for them, and you. They cannot know your experiences, because they haven't been inside your brain. Some of these relationships may fall away, and that's okay - we don't have to stay in situations that don't serve us.

Many of these people will be neurodivergent themselves, but they aren't in the position to know that. We cannot make other people accept help, but we can model this difference this makes for them, empowering them to do the same when they're ready in the ways that work for them.

For me, my own AuDHD diagnoses helped me to eventually understand and accept the people in my life who I'd always struggled with for various reasons. I took some space from these relationships, but the more I learned about AuDHD, the more I realised that they were struggling without the luxury of living in a world where more is known about neurodivergence. I accepted that for them, recognising this within themselves would mean that they'd have to look back on their entire lives, which can be very painful to do.

I understood why they did certain things that they did, and that these things weren't about me - they were about them. This helped me to understand and forgive them, accepting that they'd probably never be able see things in the same way as me, but that doesn't make them bad people. Ultimately, this led to me being able to have stronger relationships with them overall, accepting them as they are, instead of how I'd like them to be.

Turning your pain into purpose will empower you to take action. The world needs different ways of thinking, compassion, and human connection more than ever before. Accepting yourself, and understanding your own experiences, perspectives, needs and boundaries, will enable you to do the same for others. Instead of trying to be 'selfless' - to literally not have a self - try to be responsible for your own happiness, and watch how much easier life becomes.

How to help yourself - no matter who you are

- Take your time to process your experiences of AuDHD, recognising that this may be a significant shift in your identity, regardless of whether it's your journey or somebody else's.

- Notice any strong reactions or emotions, and take your time to understand where they come from.

- Identify what you'd like to be different, including what you can control - and what you can't.

- Protect your energy in the ways that you need to, recognising that this is a lifelong learning about what you need and who you are.

- Notice when you hold yourself back from being yourself, and ask yourself what the reasons are for this.

- Identify the environments and relationships that enable you to feel safe as yourself, and those that don't, and make changes accordingly.

- Turn your pain into purpose by identifying broader causes of challenges, and taking action. It only takes one voice to make a difference.

Acceptance

- Recognise that you cannot control or change anybody, as we all have our own autonomy in life.

- Take the time to listen to the people in your life, without simply waiting for your turn to talk, and notice how different it feels.

- Spend your limited time on this planet chasing the things that bring you joy.

Thank you

A huge, gigantic thank you to everybody who has read this book. Thank you to Dr Becky Quicke for giving up her entire weekend to read my writing at short notice, sharing a deeply validating foreword that reminds me that maybe, over-sharing my life could actually help someone.

Thank you to Iona Sinclair, who not only has trained as an AuDHD coach with ADHD Works, but who went above and beyond to help turn this book into reality. This was along with the support of Mayer Brown, Mehreen Malik, and Daniel Fahey, who helped me to feel brave enough to hit 'publish'.

Thank you to Professor Nancy Doyle, who's sharing of the referencing tool Zotero saved me many tears. Thank you to Ella Davis (and everyone at the Book Publicist) for always being so inspirational to work with, cheering me on, and keeping me busy!

Thank you to Jessica Killingley for her brilliant advice, and for sitting in her car to read the book straight on her phone for 2.5 hours. I am really glad it surpassed your expectations!

Thank you to Leah Feltham, who helped me to pause and not publish my first draft the day after I'd wrote it, along with refining my ideas. Thank you to Catherine Asta for very acutely pointing this out back when I was freshly diagnosed - there were things I didn't want to include, after all.

Thank you to Helen Calvert, who reminded me of the importance of just going ahead and publishing it as I am. Thank you to my family, who have always been there, in their own way.

Thank you to my best friend, Josephine McGrail, who has always inspired me with her self-confidence in being an energy healer and wellness coach to remember that I can do anything!

Thank you to my first ever coach, Stephanie, for changing my life and those of so many others'. Thank you to every coach I've been fortunate enough to work with since then. Thank you to those who took a chance on hiring me, seeing things in me that I didn't see in myself at the time.

To the ADHD Works' team, especially Charlie Champion, Sarah Hardy, Gina Cory and Ellie Perkins, a million thank yous for being the best quasi-editor group and general superstar team that any author could wish for. Ellie, thank you for a book cover that sums up the 53992020 sunflower images I sent you on Pinterest.

Thank you to my wonderful clients, who I have been so incredibly lucky to coach and train over the years. It is a real honour, joy and privilege to be able to hopefully help you to see how brilliant you already are.

To the many people who have shown me kindness over the years, thank you. You may not have even noticed how much little things like joining my Scrabble game at the Christmas party meant, but they really helped.

To the people who have been less so, as Taylor Swift says, 'there wouldn't be this if there hadn't been you', so thank you too.

Resources & Recommendations

The resources chapters at the end of books are often pretty generic, so I wanted to make some personal recommendations - although I don't take any liability for services provided! Please make sure to do your own research before engaging with any of my recommendations, and ultimately, trust your intuition.

WHO'S HELPED ME
1. Coaches
It feels important to add here that many of the below coaches have zero 'training' or 'qualifications', and that's what was so brilliant about them! They worked in the ways that worked for my brain, and I found them exactly when I needed them.

- **Stephanie Camilleri** - the ADHD Advocate - my first ADHD coach! Stephanie has a legal background.
- **Josephine McGrail** - Josephine McGrail - my best friend, energy healer, wellness coach, yoga teacher, retreat facilitator, and all around incredible human being. Josie works with both children and adults, changing lives with her holistic and irreplaceable magical energy.

- **Jacqueline McCullough** - We Make Space - Jackie coached me on everything from setting up ADHD Works to finding somewhere to live, with her magic Notion Operating System framework.
- **Kat Sorbello** - the Stella Way - Kat helped me to *actually finish* creating and launching online courses, after years of procrastination. The best investment I have ever made!
- **Ari Scott** - the ADHD Entrepreneur - I woke up at 6am to have coaching with Australian-based Ari, and it was so worth it! Ari helped me to overcome my RSD related to sales and making any kind of money for my work.
- **Georgia Fitzgerald** - Lead Brave - Georgia coached me on creating the ADHD coaching course, overcoming my RSD about it being 'different' from 'normal' training, and has been instrumental in helping me to hire the right team.
- **Tanisha Cro** - Tanisha Cro - who was enormously helpful as a finance coach in helping me to go from a million bank accounts to.. a few!
- **Jane Tarrant** - Link Breathing - Jane helped me to learn how to breathe properly, which was very useful during the stress that running ADHD Works has involved!
- **Sam Bramwell** - the ADHD Leader - Sam not only first invited me to speak at Microsoft all those years ago, she's also coached me on leadership and management (as an ADHD Works trained coach!).
- **Saskia Mardi** - the Business Minimalist - Bali based, Saskia has been instrumental in helping to build a functioning back-end for ADHD Works as a ClickUp magician.
- **Helen Calvert** - Happier Life - Helen has provided incredibly helpful autism coaching during my post-diagnostic search for help. I came across her speaking

Resources & Recommendations

in an event and begged her to step outside of her life coaching arena to help me - and she did!

2. Therapists

Therapists have been a bit more of a 'mixed bag' than coaches, ironically - although I have had a LOT! However, I have a few recommendations who have been absolutely incredible (probably due to embracing their own neurodivergence!):

- **Catherine Asta** - Catherine Asta - Catherine has been by far the best therapist I have ever worked with, with such a deep sense of integrity, wisdom and boundaries that it's been transformative.
- Catherine also runs a '**Late Discovered**' support group for autistic women, which I found to be a lifeline after my diagnosis.
- **Kazzy Whiting** - Too Much Therapy - after years working in the NHS, Kaz runs the most incredible 'alternative' and accessible therapy, which are tailored for neurodivergent people.
- **Angela Cox** - Paseda360 - I only discovered Angela after hearing her speak at the National Coaching Awards (where I was very surprised to be given an award!), but as a therapist and coach with literally endless qualifications, she's doing amazing work at providing an integrated, blended, and creative approach for her clients.

3. Other professionals

I have worked with a *lot* of people as an AuDHD founder, and these are the best of the best (in my opinion!).

First off, those who work very closely with ADHD Works day-to-day, that I would please ask you to avoid luring away, because I need them to function:

- **Ellie Perkins** - Write and Sunny - Ellie has a magical ability to turn my chaos into clarity, which she does on our ADHD Works website, social media channels, presentations, logos, and even the cover of this book!
- **Charlie Champion** - ADHD Works - Charlie is our magnificent Client Manager, who has one of the most unique and brilliant minds of anyone I've ever met. She sees solutions and strategies in a way that blow me away on a daily basis!
- **Sarah Hardy** - SJ Hardy - Sarah is not only an ADHD Works trained coach herself, who's worked with many of our clients, but has been a crucial 'support worker' / virtual assistant in helping me to manage the chaos of my life.
- **Gina Cory** - Gina Cory VA - is a technological genius, and can do the tasks that I simply couldn't do because of my AuDHD, even if I underwent intensive training for months, including everything numbers and tech related.

Here's everybody else I'd recommend:

- **The Orenda Collective** - after many tried-and-failed accountants, this is the first accountant that has genuinely been neuro-affirmative, and as detailed as my autistic brain needs them to be!
- **Sam Walkley** - XVO Legal - the very definition of a neuro-affirmative lawyer, helping with everything contract (and stress!) related. He has been a true life-saver, and I highly suggest the rest of the legal industry follow his practices, such as offering fixed fees in advance of work!
- **Tom Haines** - InHouse It Legal Solutions - an *incredibly*

Resources & Recommendations

neuro-affirmative employment lawyer, helping *so many* neurodivergent people navigating discrimination issues at work. I'm very grateful that I can recommend everybody to him instead of trying to take this on myself!
- **Beth Lewis** - the Virtual Assisters - an incredible, mind-reading VA, who now runs her own VA company with her sister (hence the name!).
- **Victoria Nabarro** - Veda Wealth - the most neuro-affirmative financial advisor I could have found, who's focused on empowering women and makes navigating finances AuDHD-friendly!
- **The Book Publicist** - Ella and her team have been responsible for me being on everything from *Lorraine* to the cover of *The Times*. They are an exceptionally neuro-affirmative, brilliant group of people who are truly excellent at their work.
- **Jessica Killingley** - a brilliantly neuro-affirmative, passionate, and integrity-driven book agent, who I recommend everybody to!
- **Danny Lyle** - who type-set and format this very book, along with *ADHD Works at Work* - he's fantastic, and was very patient with my multiple versions of manuscripts and edits I sent across!
- **Beth Huntingdon** - Daisy Bloom - a fantastic ADHD coach and supervisor, who supervised multiple coaches at ADHD Works for over a year, helping me (and everybody else!) to manage the chaos.

4. Mentors and experts

This is the 'miscellaneous' part, for all of the many wonderful people who have helped me with advice and conversations along the way, that they probably don't even know shaped my journey so much.

- **Caroline Bielanska** - as a solicitor, trainer and author, Caroline helped kick-start my journey by giving me advice I didn't want to hear. She is one of the most passionate and determined women I've ever met.
- **Polly Sweeney** - Rook Irwin Sweeney Partner — as a public and human rights solicitor, Polly was an inspiration to me in leading the way as a lawyer genuinely helping others and 'doing good', especially in setting up her own company to do this.
- **Steve Peralta** - Unmind Co-Founder - after very fortunately *not* hiring me as a Content Creator, Steve very kindly mentored me as one of the most incredible, wise and inspiring people I've ever met. He went from being a coach himself to running a technology company helping millions of people.
- **Stef Sword-Williams** - not only did her excellent book, 'F*ck Being Humble', help me to stop living in RSD-land, her workshops and resources genuinely helped me to start ADHD Works. She also told me to go for ADHD Works instead of 'the Attention Coach'!
- **Ronni Douglas** - my biggest inspiration, as cheesy as this may sound! She encouraged me to finish writing '*the Model Manifesto*' and changed my life.
- **Sean Nesbitt** - Taylor Wessing - who provided much-needed support at one of the hardest times of my life.
- **Lucy Hendley** - Lewis Silkin - who shocked me by taking me out for lunch when I said I was becoming an ADHD coach, and has been an incredible support and all round inspiration.
- **Ellie Middleton** - a powerhouse inspirer of thousands

Resources & Recommendations

of people through her online content, Ellie also wrote the foreword for '*ADHD: an A to Z*' and went on to train in our first ever cohort of ADHD coaches! It was through Ellie that I understood I was also autistic.

- **Simon La Fosse** - not only has Simon has been invaluable in providing support and inspiration of how to run a company 'right', his company, La Fosse, was the first that hired me to do public speaking in person. This meant I got over my own limiting belief and fear, going on to talk at companies like Disney and Google!
- **Asad Raffi** - Sanctum Healthcare - Asad is genuinely passionate and ethical in his family-run psychiatrist practice, and assessed someone pro-bono who was fundraising to pay for her ADHD assessment.
- **An Nguyễn** - Founder, Practice Works - he's has provided immeasurable support through mentoring me over the years, and may be the most intelligent person I've ever met.
- **Anne-Marie Huby** - as the Co-Founder of JustGiving, Anne-Marie inspired me in ways I can't even describe, but maybe above all, the principle of 'profit-for-good'.
- **Marcus** - Body London - in addition to running quite literally the only modelling agency I'd ever work with, he's also offered me endless mentoring and support for hours on end, helping me to run ADHD Works like 'a real business'!
- **Lea Turner** - the HOLT - her self-paced course on LinkedIn made me realise it was possible to create courses, I just needed ones that worked for my brain! She's been a huge inspiration in showing up authentically online, and now runs a community for entrepreneurs.

- **Phil Anderton** - ADHD360 - Phil goes above and beyond for the ADHD-ers his company supports, going the extra mile to provide much-needed education amidst the ADHD medication shortage.
- **Alex Merry** - MicDrop - his online public speaking community helped me to overcome my own fears around this, and to actually charge money! This inspired me to set up an online community for our ADHD Works coaches.
- **Professor Nancy Doyle** - Founder of Genius Within - I was very scared of Nancy (due to an endless list of impressive accomplishments!), but when I was struggling one day, I asked for a mentoring conversation. Nancy not only provided me with invaluable support, but also shared the excellent book on leadership she was writing at the time, which helped me to learn about 'hyperlexia'. She is a true role model.
- **Lisette Schipper** - Neurodiversity Advocacy Lead at Google - who wrote a beautiful foreword for '*ADHD Works at Work*' and has driven a neuro-affirmative culture at one of the biggest companies in the world.
- **Chimen Chauhan** - Disney - who made my wildest Disney dreams come true (literally!), believed in ADHD Works, and spear-headed our ADHD Champions programme.
- **Sarah Templeton** - Headstuff ADHD Therapy - not only one of the most infectiously passionate people I've met, Sarah also reached out with compassion when I was being trolled online to invite me to a meet-up of coaches, helping me to see that there was kindness in the world!
- **Elizabeth Gilbert** - whose kindness when I met her at the 'right time, right place' enabled me to see hope and connection through the darkness.

Resources & Recommendations

- **Samantha Hiew** - Sam was one of the first people to read the *ADHD: an A to Z* manuscript, inspiring me to publish it. I also was quite jealous of her when she launched her company speaking about ADHD, which helped me to see that I needed to quit my law job!
- **Becky Quicke** - <u>Autistic Girls</u> - in providing an environment where I was able to access a neuro-affirmative autism assessment, endless support, and writing the foreword for this book!
- **Harriet Richardson** - <u>Hat.Talks</u> - by sharing content online as an AuDHD assessor herself, she helped me to see that an autism assessment tailored to my brain *was* possible, and redefined how I see assessments after the incredible support she gave me through Autistic Girls.
- **Iona Sinclair** - a brilliant ADHD coach and legal eagle, Iona did an incredible job of proof reading my first (very messy!) draft of this book, which helped enormously when I edited it. She went above and beyond to help me.
- **Mehreen Malik**, **Daniel Fahey** and **Mayer Brown** - whose incredible legal support made me feel brave enough to publish this book - a million thank yous, and I will be forever grateful.
- My dad - who has read all of my books without question or complaint, proof-reading and referencing for me when my brain had simply given up. Thank you!

I'm sure I've forgotten some people (AuDHD!), but these are some good eggs in my book - thank you so much to everybody who's helped along the way.

WHAT'S HELPED ME
1. Books
As a hyperlexic, I hope you're prepared for a *long* list!

- **Catherine Asta - 'Rediscovered: A Compassionate and Courageous Guide For Late Discovered Autistic Women (and Their Allies)'** - one of the most neuro-affirming books I've ever read.
- **Pierre Novellie - 'Why Can't I Just Enjoy Things?: A Comedian's Guide to Autism'** - honestly the best book on autism I've ever read, that made me feel so validated that I decided to go for the assessment.
- **Ellie Middleton - 'Unmasked' and 'How To Be You'** - leading books on making autism and ADHD work for you, which have changed countless lives, as I hear about from others on a daily basis!
- **Emily Katy - 'Girl Unmasked'** - I genuinely *could not put this book down* once I started it, and Emily's bravery in sharing her story so honestly inspired me to do the same in this book.
- **Charli Clement - 'All Tangled up in Autism and Chronic Illness'** - an *extremely* important book untangling the intersection of autism and chronic health conditions to be simple, the first of its kind - and written by one of the most inspiring power-houses I've ever met!
- **Alex Partridge - 'Now It All Makes Sense'** - an incredibly generous book sharing the remarkable Alex's ADHD journey, and his learnings from experts from his podcast, *ADHD Chatter*.
- **Carly Jones - 'Safeguarding Autistic Girls: Strategies for Professionals'** - a very much needed book for every autistic girl, and those who care about them.

Resources & Recommendations

- **Elizabeth Gilbert** - '**Big Magic: Creative Living Beyond Fear**' - my all time favourite book, which inspired me to start writing my own.
- **Frances Akinde** - '**Be an Ally, not a Bystander: Allyship lessons for 7-12 year olds**' - a very important book changing the mindset of future generations, empowering connection over division.
- **Pete Wharmby** - '**Untypical: How the world isn't built for autistic people and what we should all do about it**' - a groundbreaking book for autists that helped me to understand and accept my brain.
- **Nancy Doyle** - '**Neurodiversity Coaching**' and '**Learning from Neurodivergent Leaders**' - two of the best books I've read on these topics, which changed how I work.
- **Devon Price** - '**Unmasking Autism**' - an excellent book which I devoured in one sitting, and have returned to repeatedly.
- **Gabor Mate** - '**The Myth of Normal**' (and all of his books!) - everything Mate writes is so eloquent, helpful, and insightful into minds that work differently.
- **Amanda Kirby** and **Theo Smith** - '**Neurodiversity at Work**' - an amazingly knowledgable and accessible book that helped me to understand my own brain in workplace contexts.
- **Beverley Engel** - '**The Nice Girl Syndrome**' - finding this by chance was a turning point in my life, as it taught me how to start standing up for myself.
- **Edward Hallowell** and **John Ratey** - '**ADHD 2.0**' - quite simply, an excellent bible on ADHD.
- **Barbara Sher** - '**I Could Do Anything If Only I Knew What It Was**' - the first book I read that made me feel 'seen' and understood in the maelstrom of trying to figure out my 'purpose'.

337

- **Jess Baker** and **Rod Vincent** - '**The Super Helper Syndrome**' - this completely changed my own coaching approach, in addition to helping me navigate compassion fatigue and burnout.
- **Steve Chandler** - '**The Prosperous Coach**' - the book that helped me overcome my RSD about charging for helping people and 'doing good'.
- **Steven Bartlett** - '**The Diary of a CEO: The 33 Laws of Business and Life**' - the book that helped me to understand how to run ADHD Works, instead of be run by it!
- **Sarah Wilson** - '**First, We Make The Beast Beautiful**' - the book that made me realise anxiety was ruining my life, and how to stop this from happening (at least, all of the time!).
- **Stephanie Foo** - '**What My Bones Know: A Memoir of Healing from Complex Trauma**' - an incredibly helpful and important book on navigating C-PTSD that made me feel seen.
- **Pete Walker** - '**Complex PTSD: From Surviving to Thriving**' - the first book I read that made me understand that I experienced C-PTSD, helping me to feel much less alone in the world.
- **Helen Calvert** - '**The No Bullsh*t Guide To A Happier Life**' - this book summarises the way I see the world, especially in terms of business!
- **Glennon Doyle** - '**Untamed: Stop Pleasing, Start Living**' - a book that redefined how I saw the concepts of 'selflessness' and 'selfish'.
- **Elizabeth Gilbert** - '**Eat Pray Love**' - a book that saved my life by helping me to realise that the only thing I needed to do was eat chocolate almond croissants and enjoy it.

Resources & Recommendations

2. Podcasts

There's so many fantastic podcasts on neurodiversity that are all well worth listening to. Here's some of my favourites:

- **ADHD Chatter** - **Alex Partridge** - one of the most highly respected and listened to podcasts on ADHD, Alex has used his platform to make millions of people feel heard and seen.
- **ADHD Untangled** - **Rosie Turner** - ADHD Coach Rosie is infectiously passionate and enthusiastic, which helps listeners of her excellent podcast feel uplifted and empowered.
- **The Hidden 20%** - **Ben Branson** - an incredibly powerful podcast that features neurodivergent experts, helping to show the power of neuro-inclusion.
- **The ADHD Women's Wellbeing Podcast** - **Kate Moryoussef** - a wealth of much-needed information for ADHD women on everything from hormones to hypermobility.
- **No Bullsh*t Talks** - Sabrina Chevannes is one of the most intelligent people I've ever met (a *literal* chess master), who interviews entrepreneurs to make education accessible and interesting.
- **ADHDAF** - **Laura Mears-Reynolds** - this excellent podcast is also a real-life community, with live events and endless relatability.
- **Mad About Money** - **Maddy Alexander-Grout** - a very important podcast talking about finances and ADHD, with no-filter and no-nonsense.
- '**Yes, Black women have ADHD too and need your attention!**' - Abigail Agyei TedX - technically not a podcast, but one of the most important talks I've ever heard that everybody should listen to.

- **Skip The Small Talk with Ellie Middleton** - the perfect podcast for whizzy brains, Ellie shares her wisdom in accessible, yet highly knowledgeable, AuDHD-friendly shorter episode formats.
- **Late Bloomers** - by Richard and Roxanne Pink (who also have a great book and app) - this is a great podcast to see inside the reality of neurodivergent relationships.
- **It's Just AuDHD** - **John Blanco-Slingerland** and **Tarah Peltz** - our US based ADHD Works trained coach Tara and John do an incredible job of bringing neuroscience and accessibility together in this podcast.
- **All Aboard ADHD** - **Claire Quigley Ward** - ADHD Works trained coach Claire runs an excellent podcast for parents and caregivers of children with ADHD.
- **Diary of a CEO** - Steven Bartlett - technically not a neurodiversity podcast, and some episodes I don't agree with, but overall, probably one of my favourites to exist.

3. Miscellaneous

Here's some random bits that have helped me, that don't really fit into one category:

- Long songs, specifically '**All Too Well**' by Taylor Swift (10 min version), '**Defying Gravity**' by Cynthia Erivo ft Ariana Grande, and '**Burgs**' by Mt. Wolf. It's very helpful to put them on to motivate myself to do something for a limited period of time, such as cleaning!
- The 'ADHD chair' from **Pipersong** - expensive, but incredibly useful as a spinning chair to handle my endless changing of position whilst sitting at my laptop.
- A **tabletop dishwasher** - honestly, the best money I have ever spent - in addition to on a cleaner, who is my favourite human being to exist (shout out to Magda!).

Resources & Recommendations

- **Apple AirPods** - these were so game changing that when I lost them 2 days after buying them, I immediately bought some more (ADHD tax!). They have honestly saved me during periods of noisy neighbours and construction.
- **Oura Ring** - I was quite against jewellery, as I inevitably lose it all, but I've managed to keep the Oura Ring for a good few months so far. As it tracks data like sleep and stress, it's incredibly useful to be reminded of how unhealthy I am, and genuinely motivates me to do something about it.
- **ClickUp**, **Wispform** and **Notion** - these have been incredibly powerful platforms, hosting my endless ideas and helping me to turn them into action.
- **ChatGPT** - my emotional support technological virtual buddy, who helps me do everything from draft emails to understanding if I am overreacting.
- **Dubbii** - I don't really believe in ADHD apps (given our tendency to move on quickly!) but this one was created by Rich & Rox of @adhd_love_ and is AMAZING. Its a body doubling app, breaking down tasks from showering to making the bed with step-by-step instructions.
- **Weighted Blanket** - this honestly changed my life, meeting all of my sensory needs in a gigantic hug - basically all of the time.
- **Electric Blanket** - as someone who is always cold, this has helped me to unfreeze and experience immense joy!
- **SHOUT charity** - who have saved my life on more than one occasion with their text helpline for people experiencing suicidal thoughts (text 85258).

CHARITIES
- **Autistic Girls Network** - who ADHD Works donates to regularly, as they do extremely important work and make clear where the money goes on their website.
- **ADHD charities**, such as ADHD UK and ADHD Foundation
- **Autism charities**, such as the National Autistic Society and Autistica
- **Mental health charities**, such as SHOUT, Mind, and the Samaritans
- **Domestic violence charities**, such as Refuge and Women's Aid

ADHD WORKS COACHES
This one is a special shoutout to the coaches currently listed on our directory at the time of writing this book[1], separated by expertise (in my opinion!). I'll update it when our first AuDHD Coaches have graduated!

Body Doubling
- Ed Taylor - with a background in safeguarding, Ed combines coaching and body doubling to help people 'do what they know'.

Burnout
- Michelle Hurst - who after having built a successful career in managerial positions, experienced burnout and is passionate about supporting others in similar positions.
- Ellie Starkwood - who supports ADHD mums through returning to work, having experienced complete burnout herself.

---

1 February 2024 - coaches are listed on our website following passing their assessment, and then if they choose to renew after a year.

Resources & Recommendations

- James Stephenson - after being diagnosed with ADHD whilst recovering from corporate burnout from 15 years in a director role in a finance industry, James now helps others to do the same.

Children
- Justine Graham - specialises in working with teenagers
- Alice Stern - with an MSc in Child Development and holistic coaching style as an origami and sushi artist!
- Emily Keating-Bell - who was a primary school teacher before training as an ADHD coach
- Aisling Demaison - based in France, Aisling is a school counsellor and youth development specialist, with expertise in youth resilience

Celebrant, Bereavement & Grief
- Rebecca Stone - a past In House ADHD Works Coach, Rebecca has expertise in health and management, but especially unique is that she's also a practicing Civil Celebrant, supporting people navigating grief and bereavement.

Chronic Pain / Illness
- Abigail De Munnik-Geerads - who also speaks Dutch, and lives with chronic illness
- Laura Jones - perinatal peer support who is AuDHD and has a chronic pain condition
- Tracey Lomax - who has been living with chronic pain for over 10 years, including EDS, POTS, MCAS and a mix of MSK diseases. Tracey is also AuDHD, Dyslexic, and has PDA, Dyspraxia, and Sensory Processing Disorder.

Creative
- Fran Hughes - experience of self-employment as a Creative Retoucher, with a new hobby each year
- Emma De Nege - a Graphic Designer and Creative Artwork
- Ivan Pope - a writer, artist and entrepreneur who specialises in coaching creatives
- Jack Lloyd - a photographer and writer, specialising in ares including dating and relationships
- Lana Granley - a documentary filmmaker for streamers like Netflix, with a background in psychology
- Sian Parker - with years of experience as a photographer, sound operator and head of production, Sian has extensive knowledge of the creative industries.
- Chris Sayburn - a Pastoral Lead in the church, and a Christian songwriter/producer.
- Gillian Johnson - writer, editor and illustrator
- Tricia Salt - an artist and creative project worker based in Cornwall
- Emma Wright - freelance product designer with extensive experience in companies such as Sky
- Angeline Newman - who also has a custom laser engraving business (and blue hair!)
- Anna-M Weber - photographer, writer, and creative based in Germany.

Diversity, Equity and Inclusion
- Em Roberts - who has a focus on teams, inclusion, and business growth as a strategist
- Jamie Conway - EDI Manager in the NHS, with extensive experience in working with public bodies such as the emergency services.
- Hel Straker - a neuroinclusion coach and trainer with extensive experience in talent strategy

Resources & Recommendations

- Jennifer Griffiths - who runs a company advising organisations on neurodiversity inclusion initiatives and collaborating with HR teams, also assessing needs.

Education
- Holly Bristow - who has a specialism in SEN education, as a co-headteacher.
- Malea Stanton - SEND Learning Assistant and previous professional volleyball player
- Lilli Landau - a professional tutor, with an extensive background in teaching
- Llinos Williams - a highly experienced SEND teacher and Master's Student in autism and neurodiversity
- Caitlin Whitmore - who's a qualified maths teacher and psychological researcher
- Emily Sinclair - English teacher and PhD candidate
- Kristen Nairn - a teacher who works with neurodivergent children / teens, teachers, and parents
- Jan Hanson - neurodivergent AuDHD tutor with additional expertise in dyslexia
- Charlie Kiley - an AuDHD student inclusion and engagement specialist
- Ria Taher - with a 15 year career supporting children and young people, specialising in SEND and mental health.
- Dave Bedford - with a background in engineering, David is autistic and ADHD, raising awareness in schools and the community

Emergency services
- Mimi El Azizi - an ex-Metropolitan police officer specialising in coaching employees of the emergency services and armed forced.

AuDHD: Blooming Differently

Entrepreneurship
- Ellie Kay - founder of million pound recruitment businesses
- Jay Lefevre - who is not only an entrepreneur, but also a hairdresser!
- Beth Errington - a self-employed farmer based in Scotland, with a passion for the outdoors
- Cameron Marrett - Amsterdam based Cameron specialises in supporting entrepreneurs and high performers, coming from a trading background.
- Julia Crawford - an 'on-demand' HR Director coaching tech business owners
- Pablo Cifuentes - with a background in e-commerce, Pablo has created a leading marketplace for beauty and wellness services on demand in all of the Spanish speaking countries.
- Kirstin Stevens - an exited founder of an online school for neurodivergent children, with a background in teaching and a passion for AI and education innovation. Kirstin was part of our first ever cohort of ADHD coaches, and joined us on the first ever ADHD retreat!

Exercise and Fitness
- Peter Mullin - an expert in cycling mechanics, with a background as a Sports Advisor.
- Jess Lindo - a qualified personal trainer, nutritionist, and menopause coach in training.
- Beccy Rogers - who takes a holistic approach to coaching, incorporating cold water approaches, yoga and breath work
- Kathryn Williams - a fitness and nutrition coach for women 40 years+
- Sue Mahoney D'Eye - a founder of London based dance studios.

Resources & Recommendations

Health and Nutrition

- Emily Fawell - a practising Nutritional Therapist with 15 years of experience
- Jo Berry - Paediatric Dietician with NHS experience and a passion for diversity and inclusion
- Emma Ward - currently an exclusive ADHD Works In House Coach, Emma has decades of experience coaching people on diet and health, with a holistic approach
- Heather Withers - a nutrition coach focused on holistic health
- Katie Stibbs - with a background of hypnotherapy and mindfulness
- Sheena Skinner - who runs events and retreats, with a focus on natural wellbeing, incorporating healing and yoga
- Nicky Wilson - with years of experience in coaching people on wellness and health

HR and People

- Ben Emmett - ADHD-er with a wealth of experience in HR
- Bisayo Erikitola - with an impressive career at PwC and as a People Development Specialist
- Maria Rogers - HR consultant with years of experience, who now runs her own business
- Sarah Barkwill - women's business coach and HR consultant
- Karen Otton - a chartered HR professional with extensive experience in people strategy and HR
- Louise Kennedy - Managing Director of a HR management company, with an extensive background in learning and development.

AuDHD: Blooming Differently

- Jean-François Forgeot d'Arc - based in Spain, Jean-Francois has over 25 years of international experience in HR.
- Olivia Streatfield - with a background as a lawyer, before moving into marketing and circulation in the media industry.
- Victoria Lovatt-Smith - a Director of People in the non-profit sector, who also teaches yoga and bodywork
- Meryl Bengtsson - with decades of experience as a HR Director, Meryl now helps other businesses to make neurodiversity work at work.

Imposter Syndrome
- Cym Glasheen - US based Gym is a ray of sunshine who helps people to overcome imposter syndrome and was part of our first ever cohort of ADHD coaches!

Intersectionality / Identity
- Dhruti Patel - passionate about unravelling the impacts of neurodiversity as a South Asian woman
- Winnie Wong - born and raised in Singapore, Winnie brings an Asian Chinese perspective to ADHD, tackling the pressures of high-achievement cultures (and is Singapore's first Modern Kitsungi artist!)
- Amelia Harris - a neurodivergent black woman with a passion to advocate for diversity, equity, and inclusion, with lived experience of dyslexia and ADHD
- Beaux Miebach - Inclusion & Belonging Lead based in Denmark (previously a pastry chef!) - queer, trans, AuDHD and white.
- Carine Jonchere Ponin - with a logistics consultancy background working for companies such as Google and

Resources & Recommendations

the Department of Health and Social Care, with LBGQTI+ expertise

Law
- Iona Sinclair - a lawyer and head of learning and development at leading US law firm Mayer Brown, who's successfully taken her local authority to the SEND tribunal twice
- Paul Mosson - currently an ADHD Works exclusive In House coach with decades of experience in senior leadership in the legal industry
- Lisa Lawrence - who has years of experience in leadership recruitment roles at Amazon and a former lawyer.

Leadership
- Alison Traboulsi - with 20 years of experience in marketing and leading cross-functional teams
- Joe Elliott - with an impressive corporate background leading commercial teams at global organisations, also providing training.
- Tony Clark - who became an ADHD coach after retiring from a 38 year corporate career in the medical industry
- Yasmin Wills - with over 15 years as a senior leader, and significant experience in the NHS.
- Jonathan Barker - Dublin based Deputy CEO and Commercial Director at Sunshine 106.8, and self-described 'consistent over-achiever'
- Kay Johnson - Human Resources Director with decades of experience, specialising in ADHD for women in business.
- Clare Yelland - Managing Director of a PR and marketing agency within the construction industry, having previously worked at Google.

AuDHD: Blooming Differently

- Gary Hammond - based in Spain, Gary has extensive experience in Directorship roles within the tech sector, also offering business training
- Jane James - with vast experience of directorship roles, Jane's also passed our Neuro-Affirmative certification programme, supporting businesses to thrive with neuro-inclusion.
- John Massey - who has a daughter with ADHD, and decades of successful experience as a founder and director in the finance industry.
- Sarah Croxford - a leader at Microsoft, Public Governor of Berkshire NHS Foundation Trust, and Trustee of Parenting Special Children
- Clare McHatton - UK Sales Director at IRB with expertise in market research and business development
- Sam Bramwell - with 25 years of leadership in the global tech industry, including Microsoft, Sam even has written a book on ADHD leadership coming out soon!
- Simon Walter - after a 22 year executive career at Deutsche Bank, Simon transitioned to coaching leaders. He trained with us after finding himself as a crossroads when approached to coach a client with ADHD.

Management
- Sarah Castor-Perry - with a successful career as a Senior Manager at companies such as PwC
- Melanie Carr - who's had decades of experience as a manager (and studied jazz flute!)
- Sarah Ode - leadership and management specialist with 20 years of experience in learning and development
- Rowan Ahmadi-Nameghi - with a background in senior communications roles, Ro has expertise in management and ADHD, building genuine inclusion.

Resources & Recommendations

Marketing, PR and Events
- Fran Droege - my ex-flatmate, who helped me to navigate ADHD, but also a marketing expert with a wealth of experience in the creative industries.
- Rhiannon Bloomfield - Australia based, with additional qualifications in Applied Neuroscience and decades of experience in creative industries.
- Dasha Zumwalt - with an impressive career as an event producer, organising large-scale events
- Laurence Heine - Germany based, with a wealth of experience in marketing, communications and events
- Laura Scott - a marketer with expertise in copywriting and content creation
- Paula Simcoe - with experience in marketing within the technology sector for over two decades.
- Siobhan Brady - Product Marketing Manager and previous In House ADHD Works Coach
- Jess Percival - a senior communications and content executive

Medical Expertise
- Maria Khan - a Physician Associate in the adult ADHD NHS service
- Anne Gledhill - a registered midwife, nurse, and acupuncturist, with specialism in fertility
- Carrie Rochford - an advanced nurse practitioner and ex-RAF nurse, with over 18 years of experience.
- Nikki Read - neurodevelopment practitioner certified to undertake autism assessments
- Rachel Timmoney - with extensive experience in nursing as a Health Visitor in the NHS (and a passion for organising travel!)
- Fleur Poynts - ADHD Practitioner in the NHS

- Gabriel Kelly – psychiatric mental health nurse practitioner student based in the US

Hormones and Menopause
- Caroline Ross – specialising in supporting women navigating the perimenopause and beyond
- Sarah West – registered nurse with expertise in perimenopause and menopause
- Sarah Azadian – a certified menopause coach empowering 'women of a certain stage!'

Operations
- Natasha Scott – who has an extensive background in operations and strategy, including within the NHS.
- Claire Jenks – an operations implementation sidekick for Managing Directors and CEO's
- Ancy Archana Vidyadharan – a business process improvement specialist based in Norway
- Laura Gaworska – Operations Manager at Amazon specialising in supporting neurodivergent individuals and organisations.
- Abi James – building teams, operations, and managing talent at Oliva therapy platform
- Becca Edwards – a DEI expert with experience in the cyber-security sector and operations
- Jo Hills – a data literacy and culture manager at PwC, with experience in managing change across organisations
- Joanne Hill – a regional manager with 24 years of experience leading financial companies and operations
- Tanya Koekkoek – Netherlands based, Tanya has an extensive background in global operations

Resources & Recommendations

Parenting and Families
- Kate La Trobe - currently an exclusive ADHD Works In House coach, passionate about supporting parents and families navigating ADHD.
- Karen Cooke - People Partner in the NHS who is passionate about helping other parents and educating schools.
- Vikki Rose-Carless - an ADHD and autism family coach, with 3 neurodivergent children.
- Anne Dyer - offering support for parenting with ADHD and managing co-existing conditions, such as eating disorders and personality disorders.
- Michelle Bull - parent of 3 neurodivergent children, ADHD-er Michelle supports families including parents and teenagers.
- Jeni Dobson - after working as a nurse in a Veterinary Practice, Jeni retrained as a Complementary Therapist, with an expertise in helping parents who have ADHD.
- Claire Quigley Ward - with years of experience as a Director, Claire now runs the excellent All Aboard ADHD podcast, helping parents and caregivers navigating the ADHD journey.
- Sarah Hardy - a previous In House ADHD Works coach (and expert VA!), Sarah supports neurodivergent parents (and others including myself!) to find balance amidst the chaos.

Pharmaceutical
- Briana Wukovich - US based Briana has a wealth of expertise in the pharmacist industry, and was part of our first ever cohort!
- Claire Osborn - expert in developing leaders and teams in the pharmaceutical industry

Psychologists
- Nikeeta Shah - Assistant Psychologist with a background in therapy
- Tarana Jhunjhunwala - an Assistant Psychologist within the NHS, bringing a unique perspective on cultural dynamics as a South Asian woman.
- Clare Rowe - a business psychologist with expertise in selection, assessment and career outplacement.

Supervisors
- Margaret Spencer - provider of Occupational Therapy professional supervision
- Janis Sinclair - a highly experienced psychotherapist and Clinical Supervisor
- Allison Dolnik - a Clinical Social Worker and Clinical Supervisor, with a background in CAMHS

Therapists
- Charlotte Lyng - Bioneuroemotion practitioner
- Natalie Kynoch - CBT, EMDR and creative counsellor for adults, teenagers and children
- Rebecca Dalton - a psychotherapist with additional expertise in addiction psychology, who works with adults and young people.
- Samantha Chapman-Allen - an ADHD-friendly CBT therapist
- Frances Clark - with over 11 years of experience providing Auditory Verbal Therapy to preschool children and their families.
- Olivia Jennings - an integrative counsellor / psychotherapist for children, adolescents and families.

University

- Rebeca Bowers - academic research expert and Social Anthropologist who helps students for those navigating university with ADHD
- Oscar van Zijl - who helps teenagers and university students to reach their goals
- Jennie Jordan - specialises in supporting students, academics, and creatives, as a professor and researcher herself.
- Lucy Pickford - having coached teachers and students in mainstream, SEN, and mental health settings, Lucy works at a boarding school.
- Sara Hannak - with extensive experience supporting disabled students, including assessing student need for Disability Student Allowance, enabling them to access education.

Women in Tech

- Andreia Dos Santos - who's a women in AI analytical lead, VC, startup & scale-up advisor, with a background at Google, based in Amsterdam.
- Susi Bauer - with years of experience in the gaming industry, Susi offers training and designs digital ADHD-friendly spaces to organise education
- Tarah Peltz - US-based, Tarah is a product manager for Xbox, with a background in engineering and coding. She also runs the podcast 'It's Just AuDHD'.
- Rhiannon Hill - a current exclusive In House ADHD Works coach, AuDHD-er Rhiannon has a background in engineering

AuDHD: Blooming Differently

Workplace
- Colette Horn - neurodiversity in the workplace trainer and Trustee at York Mind
- Roy Banks - with 25 years of experience in corporate business roles and councils
- Freddie Howell-Jones - with extensive experience as a Chartered Accountant
- Isobel Lepist - with 3 decades of professional success in the corporate world, and personal experience of autism an ADHD
- Maurice Gabbay - an audit consultant with impressive corporate experience at companies like Visa and Deloitte
- Nicki Strouts - Scrum master with a focus on productivity using agile project management techniques
- Tom Burns - with a background in engineering, customer service and learning support.
- Azreen Abdulla - who has years of experience as a professional coach in the workplace
- Yann Ghisalberti - Netherlands based, Yann has decades of experience as a senior manager
- Jessica Partridge - with an extensive background in the property industry
- Rebecca Farrington - with a wealth of experience as a learning consultant, in companies like HSBC and KPMG
- Phil Rossi - who has a background in teaching, coaching, accounting, finance, and training and development. He specialises in supporting adults navigating challenges in work and education.
- Nicola Thomas - with expertise in learning and development, Nicola makes ADHD work for employees at work.
- Laurence Pratt - with a 12 year background as a User Experience Designer

Resources & Recommendations

- Sam Minchin - with 15 years of experience in systems engineering and IT
- Katie Campbell Quinn - with a decade of experience in people-focused roles, Kate has expertise as the Head of Community, fostering connections.
- Veronica Sommariva - a Global Services Centre Associate with infectious passion, Veronica was part of our first ever cohort of ADHD coach training, and a previous In House ADHD Works coach.